BATTLES OF THE BIBLE

BATTLES OF THE BIBLE

Chaim Herzog and Mordechai Gichon

BOOK CLUB ASSOCIATES   LONDON

This edition published 1978 by
Book Club Associates
by arrangement with Weidenfeld and Nicolson

Designed by Charles Elton

Colour Separations by Newsele Litho Limited

Printed in Great Britain by
Butler & Tanner Ltd, Frome and London

CONTENTS

LIST OF MAPS
AND THEIR SYMBOLS

Symbol	Description
	Direction of move by Jewish (Israelite/Judean) or allied force
	Direction of move by Gentile (non-Jewish) enemy force
	Fleeing Jewish force
	Fleeing Gentile force
	Jewish capital city
	Gentile capital city
	Jewish fortified town
	Gentile fortified town
	Jewish fort
	Gentile fort
	Jewish city
	Gentile city
	Jewish town or village
	Gentile town or village
	Captured position
	Empire boundary
	Country or state boundary
	Region or superseded state boundary
	Internal administrative boundary
	Jewish commander-in-chief's camp
	Gentile commander-in-chief's camp
	Jewish camp
	Gentile camp
	Battle
	Port
	Jewish-held spring
	Gentile-held spring
	Jewish blockade
	Gentile blockade
	Chariots
	Infantry
	Cavalry
	Elephants
	Camels

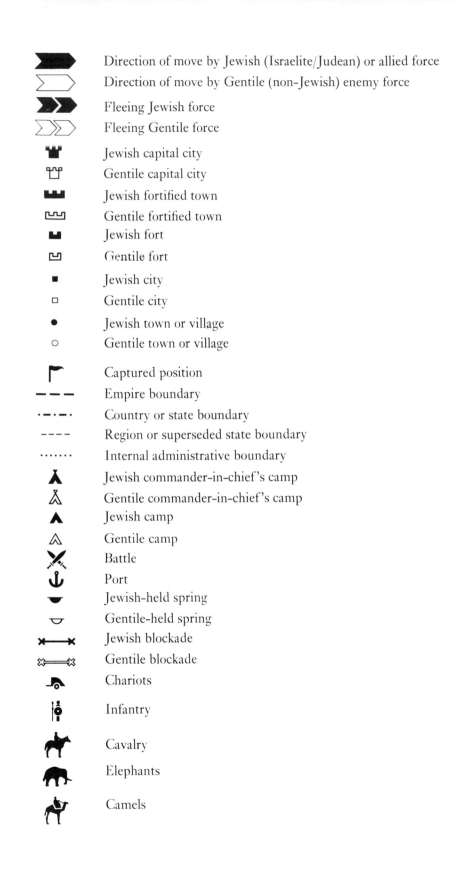

FOREWORD

This book has been written in the attempt to apply to the biblical narrative modern military thinking and understanding.

Thus we were guided by a desire to narrate the military history of the Bible in terms of modern military concepts and accepted terminology. In this manner, we felt, the military genius of many of the captains of war whose story is related in the Bible would emerge in its full scope, while the applicability of the principles of war over the centuries of history would be re-emphasized.

If there were any misgivings in our minds, when beginning our research, about the applicability of modern military logic to events two and three thousand years removed, these have been dissipated during the actual process of writing this book. Bearing in mind the quantitative changes brought about by modern weapons and equipment, the same basic laws – strategy and tactics – that apply to modern conventional warfare also applied to war in the distant past.

The very rigid and distinct factors of geography have been a principal and constant factor in commanders' considerations over the ages. We ourselves, in the course of years of military service, have had occasion to draw on the lessons of the ancient past as we contemplated the problems of the present in Israel's struggle for independence and for the maintenance of its security. The factors which influenced the generals of Judea and Israel of old continue to influence the generals of Israel today.

The Holy Land's strategic position as the main land-bridge of the eastern Mediterranean has, since antiquity, compelled those of its inhabitants who strove for independence to maintain an efficient war machine and to put it from time to time to expert use, in order to maintain their freedom. Only in this manner and by the full military exploitation of the terrain did the Jews of ancient times succeed in retaining the *de facto* mastery of ancient Israel for twelve centuries.

These military exploits of a small nation, pitted more often than not against great odds, seem to us to be worthwhile recording in modern terms. Besides offering the military background and interpretation of the events that shaped biblical history, the critical examination of wars and matters military in the Bible affords many lessons that hold good up to the present day.

This book is a joint endeavour. We have enjoyed the benefit of mutual advice and consultation. Each drew upon the specific experience and qualifications of his colleague. In writing the book, Mordechai Gichon concentrated on the period of the First Temple while Chaim Herzog dealt with the period of the Second Temple till Judah the Maccabee's death in battle with which the Bible's military account ends.

CHAIM HERZOG   MORDECHAI GICHON

PART I

1 SETTING THE SCENE

The geographical stage

Eretz Israel – the land which according to biblical tradition had been promised by God to Abraham as the permanent and particular home of the Jewish people – has been one of the main military thoroughfares as far back as written annals record. In fact, the first coherent account of any military campaign to have come down to us is held by the majority of scholars to be the narrative of an Egyptian invasion of Canaan. This is the inscription on the tomb of Uni, a general of Pharaoh Pepi I, which boasts of the conquest of the 'land of the dwellers of the sand' in a combined sea and land operation.[1] Uni's seaborne troops effected an amphibious landing behind the 'gazelle nose' ridge and overcame their enemies before the Egyptian complement marching up the coastal plain ever reached the battlefield, though the mere threat of their approach towards the defenders' rear must have contributed to the victory. The time was the twenty-fourth century BC, the 'land of the sand dwellers' was present-day Israel and the 'gazelle nose' may have been the Carmel promontory.

Uni's campaign antedates the Israelite conquest of what had become the Egyptian province of Canaan by one thousand years. Yet it provides the first picture of the geopolitical factors and properties that governed the fate of the Holy Land throughout its long, turbulent history.

Before going into details, a few words about nomenclature. As mentioned above, Eretz Israel is the Hebrew name for the Holy Land while Canaan was the name by which it was known on the eve of the Israelite conquest. After the split of the United Monarchy in about 925 BC the northern kingdom retained the name of Israel, while the southern was called Judah. Eventually the term Judah was used to designate all the Jewish dominions after the Israelites' return from exile in Babylon in 537 BC, including those of the Hasmonean kingdom within its changing borders. In its latinized form the latter has come down to us as Judea, the name later given to the country as a Roman province after its reduction by Vespasian and Titus (AD 66–73). This name was changed into Syria-Palaestina, hence Palestine, by the emperor Hadrian in his vain effort to stamp out the Jews in their homeland, after the great revolt under Bar Kokhba (AD 132–135). Throughout all its subsequent history the country continued to be known as Palestine,

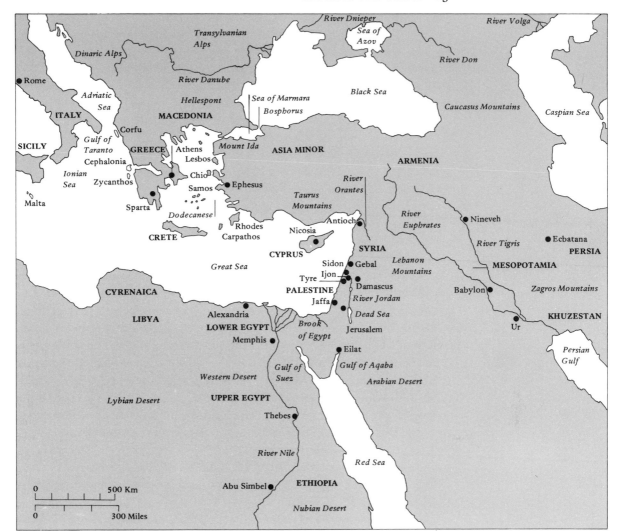

The Geographical Stage

since neither Arabs nor Turks gave it a name of their own.

In the following pages we shall use the term Palestine whenever we wish to indicate the country in a geographical sense within its geographical boundaries and without reference to the actual political constellation at any given time. Cis- and Trans-Jordan are also used in their geographical sense, meaning the country to the west and the east of the Jordan respectively.

The first and foremost of the geopolitical properties that have always governed the fate of the Holy Land is Palestine's position. The country is the sole land-bridge that connects Eurasia with Africa. There is no detour between the sea and the desert and there is no alternative but to pass along the Palestinian roads either west or east of the Jordan River. Consequently, the powers of the day usually did not refrain even from armed conflict to seize hold of this strategic area, which has proved itself absolutely indispensable both for the flow of commerce in peacetime and the movement of armies in war. Nor did the rulers of adjacent lands willingly abandon their goal of incorporating this important crossroad into their territories. Any nation aspiring to establish an independent national state on the Palestinian land-bridge had thus to accept a primary fact of life: it was destined to live under nearly constant concentric pressure from near and far, and only constant military preparedness could guarantee its survival.

It is probably no coincidence that the only people to create a national commonwealth on the Palestinian land-bridge that lasted (with only short interruptions) for an appreciable period (twelve centuries from the twelfth century BC onwards) is the Jewish people. During this long period, the Jews were more often than not forced to make up by spirit and devotion for their numerical inferiority, which was another basic factor in the geopolitical character of Palestine. The very smallness of the country set definite limits on its population. In the ancient period, when agriculture was extensive and only small portions of society were able to live by occupations other than farming, there was one major means for augmenting the national potential in manpower and food production: the conquest of foreign territory. By acquiring more arable land and sufficient tillers for its soil, a ruler could allocate a higher portion of his own people to be temporarily or permanently marshalled for war – not to speak of the auxiliaries that could be raised from the acquired territories.

Palestine, hemmed in by natural boundaries and surrounded to the north and south by much larger countries, was forced to arrive at a relatively higher standard of exploiting its limited resources than more generously endowed regions. But even after bringing the mountains under the plough and capturing large stretches of the arid south of Judea, the Negev, for sedentary, rural settlement, there was a limit that kept the 'Palestinians' numerically small compared to the nations that developed around and about the Nile, in Mesopotamia, the Syrian highlands and Asia Minor.

Although this book deals with matters material and physical, and not with the spiritual aspects of biblical history, it must be stressed that only a people imbued with religious zeal, a steadfast belief in its right to the country as its Promised Land by divine decree, and with religious tenets which make the exercise of its cult within the confines of this country one of its paramount duties, could develop the necessary moral and spiritual endurance to forge a state out of Palestine and sustain the pressure and hardship involved in its preservation.[2]

The next geopolitical factor that is evident from Uni's campaign is that Palestine is endowed with both an extended shoreline and long land borders, which impose upon any nation aspiring to dominate the country the double task of land and sea defence. One of the basic decisions of the makers of Palestine's national defence policy had therefore always been what portion of the national potential to allocate to each. From the perusal of these pages, it will become evident that the Jews of antiquity found this double task beyond their capabilities and tried to solve their naval commitments largely by alliances, treaties or coercion of the seafaring peoples who inhabited the Mediterranean coast, the Phoenicians in the north and the Philistines in the south. Both undertook, either by common understanding with the Israelites or by compulsion, the burden of sea trade and the naval protection of the Palestine coast. The weakness of this arrangement is obvious. It was exactly in times of stress, when the Israelites were in special need of naval support and the profits of maritime trade, that their naval partners or vassals tended to become lukewarm or even sever their relations with Israel.[3]

Pharaoh Uni called Palestine the 'land of the sand dwellers'. The obvious reason for this misnomer is that the name was initially applied correctly to the Sinai and the Negev, and only later, as the Egyptian horizons widened, extended to denote the northern, fertile parts of the country. But it serves to remind us of the next geopolitical factor that governed the fortunes of the Palestinian land-bridge. Palestine is a country on the border between the desert and the arable land. Its southern and eastern borders have always been wide open to major invasions by tribes attempting to settle permanently in 'the land of milk and honey' as well as to raids that created day-to-day problems of current security. The solution to these problems played an important part in the military effort of biblical Israel. Consciousness of this problem was all the keener as the Israelites themselves had initially been a tribal federation that had invaded Palestine from the eastern desert.[4]

The Palestinian land-bridge proper extends from the white-cliff promontory ('the ladder of Tyre') to the 'Brook of Egypt' (Wadi El Arish), 155 miles as the crow flies, and from Ijon (Marjayoun) to Eilat, 280 miles. From west to east, the average distance between the Mediterranean Sea and the eastern edge of the Trans-Jordanian highlands is seventy miles. The actual size of the Jewish state varied at any given time during the biblical period.

Palestine is divided in its centre lengthwise (i.e. north to south) by the Jordan rift valley, which at the Dead Sea becomes the lowest point on the globe, with an average annual temperature of 25 °C. Yet from the 695 feet below sea-level Sea of Galilee only sixty-eight miles north of the Dead Sea, with an average annual temperature of 21 °C., the usually perennially snow-capped Mount Hermon is only thirty-four miles away. Armies fighting in ancient Israel obviously had to be versed in diverse aspects of warfare, from mountaineering on one extreme to desert fighting on the other. A good example of the diversity of conditions in the Palestinian theatre of war, though from a much more recent period, is the Battle of Hattin in AD 1178. While the Crusader host was withering away for want of water on a hot summer day on the descent from Galilee to Tiberias, the Saracen army kept its commanders provided with drinks cooled by ice brought down by camel relays from the upper slopes of Mount Hermon, fifty-five miles away.

Topographically, the country to the west of the Jordan River (Cis-Jordan) may be divided into five major zones: (1) the coastal plain; (2) the Negev; (3) the central highland massif (the mountains of Judah and Ephraim or Samaria); (4) Galilee; (5) the Jordan Valley (the connecting link with eastern

Palestine, also called Trans-Jordan). Two great east–west valleys divide the western highland into its three components: the Beersheva Valley, which lies between the Negev and the central massif; and the Valley of Jezreel (Esdraelon of the Greek and New Testament sources), which lies between the central massif and Galilee.[5]

Galilee may be likened to a huge wheel, with its hub at the Merom ridge, its highest elevation (3,962 feet). From this central watershed, the rains have carved out valleys that fan out like spokes in all directions and serve as main arteries of communication – as well as centres of agriculture – while the intervening ridges divide the region into many semi-isolated sections.

While Galilee reminds us topographically of a huge wheel, Judah and Samaria are like a giant staircase leading up from the sea to the central watershed plateau and down again, though in much steeper steps, towards the Jordan Valley. From the shore, the first step, one ascends through the foothills (called the Shephelah in the Bible) to the third step (the lower slopes) and the fourth step (the upper slopes), up to the plateau. On the descent, the lowest step (from the slopes to the Jordan Valley) is a steep, perpendicular cliff of varying height. From the air, the relief of the central massif looks like a huge fishbone. The spine is the watershed, and the *wadis* (river beds) running down from the watershed towards the Mediterranean and the Jordan Valley or Dead Sea are like the bones emanating from the spine. North-to-south communications west of the Jordan River run along either the coastal plain, the plateau or the Jordan Valley, while the west-to-east communications, other than those via the great lateral valleys, are confined to the wadis descending the watershed.

The topography of the country east of the Jordan River (Trans-Jordan) may be summed up as a mountainous highland plateau with distinct high-mountain relief in parts of Edom and southern Moab. The ascent from the Jordan Valley is very steep, while the descent towards the desert in the east is so gentle and gradual that the border between the plateau and the desert is often hardly noticeable.

Four deep canyon-like gorges of the Yarmuk, Jabbok, Arnon and Zered rivers force the western arm of the main Trans-Jordanian north-to-south artery, the King's Highway, into tortuous traverses that are easily blocked. To skirt these deep gorges, the eastern arm of the King's Highway was laid out close to the confines of the desert.

Abraham and the Patriarchs

The wars of the Bible begin with the exodus of Abraham and his clan from the Mesopotamian city of Haran because of his revolutionary belief in a single god, unique creator and lord of the universe. On leaving Haran, Abraham seems to have joined the great movement of ethnic units that shook the eastern Mediterranean in the eighteenth century BC. Population up-heavals in Asia Minor and the regions to the north of Mesopotamia initiated great migrations that, together with other developments, welded together heterogeneous ethnic groups – the Semites, Horites and Indo-Iranians among them – into the so-called Hyksos nation. It was the Hyksos who con-

quered Egypt (in the eighteenth century BC) by making use of for the first time, and in great numbers, a weapon new to the area – the war chariot.[6]

As happened so often in later history, although the new weapon was soon in common use, its initial possession and deft use was decisive. Hence the Hyksos were able to build their empire and rule Egypt for about two hundred years. The Hyksos were never able, or perhaps never willing, to assimilate themselves into the autochthonic Egyptian population. To keep their hold over Egypt, as well as over the Palestinian land-bridge that connected them with related ethnic elements in Syria and Asia Minor, they encouraged the

Two warriors in combat, from an orthostat at Tel Halaf, c. tenth century BC.

settlement of these related peoples both in Egypt and in Palestine.

The upheavals created by the Hyksos caused both unrest and belligerent activity, as reflected in the account of Abraham's life in Genesis 12–25. Abraham's military exploits, and those of Isaac and Jacob, came under two categories. The first was the defence of grazing grounds – the grazing rights of his clan – on entering Canaan, the country promised to him by God. This category also included the actions taken to retrieve stolen flocks (Gen. 26ff.). The second category was participation in major wars. Such involvement was probably Abraham's obligation towards the Hyksos authorities and their Canaanite vassals, the local petty kings who governed the territories in which Abraham had established himself.[7] Exact information is lacking, but one major war in which Abraham participated, that of the four kings of Mesopotamia (?) against the five kings of the Dead Sea area, throws light on the continuity of strategic conditions and geo-military factors in Palestine from the earliest times onwards.

While the northern allies, headed by Amraphel of Shinar (in Mesopotamia), swept down the King's Highway east of the Jordan to establish control over the route leading to Eilat and the Red Sea, Abraham was free to move on a parallel line west of the Jordan. Using the watershed road on the central mountain massif, he moved in a direction opposite to that of the northern kings and arrived in good time to lay an ambush not far from Damascus on the road to Hobah, the area of the eastern foothills of the Hermon: 'And he divided himself against them, he and his servants, by night, and smote them, and pursued them into Hobah . . .' (Gen. 14:15). The site of the nocturnal ambush was of course somewhere near the convergence of the two highways which was near Damascus proper. It is tempting to suggest the Barada gorge north-west of Damascus, an ancient highway and scene of many an ambush, as the setting for Abraham's battle. It was here that, in a similar outflanking movement along the same direction Abraham must have taken, the Australian Mounted Division ambushed and annihilated the retreating Turkish Fourth Army on the night of 30 September 1918.[8]

The sojourn in Egypt

Jacob's migration into Egypt and the subsequent sojourn of the patriarchal clans in the district of Goshen is also to be understood as having taken place in the Hyksos period. The 'new King of Egypt, which knew not Joseph' was either Amosis I or one of his successors. Amosis I (reigned *c.* 1580–1557 BC) was the founder of the Eighteenth Dynasty and a native Egyptian prince. He succeeded in dislodging the Hyksos from the Nile Valley and laid the foundations for the subsequent Egyptian conquest of Canaan. After this 'reconquest', the Hebrew tribes in Egypt remained an alien element suspected of sympathizing with the last Hyksos strongholds in Palestine and Syria and other non-Egyptian elements in the north. They became what a twentieth-century military planner would call 'a permanent potential security risk'.

There have always been two ways of dealing with a problem of this nature.

The first is to try to induce the alien populace to assimilate and thus join it to the body of the nation. This was the policy of Alexander the Great during his eastern conquests. The other more frequently applied though often 'counter-productive' approach (to use another recently coined political term) is the subjugation of the alien elements. The Egyptians chose the latter option to deal with the Hebrews, '. . . lest they multiply, and it come to pass when there falleth out any war, they join also unto our enemies, and fight against us . . .' (Exod. 1:10).

During the subsequent persecutions, the Exodus and the 'forty years' of wandering in the deserts of the Sinai Peninsula under the inspired leadership of Moses, the liberator and lawgiver, the Hebrew clans were welded into a coherent and consciously national nucleus that became the Jewish people. The common patriarchal traditions, religion and laws, as laid down by Moses, and – last but not least – the common experience of struggle during the Exodus and for a first foothold on the east bank of the Jordan, were the forces that forged the Hebrew clans into the people of Israel.

The military organization of the Israelites was, like that of all nations emerging from tribal status, based on the duty of every able-bodied male to bear arms and serve, whenever necessary, in his tribal contingent in the national host. According to the Bible, Moses and Aaron organized the first Israelite army when leaving the Egyptian bondage:

Take ye the sum of all the congregation of the children of Israel, after their families, by the house of their fathers, with the number of their names, every male by their polls; from twenty years old and upward, all that are able to go forth to war in Israel: thou and Aaron shall number them by their armies. And with

Egyptian guards with their (bearded) Syrian prisoners, from a fourteenth-century relief at Memphis.

you there shall be a man of every tribe; everyone head of the house of his fathers. (Num. 1:2–4)

From this passage as well as the rest of chapter 1 of Numbers, we learn that, as in the emerging Greek, Roman and Germanic societies, the tribal heads were leaders in peace as well as in war – a warrant inherited later by kings, princes, archons and consuls – whereas the people in arms formed the national assembly of the initially sovereign peoples. It is an interesting sidelight that, whereas in Western societies the basically democratic rights emanating from the various early national assemblies withered away in time, ancient Jewish society, even in the heyday of monarchy, never gave way to absolutism. The 'people' always remained, directly and indirectly, a body with influence on the affairs of state. This fact was instrumental not only in the preservation of the people in arms as the mainstay of the Israelite armed forces until the destruction of the First Temple, as we shall see in the following pages, but also in the apparent readiness of the Israelites to bear the constant burden of military preparedness.[9]

From a famous wall painting in a tomb at Beni Hasan, Egypt, we get a vivid and authentic picture of a Semitic clan that entered Egypt at about the time of Abraham (nineteenth–eighteenth century BC).[10] We may well presume that no great physical difference existed between the tribe portrayed there and the Israelites at the time of the Exodus (fourteenth–thirteenth century BC). Like this clan, the Israelites were donkey nomads. They moved and fought on foot, while their few heavy goods – including tools and tents, the old, the feeble and the very young – were carried on backs of donkeys. This meant that if the whole congregation moved together, its average speed, including the cattle, was no more than three miles per hour. The men, of course, were subjected to strenuous exercise and undertook long marches when they moved out for action, unencumbered by their families and belongings. For security reasons the tribes moved and encamped according to a fixed and well-regulated pattern.

The Beni Hasan mural depicts the tribal arms: spear, javelin, bow and sword. A bard playing a lute during the progress of the caravan is reminiscent of the Levites, while the bellows carried by asses prove that these nomads, like the Israelites, were their own smiths and craftsmen and consequently self-reliant as far as maintenance of their personal armoury was concerned. Their independence assured maximum flexibility to their military manœuvring, so that if they were led well, the tribal hosts could neutralize some of the advantages of better equipped and regular forces.

The Israelites, though exclusively foot-soldiers, did not carry an arbitrary assortment of the above-mentioned weaponry according to each individual's whim. Before, during and directly after the Exodus, typical tribal proficiencies came to be established. In the following pages we shall trace the development of the Israelite army, composed of variously armed and trained tribal contingents that formed a well-balanced, mutually complementary

and supporting whole.[11] From the outset, however, there had to be a funda-
mental organization, a basic chain of command and discipline. These factors
make all the difference between an army, however primitive and unsophisticated, and an armed rabble. Many a tribal society never, or only very gradually, succeeded in transforming itself from a collection of clan gangs fighting
in a compact mass into a force with tactical divisions and a proper chain
of command. The Bible attributes all these accomplishments to Moses.
'Moses chose able men out of all Israel, and made them heads over the
people, rulers of thousands, rulers of hundreds, rulers of fifties, and rulers
of tens' (Exod. 18:25).

So far no satisfactory solution has been offered to the many problems and
the seemingly conflicting evidence that can be gleaned from the biblical
accounts of the Exodus and its battles. We are very much tempted to follow
the former British governor of Sinai, Major Jarvis, in identifying the narrow
tongue of land between the Mediterranean and the brackish lagoon called
the Serbonian Sea, halfway between Port Said and El Arish, as the site of
the encounter between the Israelites and the pursuing Egyptians.[12] Having
followed in the footsteps of Jarvis, we could well imagine how he was caught
in a sudden gale while standing in the wet sand, swept by the angry waters
of the Mediterranean, and thus became convinced that this was the spot
where the 'Red Sea crossing' had taken place. It needs little imagination
to transfer to these parts the account of Exodus 14:22–8: 'And the children
of Israel went into the midst of the sea upon dry ground.... And the Egyptians pursued and went after them.... And the waters returned and covered
the chariots, and the horsemen, and all the host of Pharaoh.'

The crossing of the Red Sea

The identification of this area is all the more tempting as two similar
occurrences were recorded as having taken place on this sand bar between
the sea and the lagoon. The first-century BC Greek historian Diodorus
Siculus relates that during Xerxes' invasion of Egypt in 340 BC, part of his
troops drowned there.[13] Strabo, writing during the same period, informs
us: 'During my stay at Alexandria in Egypt, the sea rose so high near
Pelusium and Mount Cassius [in the centre of the sand bar] as to overflow
the land and to convert the mountain into an island.'[14]

Moses thus set an example for all later Israelite commanders in minimizing his adversary's superiority by making the geographical features of his
theatre of war his ally. This 'discerning eye' is the gift of great captains to
divine the tactical qualities of the battlefield.[15] Moses' choice of the route
along the seashore was dictated by his appreciation that the pursuing Egyptians would have little room for a full deployment of chariots or any other
troops, and that the terrain abounded in features that could be used to en-
snare the Pharaonic regulars. Archaeological investigation has established
another fact: at the time of the Exodus, the strongholds along the sea route,
such as the fortress of Mount Cassius, were not permanently manned,
whereas the main highway (which is followed both by the railway line built
by the British in World War One and the present-day asphalt road) was

occupied by Egyptian garrisons stationed in fortified road-posts close to all the water sources. The desire to avoid these road defences adds likelihood to the choice of the shore route, despite the fact that it is quite different from the route of the Exodus that had already become a deeply rooted tradition as far back as the Byzantine period (fifth–sixth century AD).[16] Whatever the actual scene of the clash, however, Moses surely heeded the proverb, 'With ruses make war' (Prov. 20:18), long before it was put down in writing.

The background to the conquest

Much like the Exodus, the stages of the conquest of Canaan are shrouded in obscurity. The Bible was not interested in martial affairs *per se*, nor did the chroniclers who compiled the historical reports of the conquest of Canaan, as told in the books of Joshua and Judges, attempt to check their sources. Consequently, sometimes divergent or even conflicting versions of the course of the conquest have crept into these accounts, and modern research has not yet arrived at a commonly accepted formula in these matters.[17] Nonetheless the view held by most scholars is that the conquest of Canaan took place in the following stages: (1) the Exodus from Egypt; (2) the 'forty years'' migration in the Sinai Peninsula; (3) the invasion of Trans-Jordan and the occupation of parts of Moab and Gilead; (4) the conquest of the central mountain massif by Joshua; (5) the conquest of southern Canaan and the northern Negev by tribal penetration both southwards from the central massif and northwards through the Negev; (6) perhaps simultaneously with the above stage, the conquest of Galilee.

The conquest of both Cis- and Trans-Jordan was helped by the fact that the Egyptian Empire was no longer able to detail enough forces to safeguard the province of Canaan, which it had acquired in the wake of the retreating Hyksos. By the mid-fourteenth century BC the New Kingdom had temporarily lost its superiority and, moreover, was burdened with internal problems and challenges to its security on frontiers other than Canaan. The Hebrew tribes were therefore able to get a foothold in the Promised Land, partly by military conquest and partly by more peaceful infiltration. Egyptian sources, as well as biblical allusions, point to the probability that not all the clans connected with the Patriarchs had followed Jacob into Egypt. Moreover, several other clans, which had not initially belonged to the Hebrew tribal association linked to the Patriarchs, had joined the 'twelve tribes' and amalgamated with them during various stages of the conquest.[18]

Although we lack precise information on the initial entry into Trans-Jordan, we do have a most interesting account of one of the major events that took place during the planning stage. One of the most important staff functions from the first days of primitive tribal wars onwards has been military intelligence. The great captains of history have, each in his day, devoted much of their time to outguessing and outwitting their foes by acquiring as accurate a picture as possible of their intentions, capabilities, strength, deployment and terrain. Wellington put this major mental effort very succinctly. When asked what it was that he was thinking of during his long hours of seclusion and silent ponderings, he answered: 'I am thinking about the other side of the hill.'

'The other side of the hill' was to Moses, encamped at the oasis of Kadesh-barnea, the land of Canaan beyond the miles of barren rock and sand of the Negev. To find out how best to go about conquering it Moses sent out twelve spies. The Book of Numbers, chapter 13, records the briefing Moses gave his reconnaissance troops. The need for a detailed briefing of the intelligence officer (10) by his commander, or of the intelligence-gathering agencies by the 10, has become one of the basic tenets of any modern intelligence operation. The items under discussion and their emphasis change from mission to mission but, according to one modern official handbook, 'The subject matter of strategic intelligence may be considered from two aspects: (1) the capabilities of nations; (2) the intentions of nations.' Moses' business was clearly with the former. Our handbook goes on: 'The capabilities of nations in war and peace are based on their natural and industrial resources, their political stability and demography, the character and stamina of their populations, their armed forces, their scientific endeavour, their topography and infrastructure.'

Compared with this guideline written over three thousand years later, Moses' briefing seems surprisingly modern and in line with present-day requirements:

And Moses sent them to spy out the land of Canaan, and said unto them ... and see the land what it is; and the people that dwelleth therein, whether they be strong or weak, few or many; and what the land is that they dwell in, whether it be good or bad; and what cities they be that they dwell in, whether in tents or in strongholds; and what the land is, whether it be fat or lean, whether there be wood therein, or not. (Num. 13:17–20)

One of the weaknesses and potential failings of intelligence reports has always been the fact that the recipient must base his planning and action upon the estimates and interpretations of others. And others, by character, training or inclination, might arrive at conclusions different from those the commander would have deduced had it been in his power to take a personal look at 'the other side of the hill'. Frederick the Great's defeat at Kunnersdorf in 1759, Napoleon's reverse before Acre in 1799 and the British disaster at Arnhem in 1944 probably would not have occurred had the commanders-in-chief been able to assess for themselves the facts on which their intelligence was based.[19] Hence it is only natural that commanders have always impressed upon their intelligence-gathering agencies the need to provide them with as much tangible proof as possible to confirm their reports. Moses was no exception, for he terminated his briefing with the following injunction: 'And be ye of good courage and bring of the fruit of the land' (Num. 13:20).

The spies heeded Moses' words and substantiated their report about the natural products of Canaan by carrying with them samples of the rich fruit that grew there. Most probably, this evidence did much to enhance the credibility of those items in their report for which tangible proof could not be obtained: 'The people be strong that dwell in the land, and the cities are walled, and very great: and moreover we saw children of Anak there . . . and we were in our own sight as grasshoppers, and so we were in their sight' (Num. 13:28, 33).

Another means of minimizing the dangers inherent in basing one's estimate upon the appreciations of others has always been to choose the most capable officers for crucial missions. In the seventeenth century, when it became customary to accredit ambassadors as permanent gatherers of intelligence at foreign courts, the French handbook stressed the importance of choosing a general of the highest calibre, as 'he would be in a better position than anyone else to render good account of the forces of the country where he resided, the quality of the troops . . . the state of the fortified places, the arsenals and magazines'. Moses had already acted accordingly in his own day. According to Numbers 13:1–2: 'The Lord spake unto Moses saying, Send thou men, that they may search the land of Canaan . . . of every tribe . . . shall ye send a man, every man a ruler among them.' In this way, the more optimistic appraisal of Joshua and Caleb was effectively overruled by the voices of the ten other scouts, representing the highest leadership in their respective tribes.

Their evaluation was sustained when the attempt to push straight north from Kadesh-barnea through the Negev into the Promised Land was foiled by the king of Arad. The tribal warriors were also incapable of assailing the walled cities in the Beersheva Valley (archaeological research has revealed their pattern) and unable to stand up in open country to the heavily armed regulars, who probably included a unit of the dreaded war chariots. The scouts were vindicated, and Moses therefore changed his plan from a direct to a more indirect approach. By a great detour he skirted the well-defended kingdoms that had been established on the Trans-Jordanian highlands some generations before the Exodus and, moving on the fringes of the desert, he turned westwards to assault the only weak link in the chain of desert-border kingdoms: the realm of the Amorite king, Sihon. The Israelite intelligence service must have worked well among their kinsmen, the Edomites, Moabites and Ammonites. It did not take them long to find out that Sihon had recently carved a kingdom out of the Moabite lowlands north of the Arnon River. His conquest had been achieved with great effort, and he had not yet had the time to fortify his kingdom sufficiently. Thus the Israelites were able to invade and conquer Sihon's country and to push out from there northwards into Gilead, which was at that time only sparsely settled. There they linked up with local Hebrew clans and forged their still rather loose tribal structure into a semi-sedentary society of militant tribes, with the goal of capturing the whole of their Promised Land.[20]

2 THE CAMPAIGNS OF JOSHUA

The credit for gaining a foothold in the Judean heartland west of the Jordan goes to Joshua. If his exploits had followed a planned schedule, they would fit into the following grand design: phase one – the establishment of a bridge-head west of the Jordan; phase two – the gaining of a foothold in the mountains; phase three – spreading out from the secured base on the central ridge to widen the area of occupation for permanent settlement.

The plan of the conquest

Phase one was divided into two stages: the river-crossing and the securing of the bridge-head. The place chosen by Joshua for crossing the Jordan was the sector of the river closest to the Dead Sea. His choice was influenced by a number of considerations. First, the approaches to the Jordan in that sector were secure, since the river skirted the part of Moab occupied by the Israelites. In the event of a reverse, Joshua could retreat into friendly territory or gather reinforcements from Gilead and the Moabite lowlands. Secondly, the river could be forded in many places in this sector, which gave the crossing parties the choice of different routes according to potential hostile interference. Moreover, a large number of tracks led from the fords up to the central Judean highlands and presented the Israelites with a number of alternatives for the second phase of the conquest after the bridge-head had been secured.

As far as the prospective bridge-head was concerned, there was only one real option. On the western side of the lower Jordan were the plains of Jericho; in their midst stood the oasis city of Jericho, possibly the oldest city on earth and certainly the oldest walled town known to us so far. Five millennia before Joshua, the spring that watered the rich alluvial soil (Ain el-Sultan) had already converted the otherwise barren rift valley into a lush tropical garden that supplied the needs of the caravans and travellers commuting between the two banks of the Jordan, as well as those who travelled along the river. Hence, the capture of the oasis of Jericho meant the acquisition of a fertile base abounding in fruit and water, as well as control of the water source, which was vital for all movement in the area.

The great problem for the Israelites, who were inexperienced in siegecraft and devoid of any siege train, was, of course, the capture of the town, secured as it was behind its walls, towers and battlements. Joshua therefore

commanded his scouts to reconnoitre the other side of the Jordan for the best possible bridge-head, with special emphasis upon Jericho, and their exploits are common knowledge: 'And they went [into Jericho] and came into a harlot's house, named Rahab, and lodged there' (Josh. 2:1). There is no doubt that in later Hebrew usage the word *zonah* meant harlot. But the verb from which it was derived, *zan*, means to feed and to provide with victuals. Rahab might well have been a hostess who kept an inn for wayfarers passing through Jericho. This seems to fit her standing as householder, an accepted member of a large family to whom even the messengers of the ruler of the town spoke with a certain civility. Inns have always been excellent sources of information. The careless talk of guests and the sharp ears of hosts have combined to make them a coveted intelligence objective. Frederick the Great advised his heirs to have an innkeeper in their pay in every region of interest.[1]

One of the subjects learned from listening to conversation in inns is the true morale and opinion of the population. Thus the report of Rahab's words – 'For we have heard . . . what ye did unto the two kings of the Amorites . . . whom ye utterly destroyed. And . . . our hearts did melt, neither did there remain any more courage in any man because of you' (Josh. 2: 10–11) – must have strengthened Joshua in his conviction that the proper psychological moment for the attack upon Jericho had come.

The actual conquest was envisaged in two waves. The spearhead was to be the armed warriors of the tribes of Reuben, Gad and half the tribe of Manasseh, which had already settled permanently in Trans-Jordan. They were to be followed by the bulk of the people, who would arrive with their families and all their possessions immediately to settle every parcel of conquered land. By means of this arrangement, a *fait accompli* was to be established, and the occupying clans, if faced with Canaanite attempts at reconquest, would be spurred on by a desire to defend their new homes.

Before the beginning of the campaign, Joshua was invested with supreme powers, including the meting out of capital punishment. In the text of his investiture, we find the following passage: 'Whosoever he be that does rebel against thy commandment, and will not hearken unto thy words in all that thou commandest him, he shall be put to death: only be strong and of good courage' (Josh. 1:18). The healthy instinct of the tribal elders induced them, before the fateful attempt at crossing the Jordan, to forgo some of the jealously guarded rights so as to enable their chosen leader to accomplish his mission. At a later stage of history, the Romans similarly invested their supreme commander with the *imperium*. And just as the permanent powers and prerogatives of the Israelite kings evolved out of the temporary supreme authority of the Judges, who were chosen and invested in the image of Joshua, so was the supreme authority of the Roman emperors based upon the permanence of the *imperium*, which had formerly been granted to the supreme military commanders in times of war. While Moses had been the prototype of the divinely inspired leader – one of those few throughout history who, by their awe-inspiring charisma, laid down the laws by which

(*Opposite*) The remains of a round tower at Jericho.

The fall of Jericho

they were obeyed – Joshua was the first leader elected by the general assembly of Israel. Men of religious bent may see more than mere coincidence in the fact that the precedent for the evolvement of later forms of government in Israel was created on the eve of the landing west of the Jordan.

The actual crossing of the Jordan was facilitated by an earthquake:

> And it came to pass, when the people removed from their tents, to pass over Jordan . . . that the waters which came down from above stood and rose up in a heap very far from the city Adam, that is besides Zaretan . . . and all the Israelites passed over on dry ground. . . . (Josh 3 : 14–17)

Adam (today's Tell Damiyeh, near the Damiyeh Bridge over the Jordan) has been reported several times as the place where the course of the river was blocked when the perpendicular banks of soft soil caved in as a result of earth tremors. In AD 1267, when the lower river temporarily dried up as a consequence of a similar blockage, the Mameluk sultan Baybars was able to exploit sixteen hours to lay the foundations for the predecessor of the present bridge, and it served him as main artery during his subsequent campaigns to wrest the Holy Land from the Crusaders. A more recent instance of the phenomenon was reported by Professor John Garstang, who related that in 1927 'a section of the cliff, which here [at Damiyeh] rises to a height of 150 feet, fell bodily across the river, and completely dammed it, so that no water flowed down the river bed for $21\frac{1}{2}$ hours'.[2]

It is a moot question whether Joshua used his knowledge of seismic conditions in the Jordan Valley to wait for the resumption of the earthquake which had begun some time before to facilitate the crossing or the assault upon Jericho, or both. At all events, when the earth quaked, the tribes made ready to move. The astonishing occurrence was regarded by the Israelites as divine intercession on their behalf, and in its timing it may indeed be regarded as miraculous even today.

Thus convinced of God's assistance, the Israelite host surrounded Jericho:

> And the Lord said unto Joshua . . . ye shall compass the city, all ye men of war, and go round the city once. Thus shalt thou do six days. And seven priests shall bear before the ark seven trumpets of rams' horns: and the seventh day ye shall compass the city seven times . . . and when ye hear the sound of the trumpet, all the people shall shout with a great shout; and the wall of the city shall fall down flat. . . . (Josh. 6 : 2–5)

Joshua meticulously kept to the above procedure and, according to the biblical narrative, '. . . the wall fell down flat, so that the people went up into the city, every man straight before him, and they took the city' (Josh. 6 : 20).

Scholars have searched widely for a 'rational' interpretation of the conquest of Jericho. Many a bizarre explanation has been offered, from the wall-breaching effect of the rhythmic trampling of the besiegers' feet while marching around the city seven times to the wall-shattering blast caused by the combined trumpets and outcry of the Israelite host. More realistically, archaeological evidence has been marshalled to prove that the walls of Jericho in Joshua's time must have been in a rather negligent state of repair. Yet even granting the existence of cracks in the walls, feasibly caused by the same earthquake that accounted for the dry passage across the Jordan, explanations of this type are nonetheless untenable or insufficient. Unfortunately, the walls of the Late Bronze Period Canaanite Jericho had largely been washed away before the town's reconstruction by Hiel, the Bethelite, in King Ahab's time. Consequently, there is practically no archaeological evidence to be gathered on the period of the conquest from the three great and extensive digs at the mound of Jericho.[3]

The solution to the enigma seems to come not from material evidence but from a comparison with ancient military devices and stratagems. In the collection of stratagems published by Sextus Julius Frontinus before the close of the first century AD, we read:

When Gnaeus Pompey on one occasion was prevented from crossing a river because the enemy's troops were stationed on the opposite bank, he adopted the device of repeatedly leading his troops out of camp and back again. Then, when the enemy were at last tricked into relaxing their watch on the roads in front of the Roman advance, he made a sudden dash and effected a crossing. (*Strategmata* I.IV.8)

Indeed, the principle sounds familiar. For six days the entire Israelite host solemnly filed around the walls of Jericho in full array. And for six days the good burghers of Jericho sprang to their weapons and manned the ramparts, at first in uneasy expectancy, afraid both of the marching columns and the possible magic involved in this procession headed by the priests and the Ark of the Covenant. But after the first terror and anxiety had subsided, the people of Jericho grew accustomed to the strange performance and relaxed. Precisely at this moment on the seventh day, after the Israelites had begun their by now customary manœuvre, at a sign from their leader, the silent, tranquil procession suddenly changed into a column of frenzied assault. Before the dazed and terror-stricken defenders could collect themselves, the Israelites had scaled the walls or passed through any portion of them damaged by the recent tremors and only hastily patched and 'utterly destroyed all that was in the city . . . by the edge of the sword'.

The strategy of lulling the enemy into a false sense of security by gradually accustoming him to the manœuvres that will later be used in opening and developing an attack has often served its planners extremely well. Thus the British misled their Turkish and German foes at Romani, in Sinai, in 1916.[4] More recently, the Syrians and Egyptians deceived the Israelis before the October 1973 war by the repeated mobilization of their assault forces on Israel's borders, as well as by such manœuvres as the handling of bridging equipment and the adoption of assault formations.

The capture of Jericho gave the Israelites their first real foothold west of the Jordan. Joshua's next goal was penetration into the Judean mountains.

The Ai campaign

Reshef, the Canaanite god of war: a bronze figure from Megiddo.

With his clear strategic insight, he perceived the importance of the central mountain massif for the establishment of a Hebrew commonwealth in Cis-Jordan. The Judean mountains were the natural fortress behind whose bulwarks the lightly armed Israelites could withstand the onslaught of the heavily armed Canaanite forces. Joshua had no doubt about the outcome of a pitched battle on the open plains, where his tribal host was practically defenceless against the Canaanite chariots. On the other hand, topographical conditions alone precluded the deployment of heavily armed regulars in the mountains and gave lightly armed troops a chance to make up for their deficiencies by a combination of stealth, cunning, daring and mobility. Furthermore, the mountains were only sparsely settled and therefore permitted Israelite entrenchment and colonization, whereas there was little chance of subduing the densely populated and strongly fortified cities of the plains.

Joshua also had to reckon with the prospect of interference by the Egyptians, as Canaan was still part of the Pharaonic empire. We now know from the archives of King Amenhotep IV (Ikhnaton, 1391–1353 BC), discovered at Tell el-Amarna on the Nile, that most calls for aid from the Canaanites and Egyptian officials alike had been put off with empty promises. And Joshua, though certainly not privy to the Egyptian diplomatic correspondence, did gauge the actual situation correctly. The time was ripe for a strike, and there was little danger of Egyptian interference as long as the Israelites kept to the mountains and away from the plains, the site of the Via Maris (Way of the Sea), the great trade route that connected Egypt with Syria and thus the strategic lifeline of the Egyptian empire.

The preliminary step in the campaign to penetrate the mountains was the Israelite alliance with the Gibeonites, who were themselves a rather hard-pressed, small tribal confederation that had settled, probably not very long before, around the watershed of the mountains north of Jerusalem. Their chief town was Gibeon (present-day El Jib), five miles north-west of Jerusalem. The biblical report has it that the contact with the Gibeonites was established only after the capture of Ai (Josh. 9), but a critical analysis of the text, as well as the choice of the territory of Bethel as the object of Joshua's first assault, makes it highly probable that initial contact with the Gibeonites was made after the conquest of Jericho and as a prerequisite to the attack on Ai.

Having thus secured the rear of his chosen theatre of operation, Joshua began to gather the necessary intelligence about his objective: Ai or, more probably, the terrain around Bethel, the town commanding the ascent to the Judean watershed via a number of tracks, not far from Gibeonite Beeroth (present-day El Bira near Ramallah). The reports brought by his scouts must have dissuaded Joshua from attacking Bethel itself because of its strong defences. Indeed, such an attack proved quite unnecessary as the place guarding the ascent at the edge of the watershed was not Bethel itself but Ai.[5]

Ai had been a heavily fortified town thirteen hundred years before

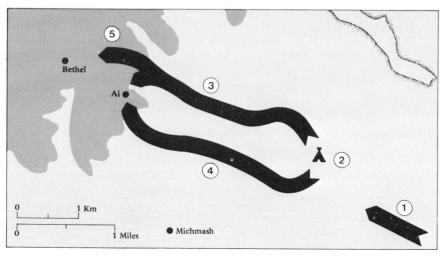

The Ai Campaign (phase one)

1 The Israelites move up towards Ai from Gibeon.
2 Joshua's camp.
3 After their initial defeat, the main Israelite force returns to attack Ai and draw the Canaanites out of the city.
4 Another force is sent to ambush Ai while the city is engaged with the main force.
5 A third force blocks any relief force from Bethel.

Joshua's time, and archaeological evidence proves that it had only recently been resettled – rather sporadically and without an orderly rebuilding of its defences – by the Bethelites. However, the biblical narrative (Josh. 7–8) leads to the assumption that to forestall the threat of an Israelite attempt upon their town, which must have seemed imminent after the fall of Jericho, the people of Bethel did prepare Ai as a fortified outpost because of its commanding position above the ascent (which was in 'dead ground' from Bethel itself).

Unlike the scouts' evaluation of Bethel, the intelligence reports about Ai were optimistic (Josh. 7:3–4), and the scouts, unfamiliar with the great strength inherent in ruins prepared as defensive positions, advised their commander that a token force of up to three thousand men would be sufficient to capture the town. At that stage, Joshua committed an error common to many a general made over-confident by repeated success, and adopted his scouts' suggestion, which was based upon an underestimate of the enemy's force and capacity. The result, in retrospect, was entirely predictable: 'So there went up thither of the people about three thousand men, and they fled before the people of Ai' (Josh. 7:4).

The tactical drawback, though severe, was not calamitous. Far more dangerous was the psychological impact and its foreseeable consequences. Not only did the Israelites lose faith in their prowess, but the myth of Israel's invincibility was about to be broken ('For the Canaanites and all the inhabitants of the land shall hear about it' (Josh. 7:9)) and the flagging spirits of their opponents to be strongly revived. Joshua's reaction proved the justice of the Napoleonic dictum that 'a great commander proves his mettle in adversity'. His decision was to renew the attack almost immediately, making the natural self-assurance of the victors the basis for a ruse which would assure success according to the following plan: (1) employment of the complete tribal host; (2) dislodgement of the garrison at Ai from its stronghold by a simulated flight of the main force of Israelite troops after

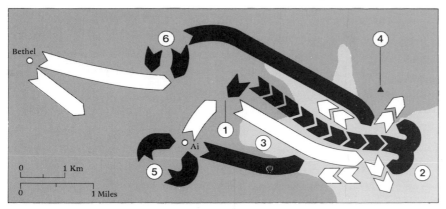

The Ai Campaign (phase two)

1 Joshua's main force attacks Ai and draws out the Canaanites.
2 The Israelites make a false retreat, but then turn and face their pursuers.
3 The enemy, tricked into chasing the Israelites, are then put to flight.
4 Joshua's signal point.
5 The ambushing force takes Ai.
6 The third force attacks and routs the Bethelites.

a head–on assault similar to the first abortive attempt; (3) detachment of a body of 'picked troops' to the rear of Ai, prior to the main assault, under cover of night, so as to capture the objective deserted by its defenders in pursuit of the supposedly fleeing Israelites; (4) trapping the pursuing enemy between the main force and the capturers of Ai; (5) detachment of a strong blocking force prior to the battle to occupy a position straddling the approaches from Bethel, so as to forestall any assistance reaching Ai from the rear.

A commander's place during battle must be where the most critical decisions are being taken. Joshua judged rightly that the most difficult task lay with the main body feinting a retreat. First, it would be necessary to return to a concerted attack immediately upon receiving the order. Secondly, it was imperative to choose exactly the right moment to wheel this force around. The combination of these two tasks was among the most difficult manœuvres of the war. Consequently, Joshua decided to take personal command over the main body of the host. After despatching the troops selected to lie in ambush in the rear of Ai, he moved into camp with his troops on the eve of battle, so as to raise their spirits by his presence. Wherever the Israelite camp was located, an approach march of no less than six hours (through either one of the branches of Wadi Muheisin or via a parallel ridge track) had to be reckoned with, climbing up-hill all the way. Zero hour was at daybreak, after the blocking force had been despatched to occupy a covered position towards the north-west.

The main force attacked and, under Joshua's command, staged its feinted retreat at the proper moment. As anticipated, '. . . all the people that were in Ai were called together to pursue after them . . . and were drawn away from the city' (Josh. 8:16). When the defenders were well drawn off and deep in the steep gorge of Wadi Muheisin, Joshua quickly mounted the adjacent slope and flashed his sword (a pre-arranged signal), whereupon the assault force rushed the practically abandoned positions and immediately set them on fire.[6] At the same time, Joshua turned his troops 180 degrees to attack. Before the pursuers could recover their wits, they were attacked simultaneously from the rear by the capturers of Ai; and though it is not

(Opposite) Ai: a view from the site towards the hiding place of the 'picked troops', background right.

explicitly stated, the blocking force would by then at least partly have joined the mêlée by charging down the slope on the desperate and undoubtedly still bewildered Bethelites. Their fate was sealed. They were completely trapped, and in later generations it was said that not a single soul escaped the ensuing rout.

The assault on the Judean mountains

The fall of Ai rang the tocsin among the Canaanite rulers of Cis-Jordan. The most immediately concerned were the petty kings who ruled the Judean highland. The alliance of Joshua and the Gibeonites was a disaster for the Canaanite cause, no less than the fall of Ai.

Wherefore Adoni-zedek king of Jerusalem sent unto Hoham king of Hebron, and unto Piram king of Jarmuth, and unto Japhia king of Lachish, and unto Debir king of Eglon, saying, Come up unto me and help me, that we may smite Gibeon: for it hath made peace with Joshua and with the children of Israel. Therefore the five kings of the Amorites . . . gathered themselves together, and went up, they and all their hosts, and encamped before Gibeon, and made war against it. (Josh. 10:3–4)

The moment of truth for the newly formed alliance had come, perhaps earlier than expected. But when the Gibeonite call for assistance arrived at the Israelite camp at Gilgal, Joshua did not waver. He sensed that to leave the Gibeonites to their fate would mean losing his newly gained position of strength along with his foothold in Cis-Jordan.

So Joshua quickly prepared for battle, and at nightfall – in order to neutralize possible enemy observers – he started out on a march of about fifteen

Gibeon: the ancient town was situated on the hill in the centre of the picture. The main Amorite encampment was in the valley, and Joshua's forces took up positions on the surrounding hills.

miles and the Israelites reached the region of Gibeon without having been observed. The hilly, wooded and sparsely settled terrain gave them ample cover, which Joshua probably used to allow his warriors some rest and time for the necessary last-minute preparations for battle. Meanwhile, he was able to reconnoitre his objective for the first time, either from Nebi Samwil (Mizpah of the Maccabean era?[7]) or from an adjacent height, and noted that Gibeon was built upon a low rise in a pleasant mountain dale and was overlooked by the surrounding ridges. The Amorite allies were in the process of besieging Gibeon, and their camp (or camps) was probably situated not far from one or another of the springs and wells in the valley.

As the Amorites had no inkling of the presence of the enemy at their rear and had neglected to send out effective screening parties to warn of any un-expected hostile movement in that area, Joshua was able to achieve complete surprise. The downward gradient of the line of his assault gave his troops additional impetus and penetrating force, and the Amorites, by then obvi-ously harassed by the renewed strength from the battlements of the besieged city, broke and fled in utter confusion.

The route of their flight was along the Beth-horon pass, a major gateway to Judah which figures throughout the country's subsequent history both in war and in peace. The physical prowess of the Israelite host troops must be admired. After an approach march of fifteen miles over a steep ascent of more than 1,900 feet, which took almost all night, they soon went into battle. The length of the contest cannot be gauged, but after routing their

enemy the Israelites were still able to exploit their victory by pursuit.

> Then spake Joshua to the Lord . . . and he said in the sight of Israel, Sun, stand thou still upon Gibeon; and thou, Moon, in the valley of Ajalon. And the sun stood still, and the moon stayed, until the people had avenged themselves upon their enemies. Is not this written in the book of Jashar? . . . And there was no day like that before it or after it, that the Lord harkened unto the voice of a man, for the Lord fought for Israel. (Josh. 10:12–14)

For all its eloquence, the English version of this passage bears only a faint echo of the drama of the original Hebrew. Still, we may envisage Joshua, staunch and doughty, though flushed with victory, sensing in the midst of the pursuit that, if he did not crush the Amorite armed forces completely, much of the decisiveness of his victory would be lost.

Many a victory has been robbed of its fruits by the victor's obvious inability to exploit his success. Thus the Swedes could not, or would not, prevent Wallenstein's safe disengagement after the battle of Lützen (1634); Wellington was without means to prevent the orderly retreat and regrouping of the French after the battle of Talavera (1805); nor did Napoleon follow up his victory at Ligny in 1815 by destroying Blücher's Prussian forces, thus allowing the old marshal to reinforce the allies two days later at Waterloo, and thereby bringing about his own defeat soon after.[8] Modern military doctrine therefore stresses planning for the exploitation of a victory, which has become an integral phase in any operation, including the allocation of troops and means for this purpose as early as the planning stage.

In ancient times, exploitation was usually achieved not by fresh forces, which were more often than not unavailable, but by sheer surplus of moral stamina and physical force, enhanced by the natural elation that resulted from victory in battle.

In Joshua's case, the problem was to achieve maximum success while the moon was still visible in the west (the direction of the Valley of Ajalon) and not completely outshone by the sun rising in the east (the direction of Gibeon). In other words, he wanted to crush his foe before dawn had given way to full day and the enemy had cleared the defiles of the Beth-horon pass. Besides, the physical strain must have been almost beyond endurance by then, since after the former night's approach march and the day's battle, another night of an eleven-mile pursuit followed.

Joshua's prayer was heard, and under his leadership the pursuers drove themselves on and gave their foe no respite until the Amorites were totally dispersed. The last phase of the contest brought the Israelites through the Ajalon Valley, as far as the gates of Azekah, the Canaanite stronghold that later became one of the main fortresses of Judah. Altogether the Israelite warriors had traversed about thirty miles in forty-five to forty-eight hours, two-thirds or more of the time under battle conditions.

As the initial stretch of the Amorite flight was past Gibeonite territory, the Gibeonite farmers undoubtedly turned out in force to harass the fugi-

tives. The Bible speaks of the great stones from heaven that were cast down upon the escaping Canaanites. It is difficult to avoid an analogy with the retreat of the Austrians and later of the Burgundians in their wars against the Swiss (1386, 1474–7 respectively) and of the French in their efforts to quell the Tirolean resistance in 1809 (to cite only a few examples), when the population rolled large numbers of stones and boulders down into the defiles, killing and maiming some of their foes and blocking the retreat of the others. All these harassing actions go a long way towards explaining the length of this running battle. Both sides were probably driven more than once to a temporary standstill, caused by the enemy or by sheer exhaustion. If, on the other hand, we do not adhere to the text literally and take the stones to be a hailstorm, even this could have seriously impeded the Amorites' escape. Anyone who has had to brave a severe hailstorm in the Judean mountains in the open knows its disruptive effect.[9]

After Joshua had repelled the Canaanite counter-offensive in Judah, the Israelite tribes began to take possession of the sparsely settled mountain lands. From central Judah, Joshua fanned out in all directions and, according to the biblical account, we have to credit him with both the complete conquest of the central mountain massif and its western foothills, and the conquest of Galilee.[10]

Following the Bible's account, we learn that Joshua smashed the alliance

The Ajalon Valley, scene of Joshua's pursuit of the Amorites as well as of many subsequent Philistine–Israelite encounters in the time of the Judges and later.

Crushing the rulers of Galilee

A drawing of Canaanite war chariots, from a Late Canaanite stone relief.

of all the northern Canaanites, headed by Jabin, king of Hazor, the foremost city in these parts, at the Waters of Merom:

And when all these kings were met together, they came and pitched together at the Waters of Merom, to fight against Israel . . . So Joshua came, and all the people of war with him, against them by the Waters of Merom suddenly; and they fell upon them. And the Lord delivered them into the hand of Israel, who smote them . . . until they left them none remaining. And Joshua did unto them as the Lord bade him: he houghed their horses, and burnt their chariots with fire. (Josh. 11:5, 7–9)

This account is the first to mention the war chariot. This forerunner of the modern armoured fighting vehicle was one of the main armaments from the time of its introduction by the Hittites and Hyksos in the eighteenth century BC. It seems that its tactical employment was in many ways similar to that of medieval cavalry. But while the mounted and armoured knights relied mainly on the effect of shock, the ancient chariot – much like the modern armoured fighting vehicle – already combined shock with fire power, by mounting bows and javelin men alongside the charioteers. These were drawn from the *marianu*, who – like the medieval knight – formed a privileged caste of warriors in Canaanite society and were able to spend much of their time in the exercise of arms.[11] They thus formed the main offensive troops in what was otherwise an army of foot-soldiers. If it was difficult for the Israelite tribal contingents to face the Canaanite infantry on open ground in set battle, there was no way at all for the Israelites to counter their chariots by conventional methods. In the mountain campaign to take Gibeon, the southern kings had probably left their chariots in the plains, since they were not mentioned in the account of the fighting. On the other hand, Joshua's fervent prayer for an extension of the dawn makes additional sense if we add the possibility of an encounter with the chariots to his other worries.

In the campaign against the northerners, there was no escaping such an encounter. Joshua solved the problem in a way that was to set a precedent for subsequent Israelite commanders, as long as they were unable to pit chariots against chariots – or at least troops well- and long-versed in anti-chariot combat. He bided his time until he was able to surprise the Canaanites while they were encamped in the narrow gorge of the Merom brook. With no space to deploy their chariots, the vehicles were only a nuisance. If the horses were unharnessed either before or after watering, the chariots were actually a hindrance. Harnessed and frightened, the horses might even endanger the close ranks of foot-soldiers. With the chariots thus neutralized and temporarily out of action, Joshua came charging down the adjacent slopes and won another complete victory. This time surprise was probably achieved no less through stealth than through sheer speed.[12]

The choice of the valley of the Waters of Merom as the concentration point for the Canaanite allies and staging area for their combined offensive to oust the Israelites from their possessions west of the Jordan – and, more particularly, to stop them from infiltrating Galilee – was a good one. In the geographical introduction, we mentioned that the major axes of communication in Upper Galilee all converged upon the central ridge of Mount Merom and that from this pivot the roads radiated in a compass of 360 degrees all over the countryside. Therefore, by concentrating on Merom, the allied forces from all over Galilee met at a common, central crossroads. Moreover, they were able to direct their offensive in whatever direction they thought fit, which in itself would make pre-emptive defensive measures by Joshua difficult.

There remained but one course, which Joshua chose either by instinct or, according to the tenor of the biblical narrative, with due calculation and foresight: to wrest the initiative from his foe by lightning action. Thus, while the Canaanites were still preparing for the offensive, Joshua's counter-stroke, the prototype of a pre-emptive offensive, caught them off balance, before they could deploy on more open ground.

Since Joshua had no means whatsoever of using the captured chariots, he had no choice but to destroy them and their horses. This is a good indication of the technical and administrative backwardness of the conquering tribes compared with the Canaanites. It was not until the latter days of David's reign that the Israelites reached a stage when they were able to

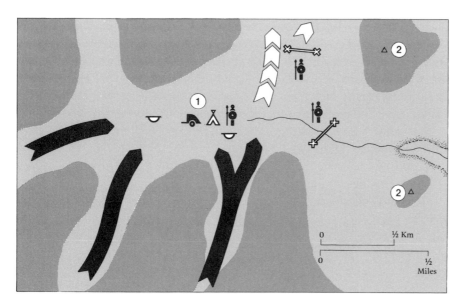

The Waters of Merom Campaign

1 Canaanite encampment.
2 Probable Canaanite observation posts.

operate chariots. Another weak spot in the military capabilities of the Israelites during the first stages of the conquest was their lack of siegecraft: 'But as for the cities that stood still in their strength [the fortified cities], Israel burned none of them' (Josh. 11:13).

These two factors made the Israelites concentrate first upon capturing the mountains, descending only gradually into the plains. This strategy is evident from the following passage:

The children of Joseph said, The hill is not enough for us: and all the Canaanites that dwell in the land of the valley have chariots of iron . . . And Joshua spake unto the house of Joseph . . . but the mountain shall be thine; for it is a wood [uninhabited woodland] . . . and the outgoings [the slopes] shall be thine: for thou shalt drive out the Canaanites, though they have iron chariots [which may be neutralized in these areas], and though they be strong. (Josh. 17:16–18)

Modern research does not support the idea that Joshua was the leader of the war against the northern Canaanites. It is quite possible that this achievement belongs to the following generation, or the one after it, which exploited Joshua's victories by further expansion. If so, the identity of the actual but anonymous leader was overshadowed in later annals by Joshua's surpassing renown. In either case, the military implications of the war are the same and our appreciation therefore holds good.

There has also been considerable argument in favour of dating the Waters of Merom campaign subsequent to Deborah's war, as an appendix to it or another version of the sagas that were later spun around the same general struggle.[13] The biblical narrator's mention of Hazor as the head of the anti-Israelite league in both the wars of Joshua and of Deborah, as well as the naming of Jabin as Hazor's king or military chief in both these instances, has been taken as evidence against the correctness of the biblical account. Even archaeological finds have not been able to settle the controversy decisively, although the excavator, Professor Yadin, maintains that there is proof that Hazor was destroyed both by Joshua and after Deborah's victory. To us it seems that as long as there is no clear archaeological proof against the claim that Joshua destroyed Hazor – and there seems to be a lot of evidence in favour of that reading – there is no logical reason to change the order of the two campaigns or to merge them into one. Deborah's war, as will be seen in the following pages, is easily understood as a sequel to the Merom campaign. Even Jabin need not have been the same person in the two accounts, but an earlier or later bearer of this name from the dynasty that ruled Hazor.

If one were to pass a final judgment on Joshua's generalship, one would have to place him very high indeed among the great captains of history. His clear strategic insight is demonstrated time and time again – for example, in his choice of Jericho as his first objective, and of its plain up to Gilgal as the initial base for the conquest of western Palestine, or in his alliance with the Gibeonites and his swift decision to come to the assistance of

(Opposite, above) 'The sun stood still, and the moon stayed' – a medieval stained-glass window depicts the battle of the Valley of Ajalon, in which Joshua crushed the fleeing Amorite army; *(below)* a stone model of a four-horse chariot from the sixth-century BC. *(Overleaf)* The dry, inhospitable Negev, southern gateway into Judah. It was also important as the land link for trade between the Red Sea and the Mediterranean.

Als Josue in einem Streit
Zu Kriegsmit werden woll die Zeit
Auff Sein Gebott Streckt sich der dag
Schaur wass der Wahre glaubber mag

Her Haubtman Oswald   Reyenenberg des Raths
Zug Berweffer   Landtvogt der
Grafschafft   Lugaris Fr
Veronica   Eltenerin
Deinst   gmach

beleaguered Gibeon, so as not to lose his vital foothold on the Judean mountains. The latter is also a fine example of the combined application of military action and diplomacy for the attainment of a political goal. Joshua also showed great strength of mind in adversity after the disastrous first attempt on Ai, particularly as he then boldly exploited the Israelites' defeat and its effect on their opponents to lure the enemy into a second encounter, in which Israelite victory was assured. His superb handling of the divided forces during the second Ai campaign and the timely and exact execution of the intricate manœuvres involved also indicate highly developed abilities of leadership and military assessment.

As a great soldier, Joshua was fully aware of the limitations imposed on him by the Israelites' inferiority in armament and training for set battle. Consequently, he based his tactics in battles such as that of Merom on the Israelites' qualities of speed, stealth and knowledge of the terrain, and so crushed the otherwise unbeatable enemy. It was this approach which therefore became the model for subsequent Israelite commanders.

(Opposite) 'The land of milk and honey': spring flowers by Lake Chinnereth (the Sea of Galilee).

3 THE WARS OF THE JUDGES

The period of the Judges was that of the final and complete entrenchment of the Israelites in the Holy Land, both to the west and the east of the Jordan. The Canaanites, who were divided among themselves, were unable to withstand the Israelites over an extended period; and as they became compressed into smaller and smaller enclaves, they either fell or submitted to the Israelites.

The era of the Judges was thus one of the heroic struggles of a basically simple tribal society against a sophisticated, though rather decadent, foe who nevertheless was often able to put up a fierce fight. In their endeavour to stave off the Israelites, the Canaanites were aided by the desert-fringe kingdoms of Trans-Jordan, which resented Israel's ascendency. Thus the Israelite tribes were welded together under constant pressure from all their neighbours and were led by warriors who 'judged' part or all of the tribes, though without interfering in their internal affairs.

The victory at the Waters of Merom gave the conquering tribes a permanent foothold in Galilee. In the process of settling down, they were aided by close affiliation with a number of the local clans which, according to extra-biblical sources, made up the heterogeneous population inhabiting the 'Galilee of the Nations' (as it was consequently called) prior to the final Israelite conquest. Whether these clans, such as the families assigned by the Bible to the tribes of Asher and Issachar, were blood-relations of the conquering tribes from before the Israelites' sojourn in Egypt, or had been amalgamated with them immediately after their entry into Galilee, does not alter the fact that they must have been a substantial force in accelerating Israel's takeover of much of the mountainous region of northern Canaan.[1]

Against this, the plains (i.e. the coastal area and the Jezreel Valley) were still securely in the hands of the Canaanites. Although the power of the two major towns on the south-western slopes of Lower Galilee, Shimron and Achshaph, had been broken after the Waters of Merom, another local ruler, 'the King of the people in Galilee', had stepped into the void (Josh. 12:23 according to the Vatican Codex). The geographical sequence in which the names of the vanquished rulers are given in Joshua 22 points to the fact that this new ruler succeeded in uniting the diverse ethnic groups of Lower

(Opposite) A Canaanite figure from Hazor.

This Late Canaanite ivory from Megiddo shows a ruler with servants, warriors and captives.

Galilee against the Israelite intruders. From the subsequent narrative in the Book of Judges 4 and 5, on which our material is based, it becomes evident that the people in Galilee inhabited the woodland of 'Haroshet of the Gentiles', which skirts the northern fringe of the Jezreel Valley.

The natural allies of 'the King of the people in Galilee' were the rulers of the remaining towns skirting the Jezreel Valley. The most prominent of these were the kings of Taanach, Megiddo and Jokneam. The rulers of Dor on the Mediterranean coast, of Kedesh in northern Naphtali and of Hazor lent this coalition depth and additional strength. Paramount among these remained, as before, the king of Hazor, Jabin, who was the proclaimed head of this league of northern Canaanite cities.[2]

The primary strength of the Canaanite petty kings was in their fortified towns. Yet by simply remaining behind their closed gates they could not subdue the Israelites. A more active course had to be pursued. Here their main military armament, the war chariot, was invaluable. Mobile patrols of charioteers could control the plains – and more specifically the roads – affording, if necessary, protection to trade caravans and all other road traffic. Israelite raiders could be tracked down or intercepted with speed, and even in hilly country the charioteers could provide a powerful addition to the foot-soldiers. To provide more cohesion to the coalition, the overall command of the combined effort was given to Sisera, the commander of Jabin's army, and probably a chieftain in his own right.

Things came to a head when Sisera occupied Haroshet of the Gentiles, which commanded the narrow pass from the Jezreel Valley into the coastal plain north of Haifa, as well as roads connecting Galilee with the Sea of Galilee and the Jordan Valley to the south.[3]

Deborah's war

At this time the loose tribal coalition of Israel was headed by Deborah, 'a prophetess, the wife of Lapidoth ... and she dwelt under the palm tree of Deborah ... in Mount Ephraim, and the children of Israel came up to her for judgment' (Judg. 4:4–5). From Miriam, the sister of Moses, down to Salome Alexandra, who headed the Hasmonean Kingdom during its last golden days (76–67 BC), women have played a prominent and often decisive role in Jewish history. Among them, Deborah stands out as the God-inspired fighter for her country's freedom and her people's survival. The veritable prototype of Joan of Arc, Deborah was decidedly her peer in the art of strategy and tactics. While Joan of Arc provided leadership and the example

The ruins of Megiddo.

of unflinching valour, it was Deborah who called for Barak – one of the most promising, or perhaps the most outstanding, of the tribal leaders from Kedesh in Naphtali – and said to him:

Hath not the Lord God of Israel commanded, saying, Go and draw toward Mount Tabor, and take with thee ten thousand men of the children of Naphtali and the children of Zebulun? And I will draw unto thee, to the river Kishon, Sisera the captain of Jabin's army, with his chariots and his multitude; and I will deliver him into thine hand. (Judg. 4:6–7)

In other words, Deborah gave Barak the gist of a complete and multi-phased plan of battle to throw off the yoke of the Canaanite league.

Before going into detail, it is important to stress once more Canaanite supremacy in a regular set battle, because of their chariots and their regular infantry ('chariots and multitude'), which consisted at least partly of heavily armed pikemen. The number of Sisera's chariots is given as 900. This number can be verified by comparing it with the number of Canaanite chariots quoted by Pharaoh Thutmose III as making up the armoured forces of his northern Canaanite foes during the battle of Megiddo in 1468 BC. Both numbers actually tally, since 924 chariots were in the booty from the

Megiddo battle, when the Canaanite coalition was somewhat larger and more prosperous.[4] Deborah's main concern must consequently have been how to neutralize the decisive arm in the enemy's host, his chariots.

With all this in mind Deborah developed a three-phased campaign. Phase one was the concentration of the tribal contingents from Naphtali and Zebulun, a total of not less than about 10,000 men, possibly 20,000, on Mount Tabor. Mount Tabor, as the concentration area, was an easily defensible base against which the chariots had no chance of success; a flanking position *vis-à-vis* hostile movement along the Jezreel Valley, with excellent visibility in all directions; and last but not least, a perfect staging area for a surprise attack on an enemy encamped at the foot of the mountain.

Phase two was based on the assumption that, when informed of the Israelite deployment, Sisera would concentrate all his available forces to contain Barak within the bounds of Mount Tabor, to try to force him eventually to battle in the open plain. Counting on this, Deborah proposed employing the forces she had gathered in Ephraim to draw Sisera away from his vigil opposite Mount Tabor towards the swampy area of the Kishon River in the western part of the Jezreel Valley.

In phase three, near the Kishon River, where the swampy soil in the rainy season hindered men, horses and chariots alike in their movement and manœuvrability, the Canaanites would be attacked simultaneously by Deborah's forces and those of Barak (who, having been relieved of the hostile threat, would be free to follow Sisera and fall upon his rear).

The exact course of Deborah's proposed diversion is not apparent from the biblical text. Logically it must have been a movement threatening the unprotected plain on the shores of Haifa Bay or thereabouts. Only a movement of that kind, endangering a major partner of the coalition such as Dor and its dependencies, would induce Sisera to abandon his guard of Barak, break camp and move speedily in the direction of the Kishon River, to secure the narrow passage between the Carmel and the Tivon hills leading from the Jezreel Valley into the coastal plain.

Barak accepted Deborah's proposals, but he balked at the idea of shouldering the main burden himself and would only agree to Deborah's plan if she accompanied the forces under his command. Perhaps he made this demand not out of timidity but out of chivalry: he may have wanted to draw the prophetess away from the dangerous role of leading the decoy. Deborah's famous reply was: 'I shall surely go with thee: notwithstanding the journey that thou takest shall not be for thine honour; for the Lord shall sell Sisera into the hand of a woman' (Judg. 4:9). The forces from Mount Ephraim were thus placed under the command of an unnamed captain, and Deborah joined the forces that stealthily collected at Kedesh-Naphtali and from there moved to Mount Tabor.

According to the Bible, Heber the Kenite, head of a semi-nomad clan related to the Israelites, gave away their concentration point to Sisera. Yet in view of subsequent developments and the behaviour of Jael, Heber's wife,

(*Opposite*) Mount Tabor, where Deborah defeated Sisera.

Deborah's Victory Over Sisera (phase one)

1a Barak concentrates his forces on Mount Tabor.
1b Deborah leads reinforcements to Mount Tabor.
1c Sisera's initial base camp at Haroshet Hagojim.
2 Sisera moves to attack the Israelites.
3 The second Israelite force, based on Mount Ephraim.

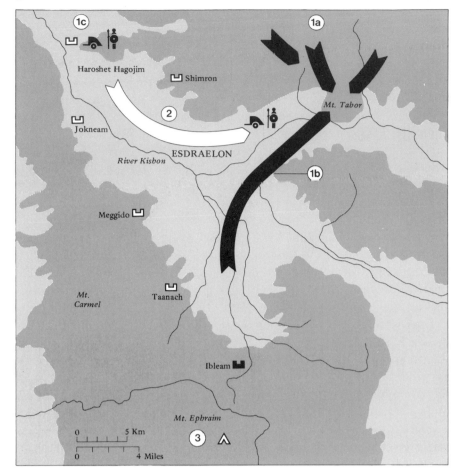

when she encountered the fugitive Canaanite commander, it seems that Heber must have been in collusion with Deborah, and his action was part of her overall plan to concentrate Sisera's attention on Mount Tabor and away from Mount Ephraim.

When Sisera learned of the Israelite concentration, he reacted as predicted and collected his entire army to oppose Deborah and Barak. The opposing forces watched each other for a few days. One may surmise that Deborah was waiting for rain to turn western Jezreel around the Kishon and its tributaries into a mire. When she received the confirmation she hoped for she gave Barak the sign to attack: 'Up, for this is the day in which the Lord hath delivered Sisera into thine hand' (Judg. 4:13). The diverting force of Ephraimites must have received the order to move some hours earlier. We do not know how far they got, but Deborah's song of victory after the battle (Judg. 5) mentions a crucial encounter with the kings of Canaan (verse 19) which took place 'in Taanach by the waters of Megiddo'. It seems that when they entered the Jezreel Valley (via present-day Jenin), the tribesmen from Mount Ephraim were intercepted by forces from the towns on the southern fringes of the valley, which had kept a constant guard against just such a contingency. A difficult encounter followed. At all events Sisera's attention was drawn to the new foe in his rear, which threatened the insufficiently protected regions in the west, and he moved to the assistance of his allies.

Some time after this, Deborah's command to attack was given. Her assault was effected from the foothills of Lower Galilee and caught Sisera's troops in the flanks or rear, or possibly both. At that point the Ephraimite force joined the main battle. 'And the Lord discomfited Sisera, and all his chariots, and all his host, with the edge of the sword before Barak' (Judg. 4: 15). A sudden downpour aided the Israelites considerably and helped turn Sisera's defeat into a rout. The Song of Deborah speaks explicitly of heavenly intervention and tells how the Kishon River rose and swept away in its torrent the enemy's horses and chariots. It should be explained that sudden rainfall, often at a substantial distance, can fill the dry river beds or turn docile streams into a roaring torrent that appears suddenly and sweeps down with deadly force on anything and anybody caught unawares. To this we must add the sudden local downpour that did much to hinder those of the much-dreaded 'chariots of iron' not caught by the torrent itself. Even the heavily

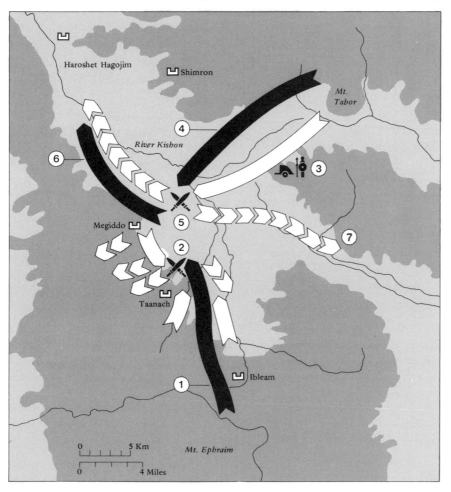

Deborah's Victory Over Sisera (phase two)

1 The second Israelite force moves to divert Sisera from Mount Tabor.
2 The diversionary force is intercepted by local villagers in the region of Taanach.
3 Sisera moves to assist the Canaanite villagers.
4 Deborah and Barak follow Sisera.
5 They overcome Sisera by the River Kishon.
6 Sisera's troops flee, pursued by Barak.
7 Sisera himself flees on foot, and is killed by Heber's wife.

armed infantry must have become bogged down and hampered in their movements.

When the Canaanite ranks became disorganized, Sisera panicked. Instead of trying to save as much as possible from the débâcle so as to fight another day, he jumped off his chariot and fled by foot to his ignominious death at the hands of Jael, wife of Heber the Kenite, in whose tent he sought refuge. 'So God subdued on that day Jabin the King of Canaan before the Children of Israel' (Judg. 4:23).

Gideon's campaign against the desert raiders

Like most of the narrative in the Book of Judges, the facts in chapters 7 and 8, which deal with the campaigns of Gideon, are overlaid with conflicting tribal traditions reflecting the inter-tribal rivalries of the age. Gideon's war against the clans located on the desert fringes was a consequence of the settlement of Israelite tribes in the area straddling the desert and the arable lands. It has become increasingly apparent that the climate of Palestine has not changed drastically from biblical times to the present. The six-inch isohyet (line connecting points of equal rainfall) passed then, as now, somewhere south of Beersheva and east of Amman (biblical Rabbath-bene-ammon), parallel to the line of the Hedjaz Railway (eight inches are the minimum for settled agricultural life other than by special irrigation). Consequently, minor fluctuations in precipitation which caused only temporary emergencies in the country north and west of the above lines might have most grave consequences in the semi-arid areas, with wells drying up, the cisterns emptying and pastures withering away.

In situations like these, the tribesmen roaming Sinai, the central Negev and eastern Trans-Jordan had no alternative but to make inroads into the fertile country. The longer the droughts lasted and the more severe their scope, the more desperate was the plight of the nomads and the fiercer became their razzias with the aim of occupying, along with their flocks and kindred, and for as long as possible, large pasturelands in the arable areas. Thus one of the primary functions of any central authority throughout the ages, that wished to guarantee safe and undisturbed life in Israel, was to organize and maintain permanent and competent border defences against the raids and invasions from the desert.[5]

During the period of the Judges, prior to the establishment of a centralized government in Israel, no such scheme could be contemplated, and consequently, as the Book of Judges puts it:

And the hand of Midian prevailed against Israel . . . And so it was, when Israel had sown, that the Midianites came up, and the Amalekites and the children of the east . . . and they encamped against them, and destroyed the increase of the earth, till thou come into Gaza, and left no sustenance for Israel, neither sheep, nor ox, nor ass. For they came up with their cattle and their tents, and they came as grasshoppers for multitude; for both they and their camels were without number; and they entered into the land to destroy it. (Judg. 6:1-5)

The answer of the southern tribes, Judah and Simeon, to these threats seems initially to have been of a passive nature. On the approach of the raiders, the Israelite farmers and husbandmen, who must have had some kind of warning system by lookouts posted with a wide field of vision, would hastily withdraw into pre-constructed lairs and refuges (Judg. 6:2), leaving their villages and fields to the nomads.

Encouraged by this state of affairs, or possibly driven by a worse drought at home, the desert tribes staged a wholesale invasion of northern Palestine, by galloping on their swift dromedaries through Gilead, east of the Jordan, and penetrating into the Jezreel Valley. At this stage of imminent disaster, the northern tribes chose a course different from that of their southern kinsmen. Apparently their policy was inspired by one single individual, Gideon, the judge-leader of the clan of Aviezer, which had settled at Ophrah (present-day Afula?). Hearing that the vast nomad host had encamped at the northern piedmont of the Hill of Moreh and around the spring of Endor, Gideon decided on offensive action and succeeded in mobilizing tribal contingents from Asher, Zebulun, Naphtali and Manasseh.

We are not told the nature of Gideon's deliberations while waiting for the concentration of his forces, but his main problems are clear. In daylight there was no chance whatsoever of luring his enemy to battle. In adverse circumstances swift dromedary-riders could easily disengage from their adversaries and press on to further looting. On the other hand if the lightly armed Israelite infantry were caught at a disadvantage, and especially if their ranks broke to enable the flexible raiders to penetrate them, they would be severely mauled.

Gideon's only chance lay in surprising his enemy while dismounted and off guard – in other words, to attack the raiders at night. To do so he needed a picked force small enough to minimize the danger of noise and premature discovery. The greater part of the force could consequently be employed to block the flight westwards of the surprised raiders and to manœuvre them into a vast killing ground between Mount Gilboa, the eastern slopes of the Samarian ridge and the Jordan. There (read 'Gilboa' instead of 'Gilead' and 'turn' instead of 'return' in Judges 7:3) those of Gideon's troops who were not engaged in the initial surprise attack could be deployed to swoop down upon the retreating Midianites, who were being driven on by Gideon's pursuit from the rear.

From the ensuing events we can gather that these were the outlines of Gideon's plan, and we find him occupied with choosing from about 32,000 men a shock-troop of 300 for his night attack.[6] By a spark of inspiration (Judg. 7:4–7) Gideon chose his small task force by observing the habits and behaviour of his men while he led them in full daylight to the spring of Harod where they might have been attacked at any time by the enemy, which could well have mounted a guard on the summit of the Hill of Moreh. The men chosen were those who, in spite of their thirst, remained cautious of the presence of the enemy nearby and did not abandon their weapons even when drinking, which they managed to do by lying down upon their bellies and lapping up the water with their tongues.

(*Overleaf*) Mount Moreh, scene of Gideon's defeat of the Midianite raiders.

After having built and deployed his forces according to plan, Gideon decided upon a personal reconnaissance of the enemy and his positions so as to ensure complete surprise. According to the biblical narrative (Judg. 7: 10–14), only Puah, his personal swordbearer, accompanied Gideon on this mission, which culminated in infiltrating the enemy encampment and listening to the conversations. Consequently Gideon made his final plans. Each soldier was provided with a burning torch hidden in an earthen jar and a trumpet (or, more probably, some carried trumpets instead of torches). The small force was divided into three parties, which approached the Midianite camp from three directions simultaneously (at least one must have scaled the summit of the Hill of Moreh and approached straight down towards the enemy encampment below). Upon reaching the hostile perimeter, Gideon gave the pre-arranged signal, and with a general shout and blowing of trumpets the attackers broke the earthen vessels and probably threw the torches at the tents of the nomads, frightening man and beast alike. In the ensuing mêlée, and blinded by the sudden glare, the raiders panicked and here and there even mistakenly attacked each other. Finally they dispersed in flight and were driven, as planned, into the gorge between the mountains and the Jordan River. Tabbath and Abel-meholah seem to have served as barrier forts denying the fleeing nomads freedom to disperse and driving them on southwards.

While the men of Manasseh had been alerted earlier to join with forces from Naphtali and Asher to harass and fall upon the enemy in flight, it was

The Spring of Harod, where Gideon selected his shock troops by observing the soldiers' behaviour as they approached to drink.

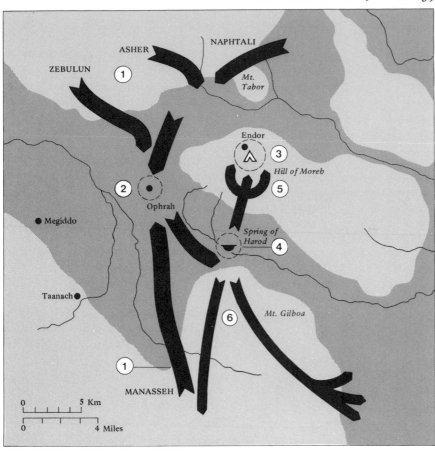

The Battle of the Spring of Harod

1 The Israelite tribes converge to meet the nomadic Midianite invasion.
2 The Israelite concentration area at Ophrah.
3 The nomad camp at Endor.
4 The Israelite army moves to the Spring of Harod; Gideon selects his shock troops for a surprise attack.
5 A sudden three-pronged assault throws the Midianites into confusion.
6 The fleeing enemy is driven into the Jordan River gorge.

only then that Gideon gave a last-minute alert to the clans of Ephraim settled around the main fords of the Jordan in the Adam area, calling upon them to occupy the fords and block the passage to the routed nomads. They did so with partial success, and in the ensuing struggle to gain the eastern shores of the Jordan, two nomad chieftains were killed. It is quite likely that inter-tribal animosity made Gideon wait until the last possible moment before calling in the Ephraimites, and had he done so sooner, the Midianite rout might have been more complete. The Ephraimites told him so, and he had a hard time appeasing their anger.

Even worse was the reaction of the people of the two great Gileadite towns to the east of the Adam fords, Succoth and Penuel, who suspected Gideon's political aspirations and refused to feed the pursuers. In spite of these drawbacks, however, Gideon pressed on and succeeded once more in surprising his enemy not far from the border of Ammon. Somewhere in the mountains near Jogbehah the exhausted desert raiders stopped to rest, assuming themselves at a safe distance from Gideon and near the neutral or, in this instance, even friendly territory of Ammon. Details are lacking, but we know that Gideon succeeded in surprising and annihilating his enemy: 'Thus was

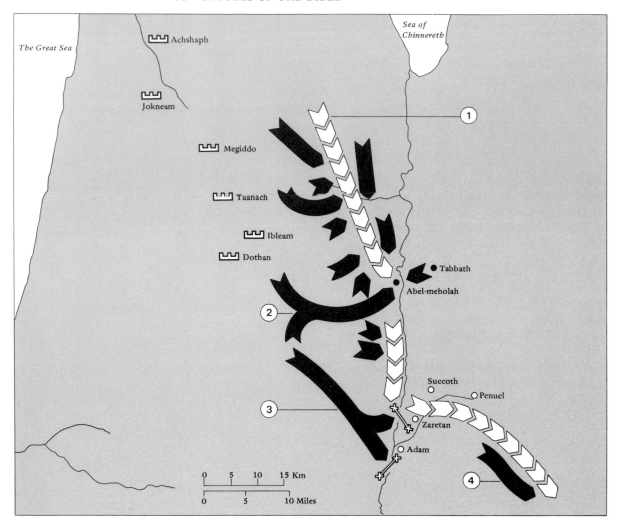

Gideon Pursues the Midianites

1 The Midianites flee after defeat by the Israelite shock troops.
2 The main Israelite army attacks them in their flank.
3 The Ephraimites secure the fords over the Jordan.
4 Gideon continues to chase the Midianites and finally overtakes and annihilates them.

Midian subdued before the children of Israel, so that they lifted up their heads no more. And the country was in quietness forty years in the days of Gideon' (Judg. 8:11).

If we look for the formula of Gideon's success, we recognize the same ingredients as in the former campaigns waged by the early Israelite commanders described in these pages: daring, swift, mobile action; taking the offensive; and an unconventional approach. Gideon showed particular astuteness by attacking at night, when his enemy was in no position to use his advantage, his mobile archers and pikemen. He was also prepared to persevere in face of all odds, including internal discord, once he had gained an initial success, so that he could turn this tactical success into a lasting strategic victory by driving home his pursuit and forcing a second, decisive battle on the retreating foe.

The decision to split his forces and to stage the attack at the Hill of Moreh with only 300 men is an early example of what military men describe as a 'calculated risk'. This decision was based largely upon exact and personally checked intelligence about the enemy's location, dispositions and morale. Since he had personally overheard the Midianites' doubts and worries at being encamped deep in Israelite territory Gideon was able to conceive on the spot the details of his attack, which aimed at playing on his enemies' superstitions and fears.

One problem remains to be solved. Why did those quick, mobile raiders give Gideon the time to concentrate his forces and prepare for battle on his terms? In other words, how did they come to remain encamped, against their custom, for at least a few days on the same spot at the foot of the Hill of Moreh, instead of pushing on westwards? The answer lies in Gideon's remark when refusing to grant the captured Midianite chieftains their lives: 'What manner of men were they whom ye slew at Tabor? . . . They were my brethren, even the sons of my mother . . .' (Judg. 8:18–19).

The following reconstruction of events seems the most feasible. When he learned of the Midianite approach, Gideon sent a hastily assembled force, conceivably small in number, to block the enemy advance in the narrow valley between Mount Tabor and the Hill of Moreh. This force, whose mission was to stop the enemy advance at all costs and gain for Gideon the time needed to gather and deploy his forces, was built largely round his own kinsmen and was probably led by his brothers. In the ensuing encounter, his brothers lost their lives, but the passage remained blocked.

By positioning themselves on the lower slopes of Mount Tabor, this small Israelite contingent also served as a decoy to ensure Gideon's move to the rear of the Midianite base in perfect concealment, as well as an effective brake on their further movement westwards. Moving westwards without at first dislodging the Israelites in their front would have opened the Midianite flank to an Israelite attack and enabled the latter effectively to block the Midianite line of retreat. This is exactly what happened to the French force of General Kleber 2,500 years later. It came close to being annihilated while unwittingly pushing through the same defile, which was held in a flanking position by the Turks. The composition and skilful handling of the small northern blocking force was thus an integral part of Gideon's planning, and an essential prerequisite for its success.

Gideon's son Abimelech has achieved notoriety for his cruel fratricide. His historical importance is that he was the first to attempt to impose some kind of centralized hereditary rule on ancient Israel, or parts of it (Judg. 9). His campaigns have to be mentioned in our context insofar as they demonstrate the progress in Israelite siegecraft. Following Abimelech's war against the Shechemites (Judg. 9:22–45), we find that it was still mainly by stealth and ruse, and contact with allies from within a besieged city, that he tried to overcome its defences. During the height of the contest he succeeded in drawing off a large number of the defenders from a city and so managed to enter through the gate. We are reminded of Joshua's stratagem at Ai, yet as late as 1799, General Reynier, lacking a sufficient siege train, could not think of any better way to capture the citadel of El Arish.[7]

Abimelech's next moves prove that he had already mastered the technique of using fire to smoke out defenders of smaller fortifications, as well as to set fire to their wooden components, especially their most vulnerable spots – the gates (Judg. 9:46–9). It was in one such operation that he met his death: 'And Abimelech came unto the tower [the citadel (?) of Tebez] . . . and went hard unto the door of the tower to burn it down with fire. And a certain woman cast a piece of millstone upon Abimelech's head and all to brake his scull' (Judg. 9:52–3). Thus Abimelech died as violently as he had lived. Yet his death did have a kind of pathos: 'Then he called hastily unto the young man, his armourbearer, and said unto him: Draw thy sword and slay me, that men say not of me, a woman slew him. And his young man thrust him through and he died' (Judg. 9:54).

4 FOUNDING THE KINGDOM AND THE STANDARDIZED ARMY

Not much later than the Israelites, another nation began its assault upon the *de facto* Egyptian province of Canaan: the Philistines.[1] The direction of their penetration, however, was diametrically opposite to that of the Israelites, as they came from the west. The Philistines were of Aegean stock and were therefore related to both the Minoan and the Mycenaean peoples of the Mediterranean islands and mainland Greece and to the latter-day 'classical Greeks'. They belonged to the family of 'Sea Peoples' that swept down the shores of the south-eastern Mediterranean in swift ships, with fire and sword, to capture new lands for settlement. Their mode of operation resembled that of the later Norsemen and Vikings. In the early twelfth century BC, the Sea Peoples attempted to conquer Egypt, and it was only after major efforts that Pharaoh Rameses III succeeded in breaking their assault in a long-drawn-out and bloody sea battle in the Delta (*c.* 1190 BC).

After that encounter, the Philistines seem to have come to some kind of *modus vivendi* with Egypt, and they settled with the blessing of the Pharaonic authorities on the south-western shores of Canaan. At first they not only accepted Egyptian sovereignty but served as garrisons to the Pharaohs in their last attempts at tying Palestine to their domains, prior to the final Israelite takeover. But soon, with Egypt's power on the wane, the Philistines became virtually independent and pushed out into the plain of southern Judah in order to guarantee themselves ample hinterland.

It was in this endeavour that they clashed with the Israelites, who were attempting to gain a foothold in the same region. The Israelites had occupied the western strategic gates to both the Judean mountains and the Judean foothills, the Shephelah. Here they clashed with the Philistines, and here, where the modern highway from Jaffa and Ramleh to Jerusalem passes the hills between Zorah and Eshtaol, the tribe of Dan faced the Philistines directly. The Shephelah was the setting for the exploits of Samson, whose final downfall reflected the temporary ascendancy of the Philistines (Judg. 13–16).[2]

While in most of Palestine the Israelites were, on the whole, victorious, by the middle of the eleventh century dark clouds were gathering on the Philistine front. The signs were all the more ominous as the Philistines were

The coming of the Philistines

(*Overleaf, top*) The sea battle between the Philistines and the armies of Pharaoh Rameses III, *c.* 1190 BC. (*Overleaf, bottom*) A Philistine iron dagger from a tomb at Tell Farah.

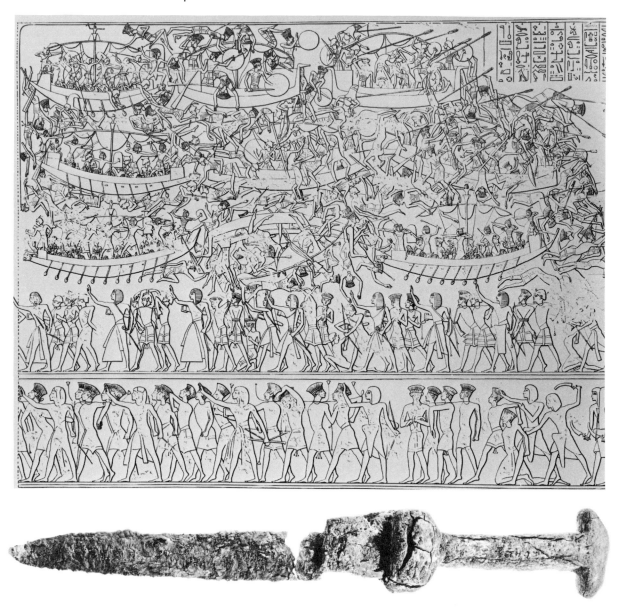

Samuel

master iron-smiths and provided their warriors with iron weapons, which the Israelites almost totally lacked.

This happened during the time of Samuel 'the Seer', who combined the attributes and tasks of priest, prophet and judge. The Philistine menace to the existence of Israel became very real during his leadership. Samuel's pious zeal notwithstanding, the loose tribal league of the Israelites proved itself incapable of exercising the enduring and concerted effort necessary to stem the Philistine tide, especially as the superiority of the Philistine armament began to outweigh the native Israelite valour. Thus, in spite of the Israelite victories under Samuel, such as the second battle of Eben-ezer (1 Sam. 7),

in his latter days we find the Philistines established in the heart of the Judean mountain redoubt. A permanent Philistine garrison was stationed in the stronghold of Gibeah (the later Gibeah of Saul), three miles north of Jerusalem, in easy striking distance of both the western and southern slopes of northern Judah and Benjamin. Small wonder that the tenor of the relevant biblical passages (1 Sam. 7:7–8) proves that the Israelites had lost much of their former self-confidence, one of the mainsprings of their victories until then. Moreover, the Philistines seem to have achieved some kind of control in Judah, as they had made the forging of iron a Philistine preserve: 'Now there was no smith found throughout all the land of Israel: for the Philistines

Excavations at Ashdod: in the foreground, remains of the Canaanite city, in the background a section of the Philistine fort.

said, Lest the Hebrews make them swords or spears: but all the Israelites went down to the Philistines, to sharpen every man his share, and his coulter, and his axe, and his mattock' (1 Sam. 13:19–20). This general state of weakness was naturally exploited by Israel's neighbours east of the Jordan as well; and shortly after, when the Judean mountains – Israel's heartland west of the Jordan – were penetrated by the Philistines, Gilead, the Israelite heartland to the east of the river, came under similar pressure from the Ammonites.

The first Jewish king

At this stage, a great historical truism – that the fortunes of nations are often shaped by their ability to stand up to challenges by breaking with their conventional modes of conducting affairs – was proved. Against the warnings and advice of Samuel, who extolled the existing order and the old Israelite political ideal of a theocratic-democratic tribal amphictyony, the tribal leaders remained adamant in their demand for change: 'Nay; but we will have a king over us; that we also may be like all the [neighbouring] nations and that our king may judge us, and go out before us, and fight our battles' (1 Sam. 8:20). In bowing to the healthy instincts of the people in quest of a permanent and single sovereign leader in war – and thus, by necessity, also in peace – Samuel proved his magnanimity no less than his wisdom. After accepting the popular verdict, he tried to choose the right leader, one whom the unruly and independent tribes would accept even after their initial elation had worn off.

His choice fell on Saul, not mainly because 'there was not among the children of Israel a goodlier person than he: from his shoulders and upward he was higher than any of the people' (1 Sam. 9:2), but because by choosing a suitable person from the tribe of Benjamin, the smallest of the twelve tribes, he hoped to neutralize the rivalry of the larger ones. We are reminded of the much later choice of the insignificant House of Habsburg to assume the throne of the German Empire following much the same reasoning. Unfortunately for Saul, one of the most tragic heroes of the Old Testament, Samuel's stratagem succeeded only in part, and much of the internal unrest towards the end of Saul's reign, as well as his quarrels with David and the latter's succession, can be understood against the background of tribal rivalries.

In his second reason for choosing Saul as Israel's first anointed king, Samuel was more fortunate. Because he came from a tribe that suffered more directly than all the others, as it was plagued by the constant presence of a Philistine occupation force on its territory, Saul had the strongest motivation to raise the banner of freedom.

Saul's first concern, however, was in the east. The town of Jabesh-gilead had been under Ammonite siege for some time and, failing immediate aid, its defenders were ready to submit to Nahash, king of Ammon, and permit a hostile settlement in the midst of Israelite Trans-Jordan. Immediate action was clearly indicated, but the demoralizing particularism of the tribes was already so widespread that Saul found it necessary to use the threat of a

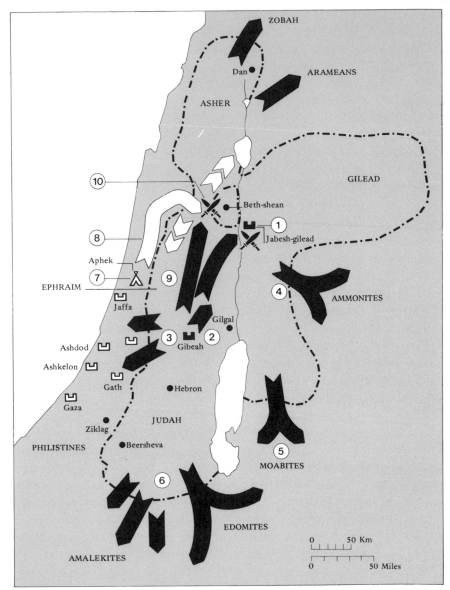

The Wars of Saul

1 Saul's first campaign to rescue besieged Jabesh-gilead.
2 The Michmash campaign.
3 The wars against the Philistines.
4&5 Wars against the eastern neighbours.
6 Campaigns to secure the southern borders.
7 Philistine concentration for the Gilboa campaign.
8 Philistine invasion of the Esdraelon.
9 Saul's last campaign: he moves to Mount Gilboa.
10 Saul is killed at the battle of Mount Gilboa.

special economic punishment to compel all the able-bodied men to join the national host: 'And he took a yoke of oxen, and hewed them in pieces, and sent them throughout the coast of Israel . . . saying, Whosoever cometh not forth after Saul and after Samuel, so shall it be done unto his oxen' (1 Sam. 11:7). The threat worked, and 330,000 men were mustered at Bezek. Incidentally, we have here a number with the ring of authenticity to it, which also permits us to calculate the total population of ancient Israel on the eve of the foundation of the Israelite monarchy at about 750,000 souls. The number 330,000 for the actual muster, never mind the force that went out to battle, is, of course, vastly inflated. It must be understood as the total male population above the age of sixteen or so, which brings us to the above estimate of the general population. Of this a conscription of ten per cent is the maximum a well-organized community was able to turn out – a number comparable with modern times. In Saul's initial campaigns, no more than half that number (i.e. 16,500) would have made up the whole host.

The details of the relief of Jabesh-gilead are not given in the biblical account, but the well-known ingredients of Israelite tactics are all there: the swift approach by quick night march, the division of forces (this time into three independent formations), the surprise to the unsuspecting enemy and his subsequent rout. It should be emphasized that the division of forces, so common in ancient and later oriental warfare,[3] presupposes, *inter alia*, confidence in the divisional commanders: sufficient means, however primitive, of guaranteeing the commitment of the divided forces to their allotted tasks; and the ability to wield a united tactical effort. As long as all the subdivisions of the force are committed to action at the same time, the commander-in-chief retains the means to influence, or even to decide, the outcome of the battle. Yet in spite of all these considerations, accepted military doctrine has often held that the division of forces into tactically independent formations is too dangerous. The Roman battle at Cannae (216 BC), with a single mass of 85,000 legionaries, is perhaps an extreme example of this attitude. Yet even the military thinking of the eighteenth century was swayed by this idea, and no less a person than Frederick II of Prussia, one of the greatest military leaders of all times, subscribed to the theory of the single, concentrated battle formation.

Creating the nucleus of a standing army

The relief of Jabesh-gilead came in the nick of time. The lesson derived from the campaign was the need for a constantly armed force, ready for immediate action, at the direct disposal of the king, to be strengthened by the tribal contingents as quickly as these could be mobilized. Accordingly, Saul created the first nucleus of a standing army, by choosing 3,000 men to serve with him permanently. This force was divided into two formations, the smaller one of 1,000 men commanded by his eldest son, Jonathan, whose first major exploit was the conquest of Gibeah and the Philistine garrison there.

The Michmash campaign

Jonathan's action was a major threat to Philistine control of the Judean heartland. Consequently, a large Philistine expeditionary force, including chariots and perhaps even a cavalry corps, was despatched to reimpose their authority and quell the Israelite attempt to establish an independent kingdom. After moving through the Beth-horon pass, the Philistines established a fortified base at Michmash. The choice of Michmash was a daring but well-calculated move. By pushing on to the eastern side of the Judean plateau, the Philistines commanded the ascents to the mountains of Benjamin from the Judean desert, the traditional staging area of the Israelite forces. Michmash straddled the eastern branch of the watershed road, the main north–south artery of the Cis-Jordanian mountains, and flanked its eastern branch, in easy distance for blocking forces. Furthermore, by making their base in the very centre of Benjamin, the Philistines openly challenged

Saul's authority and competence.

The newly regained confidence of the Israelites was again shattered by this prompt action; and although Saul had wisely chosen the difficult-to-traverse (for the uninitiated) Judean desert as the concentration area for the tribal conscripts, a general disintegration of the Israelite forces began even before the first contacts were made with the enemy. According to 1 Samuel 13–14, Saul took up a position opposite Michmash, at Geba, with only 600 men after it had been secured by Jonathan and the regulars. The Philistines must have had reliable intelligence about the open quarrel between king and priest (Saul and Samuel), and about the many desertions and the flight of parts of the populace into Trans-Jordan. Consequently, they decided to accelerate the destruction of the fledgling kingdom by despatching three flying columns to devastate the countryside on the central plateau. To counteract the weakening of their forces, they kept a blocking force at the 'passage of Michmash', the saddle that connects Michmash with Geba and, via Geba, with the western branch of the watershed road. Topography and the biblical narrative combine to fix its exact location between

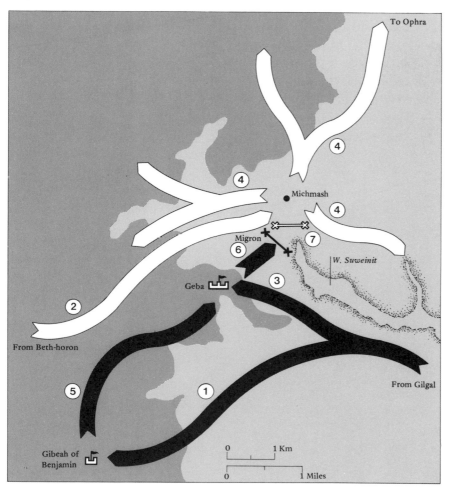

The Dislodgement of the Philistines

1 Jonathan takes Gibeah.
2 The Philistines take Michmash.
3 Saul moves his troops to Geba.
4 The Philistines send out flying columns to devastate the countryside.
5 Jonathan joins Saul at Geba.
6 The Israelites advance and set up a blocking position at Migron.
7 The Philistine blocking position.

the head of the precipice of Wadi Suweinit and the foot of Michmash hill.[4]

Saul did not dare to attack even the weakened Philistine camp, but, hoping to mitigate the extent of the enemy's raids into the Israelite hinterland, he moved his forces out of Geba into a position directly opposite Michmash, at Migron (Tell Miriam). Although his abstention from further activity cancelled out much of the initial threat exercised by this movement, the Philistine troops in Michmash, and especially those manning the blocking position in the passage, must have kept a constantly watchful eye for any telltale sign of hostile movement from the Israelite position at Migron.

Jonathan used this state of affairs for a dare-devil stratagem that by its sheer audacity promised success. Accompanied solely by his shield-bearer, he made a wide detour to the south and appeared to the men of the Philistine blocking force as a man unconnected with the Israelite host who exploited the lull in the fighting to come out of his hiding-place and attend to private matters. Therefore, after shouting some insults at 'the Hebrews [who had] come forth of the holes where they had hid themselves' (1 Sam. 14:11), the twenty-odd (?) soldiers of the Philistine blocking force returned their attention to the Israelite positions opposite. Jonathan and his shield-bearer then disappeared into the deep gorge of Wadi Suweinit, and when they reached the cliff near the Philistine positions, 'Jonathan climbed up upon his hands and upon his feet, and his armour-bearer after him' (ibid., v. 13) and, by their sudden assault from behind, both men were able to slay a considerable number of the utterly surprised enemy and beat the rest into a

Michmash: the site is the hill on the left of the picture. The Philistine blocking force was on the central low hill. The steep cliffs, through which Jonathan and his swordbearer made their approach, are at the head of the Suweinit gorge and are hidden between the two hills on the right of the picture.

wild retreat. This, in turn, surprised the garrison of Michmash so that they mistook the fugitives for charging Israelites, and general confusion and subsequent panic ensued. Saul put this confusion to good use in a general frontal assault on Michmash. Enemy resistance seems to have been broken almost immediately. Cut off from their straight line of retreat, the Philistines fled first in a northerly direction towards Bethel and only then did they turn westwards. All along the way the Israelite farmers came out of the hiding-places to which they had escaped from the enemy's raiding parties and wrought havoc upon the fugitives. Rather like the French in Spain during the Peninsular War (1808–14) or the British in Afghanistan in 1842, more Philistines must have fallen during that tortuous retreat than during the previous battle.

In retrospect, there is no doubt that the battle of Michmash was one of the most decisive in Israelite history and that it was Jonathan's 'two-man action' which paved the way for the victory that gave Saul the necessary respite from his most dangerous enemies and enabled him to establish a unified royal dominion over most of both Cis- and Trans-Jordan: 'So Saul took the kingdom over Israel, and fought against all his enemies on every side, against Moab, and against the children of Ammon, and against Edom, and against the kings of Zobah . . . and whithersoever he turned himself, he vexed them' (1 Sam. 14:47).

One of the chief, albeit unwritten, tenets of the geopolitics governing Cis-Jordan has always been that whoever wants to provide peace and security

The Battle of Michmash

1 The Israelite blocking position.
2 Jonathan and his swordbearer trick the Philistine blocking forces and then make a surprise attack on them.
3 Saul's advance guard exploits the ensuing confusion to attack the camp at Michmash.
4 The flight of the Philistines.
5 Israelite farmers harass the fleeing enemy.

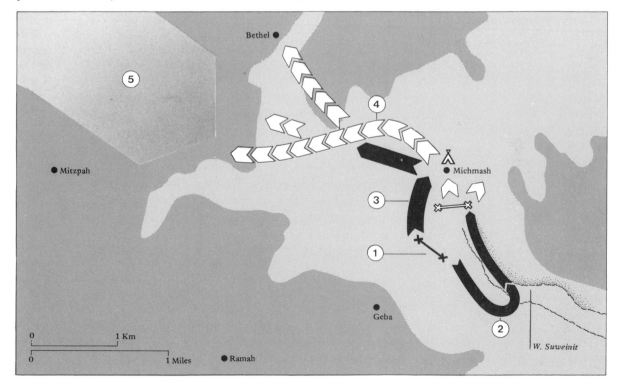

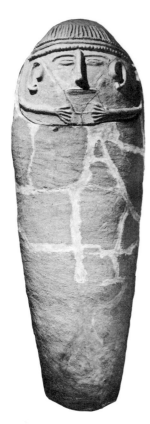

A Philistine sarcophagus found at Beth-shean.

Mount Gilboa: Saul's last battle

to those living on the arable land must fend off the inroads of the nomads roaming the desert (the Negev). Consequently, it was naturally Saul who began the continuous defence of the borders of the desert, which was later to be based upon a closely woven net of strong fortifications that lasted from Solomonic times to the Middle Ages.[5]

No details remain of Saul's war against the Amalekite nomads in the Negev. Similarly, his frequent campaigns against the never completely subdued Philistines are shrouded in obscurity. The battlefield was most probably the Shephelah, and more particularly the mouth of one or another of the valleys that led out of the mountain bastion on to the plain. A typical example was the battle of the Valley of Elah. The Israelite army had by that time adopted the construction of well-organized, semi-permanent and possibly fortified camps as bases for prolonged campaigns. By pitching their camp in the valley, they effectively barred the advance of the Philistines into the mountains. The camp was well organized with special zones for training, ordnance and supply, which were overseen by special details. In spite of these improvements, however, the Israelite host was still inferior to the Philistines in armament of all kinds, and it completely lacked chariots. Consequently, Saul bided his time and did not push out into the open plain.

This was the background of the famous duel between David and Goliath, the giant champion of the Philistines who, clad in full Homeric panoply, daily challenged the Israelites to a trial of arms. In an action similar to Jonathan's exploit at Michmash – in that it was a single-handed feat – David alone, armed only with a shepherd's sling and stones, was the cause of complete consternation among the Philistines. And again, as he had at Michmash, Saul used this critical moment to launch his general assault and rout his enemy. The Philistines were again beaten but not crushed. In the ensuing years, when revived tribal rivalries, disputes between Saul and Samuel and the break between Saul and David did much to weaken the recently unified nation, the Philistines gathered strength and plotted their revenge.

Their hour came some time after the death of Samuel.[6] The Philistine host assembled at Aphek in the Shephelah, but their plan was to try a new approach. After their many unsuccessful attempts to penetrate the central mountain massif from the west, the Philistines planned a major enveloping movement by marching northwards along the Plain of Sharon (the coastal plain) and then through one of the passes of the Carmel range into the Jezreel Valley, so as to enter the central mountain massif at Ir-ganim (present-day Jenin) and move southwards along the plateau. While manœuvring in the Jezreel Valley, the Philistines could hope for support from the Canaanite cities which had not yet been captured by the Israelites. These special ties must have existed, since the cities had formerly been garrisoned by Philistine troops in Pharaonic pay (Beth-shean being the most prominent example).[7]

Saul had the advantage of the interior lines. Accordingly, he waited to see in what direction the Philistines would move. After he was sure of their intentions, he moved his forces parallel to theirs on the plateau and then took up a blocking position that flanked the ascent to Ir-ganim in the lower foothills of the Gilboa range.

Why was no attempt made to block the Philistine passage through the difficult Carmel defiles? The answer can be inferred from the choice of Aphek as the assembly point for the Philistine host. By convening on Aphek, the Philistines posed a direct threat to the Judean mountains, which must have caused Saul to detach at least some of his observation forces to guard the western approaches. There is no mention of any planned Philistine diversionary movement, obvious as such a move would appear to any modern observer. However, there was a report of a Philistine detachment and subsequent troop movement, which – however unintentional on the part of the Philistines – must have misled the Israelite observation troops. I Samuel 29 narrates that David and his corps, who had come to Aphek to join David's liege lord, Achish of Gath, were judged unreliable by the 'tyrants'[8] and were sent back to their base at Ziklag, which Achish had allocated to David as a fief after he had escaped Saul's persecution. David's return march from Aphek to Ziklag led past some of the obvious invasion routes into Judah, such as the Valley of Elah and the Valley of Sorek, which must have kept Saul's men on their guard. Only after certifying that no stab in his back was intended could Saul rush to meet the northern threat, which gave the

Mount Gilboa, site of Saul's last battle.

Philistine host the time necessary to effect an unmolested passage through the Carmel gorges.

The outcome of the ensuing battle was decided by the Philistine chariots. Saul was forced to retreat up Mount Gilboa. But even there his position became untenable. The chariot-mounted Philistine archers followed close on his heels up the easily traversable western slope and subjected the Israelites on the flat plateau to constant and effective 'fire'. When Saul was convinced that all was lost, he chose to fall upon his sword rather than be captured by his enemy. For the moment it seemed that the Philistine goal had been achieved at last, and that the Israelite kingdom would be broken up again into its tribal components. But the Philistine triumph was short-lived. The years of Saul's reign had taught the tribes that only in unity lay strength and all the economic advantages that went with it. Although initially there must have been wide consternation throughout Israel, David, who quickly became the new focus of attention, used the story of Saul and his son's death to revive flagging spirits. His lamentation for Saul and Jonathan (2 Sam. 1:17–27), whose explicit purpose was to arouse the soldierly spirit of 'the children of Judah' to renew the struggle for freedom, has survived as one of the most moving and stirring elegies in world literature. David's words did much to rekindle Israel's energy and hope, although his initial rule may have been under some kind of Philistine overlordship.

5 THE UNITED MONARCHY

King David's reign is remembered in Jewish tradition as the first Golden Age of the Jewish people. It was David who established the Israelite empire that extended from 'the entering in of Hamath unto the river of Egypt [Wadi El Arish]' or, in another version, 'from the river of Egypt unto the great river the river Euphrates'. Although this empire disintegrated about eighty years after its foundation and was revived only for some thirty years in the days of Uzziah of Judah and Jeroboam II of Israel (c. 785–750 BC), David succeeded in welding the Israelite tribes together into a national entity of such coherence that even after the kingdom split into two, the Jewish people were established for over one thousand years – with only short intervals – as the dominant factor on the Palestinian land-bridge.

The Bible provides us with enough details to reconstruct the fascinating personality of the king. Modern Europeans might find in his nature something of a Robin Hood, a Percival, an Arthur, a Richard the Lionheart and a Lear all combined. Medieval chivalry chose David as one of its main paragons from among *les neuf-preux*.[1] Jewish lore has accorded him the epithet 'Ahuvya' (beloved of God or God's darling). Yet if we attempt to form a coherent picture of David's military campaigns, not to speak of their details, we find disappointingly little information.

David's personal exploits – first in the service of Saul, later as a leader of a band of outlaws, and still later as a vassal to Achish, king of Gath – are beyond the scope of these pages. It must be stressed, however, that these narratives provide us with a much more detailed picture of David's apprenticeship before he attained supreme command than we have for any of the other biblical captains. In those days very little, if any, schooling in theory was provided for a military leader, and whatever knowledge he acquired, or personal talents he developed, were the outcome solely of the personal experience he gained during his formative years.

Thus we do know from the Bible that David had attained proficiency as a fighter and as a commander of regular forces while still serving in Saul's army. Later he acquired first-hand knowledge, both as hunter and as prey, of guerrilla tactics; and then as independent captain of feudal mercenaries he learned all the ruses and tricks, as well as the lightning strikes, needed

King David, depicted here in a wood-engraving, was considered a paragon of knightly virtue by medieval chivalry.

The Wars of David

1 Subjugation of the Negev tribes.
2 The conquest of Jerusalem.
3 Philistine attempts to oust David in the Rephaim Valley.
4 Subjugation of Philistia.
5 Conquest of the Sharon Plain and Valley of Jezreel.
6 The war against Moab.
7 Subjugation of Edom.
8 Trade with the Euphrates region.
9 The war against the Arameans and Ammonites.
10 The defeat of the Arameans in the Edrei gap.
11 Subjugation of Damascus.
12 Extension of the empire to the borders of Hamath and the Euphrates.
13 Establishment of Israelite sovereignty in western Galilee, as far as the Phoenician border.

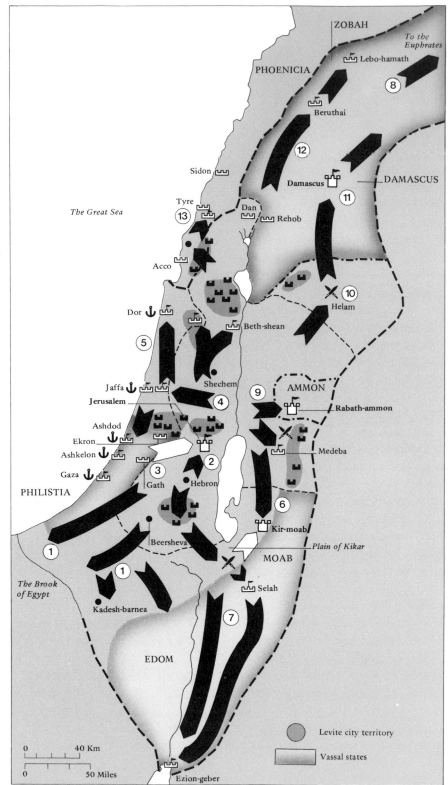

to beat the nomad raiders at their own game. Thus prepared, David was elected king over the tribe of Judah and its affiliates after the death of Saul, while Saul's trusted general, Abner, installed Saul's eldest surviving son, Ishbosheth, as king over the rest of Israel.

David's first concern was to secure Judah from the incessant inroads of the Negev nomads. He set the pattern for generations to come by settling the men of his old regiment, together with their families, among the existing settlements in the Hebron mountains. His intention was threefold: his superbly trained fighters would form the nucleus of a widespread network of resistance and head the local forces against hostile raiders, wherever they penetrated into the Hebron mountains; by settling his men among the Hebronites, who were most exposed to the raiders and the first to bear the brunt of their incursions, David assured their maximum vigilance by making them guard their own homes; finally, by allotting them land, he relieved himself of the burden of paying them.

With an eye to the needs of a united kingdom that would compass all the Palestinian land-bridge east and west of the Jordan, David next went on to capture Jerusalem as his capital. The town of Jerusalem was ideally sited in the centre of the Cis-Jordanian mountain massif. It had easy access to the sea, with Jaffa as its natural port. It also commanded the crossroads between the Jaffa–Rabbath-bene-ammon road, which was the main artery between the Mediterranean and Trans-Jordan in the centre of the country, and the watershed road, the main north–south artery of the Cis-Jordanian massif. Its defensive position was good, situated as it was on a ridge that was surrounded by valleys on all four sides. Jerusalem's climate was pleasant, and rainfall in winter was usually so abundant that it would fill cisterns and reservoirs to last the whole year. As late as 1948, in fact, when the Jewish sector of Jerusalem was cut off by besiegers from all outside sources of water, the rainwater accumulated in the city's cisterns supplied the needs of the population throughout the siege. A perennial major spring existed at the foot of the ridge, and the population had access to it by means of a covered approach, even in times of siege. An important political consideration was that Jerusalem had no Israelite tribal affiliations, and no tribal *amour propre* would be offended if it was chosen. Finally, the masters of the city at the time were the Jebusites, a small ethnic community, alien to the autochthone Canaanites, who did not command any special sympathies among most of the neighbouring peoples.[2]

The capture of Jerusalem

The capture of the strongly fortified town was nonetheless a major effort for the Israelite forces. David succeeded in securing a lodgement in the acropolis, which was in the northern portion of the elongated, narrow ridge, not only because this was the highest area but because a shallow saddle connected it to the section of the city later known as the Temple Mount.[3]

Our interpretation of the events follows the text, without additional comment: 'And the king and his men went to Jerusalem unto the Jebusites . . . which spake unto David, saying, Except thou take away the blind and

An aerial shot of Jerusalem from the south-east: the site of the Jebusite city captured by David is in the left foreground.

the lame, thou shalt not come in hither. Nevertheless David took the stronghold of Zion . . .' (2 Sam. 5:6–7). The word 'stronghold' is a free translation of *metzudah* ('fortress', though, in the parallel passage in 1 Chronicles 11:5, the word is translated 'castle'). Thus David did succeed, possibly by some *coup de main*, in capturing the citadel, but then he could not gain access to the town proper. The marshalling of 'the blind and the lame' for the city's defence has been interpreted not as a derisive gesture but as a magic spell, well understood and accordingly feared by the Israelites, which made them hold back.[4]

To give new impetus to his assault, David searched for a different approach. His keen eye discerned the *tzinor*, the rock-hewn, partly subterranean passage that led from the town down the eastern slope of the ridge to the Gihon Spring: 'And David said on that day, Whosoever getteth up to the gutter (the *tzinor*), and smiteth the Jebusites ... he shall be chief and captain' (ibid., v. 8). Having discovered the *tzinor*, David decided to launch a surprise attack through it while attention was centred upon the northern sector of the city. To overcome the fear of the magic spell, he offered a high command to the leader of the attacking party. The challenge was taken up by Joab: 'So Joab the son of Zeruiah went first up, and was chief' (1 Chr. 11:6).[5] As so often in sieges, secret passages into defended localities tend to be insufficiently guarded. They are the proverbial Achilles' heel of seemingly unassailable places. It is safe to assume that the Jebusites were taken largely by surprise when Joab and his men appeared at the head of the *tzinor*, and this enabled him to gain a secure foothold around this approach while additional men streamed in to capture the city.

The capture of Jerusalem triggered off the first of several Philistine interventions, and by the last of them Philistine power was broken and a Jewish bailiff sat in Gath. The first two Philistine interventions seem to have followed each other closely (2 Sam. 5:17–25). Both were straight incursions through the Elah Valley. Underestimation of their enemy after the battle of Gilboa, or conceit at dealing with a former vassal, made the Philistines disregard the dangers inherent in this gorge, with its steep slopes and defiles, though more than once they had already met defeat there through the Israelites' exploitation of the valley's topography.

The battles of the Valley of Rephaim

With the aim of making their defeat decisive, David each time permitted the Philistines to approach deep into the Judean mountains, as far as the Rephaim Valley (whose head extends up to present-day Jerusalem's railway station). David himself took up a covered position to the west of the Philistines, and attacked them from their rear. The extent of the defeat they suffered on their first attempt is evidenced by the fact that, in their haste to flee, the Philistines left all their sacred images in their abandoned camp.

The second Philistine defeat was again brought about by a surprise Israelite attack from the rear in the Rephaim Valley. This time, the Israelites approached stealthily through a wood in the Philistine rear or flank. Fighting in woods is considered a double-edged sword by military experts. While affording cover, forest hampers communication, command and control. It

The site of the Bechaim wood through which David's forces attacked the Philistines, recently reafforested.

The First Valley of Rephaim Campaign
(phase one)

1 The Philistines approach Jerusalem.
2 David concentrates his forces at Adullam.
3 David moves parallel with the Philistine army, towards his chosen battle site.

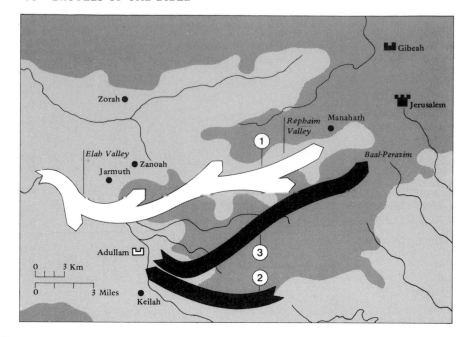

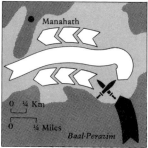

The First Valley of Rephaim Campaign
(phase two)

David ambushes and defeats the Philistine army in the valley.

restricts the use of heavy armament, and the claustrophobic influence of the forest has often had an adverse effect upon the morale of the troops confined in it. It was this feeling that led the Greeks to coin the word 'panic' after the spirit of the forests, Pan.

While these negative properties of combat in the woods made the Philistines keep their forces outside the forest of Bechaim trees (the exact botanical definition is uncertain), they probably set their flank or rear against it. The Israelites, exploiting the cover provided for their light-footed and lightly armed fighters, benefited from the tactical advantages provided by the selfsame feature. David made further subtle use of the weather. Aware of the fact that the daily breeze from the sea reaches the Jerusalem area at about noon, he timed his attack for this hour, so that the rustle of the trees would cover the steps of the stealthily approaching Israelites. The surprise was once again complete, and David had not neglected to elaborate the last phase of his battle plan: exploitation of success. This time he had taken pains to bar the Philistine retreat straight through the Elah Valley, and he was able 'to smite' the Philistines over a long-drawn-out rout of flight 'from Geba until thou come to Gazer'.

After the second Valley of Rephaim battle, David took the initiative to subdue the Philistines once and for all. Following the battle of Methegammah, somewhere in the Philistine plain, David established his dominion over the coastline from the mouth of the Yarkon River to that of the Valley of Sorek. Temporarily, at least, he incorporated Gath and its dependencies into his kingdom, whereas Jaffa became a vassal city. David contented himself with these arrangements for reasons to be discussed later. The Philistines, however, never gave up, and whenever an opportunity arose,

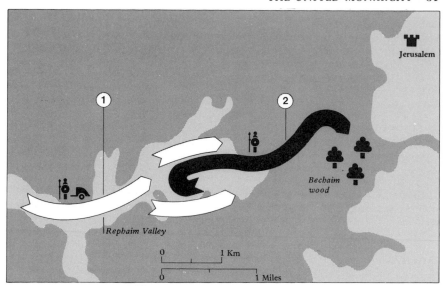

The Second Valley of Rephaim Campaign (phase one)

1 The Philistine approach march.
2 Abandoning his blocking position, David draws the enemy after him.

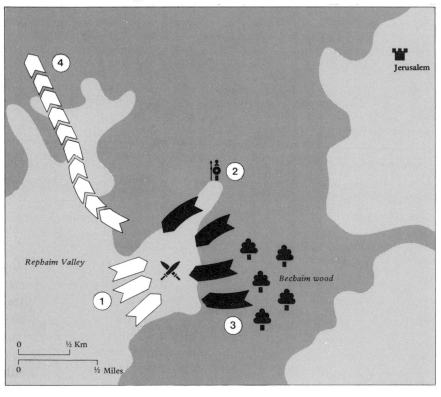

The Second Valley of Rephaim Campaign (phase two)

1 The Philistines form up to push through to Jerusalem.
2 The Israelite rearguard.
3 David's troops make a surprise attack through the Bechaim wood.
4 The Philistines' flight.

throughout the whole First Temple period, they renewed their hostilities. At least one serious, though futile, attempt is recorded in the later years of David's reign.

David's next step was the conquest of the Sharon Plain and the Valley of Jezreel, and the capture or submission of all the Canaanite enclaves that still existed. This fact is borne out by archaeological evidence from systematically excavated sites in the plains.[6]

After that, David began his Trans-Jordanian campaigns by conquering the Kingdom of Moab and reducing it to vassaldom (2 Sam. 8:2; 1 Chr. 18:2). Then he went on to Edom – or, rather, his generals, Joab and his brother Abishai, the sons of Zeruiah, did. Their main encounter was in the Salt Valley (the Kikar plain), south of the Dead Sea. The Edomites suffered a crushing defeat, but it took Joab another six months to reduce the country. Its dynasty was removed and Edom was divided into districts, each administered by a royal commissioner.[7] The next goal was the reduction of Ammon. David had hoped to preserve the amicable personal relations that existed in the days of Nahash, but the latter's son, King Hanun, understandably suspicious, rejected David's offer of peace and called to his assistance the Arameans of south-eastern Syria, north of Gilead.

The clash with the Arameans

Now came the first crucial trial of strength for the Israelite kingdom. Its eastern neighbours, Edom, Moab and Ammon, had themselves been established as centralized kingdoms not many generations earlier. The Edomites, in particular, were still partly semi-nomadic, and their defences were built to answer very much the same threat that the Israelites faced in the desert, namely the raids of tribes from the desert fringes. While the Israelites were still gaining more experience in siegecraft, all other types of armament being equal their superior military flair became decisive.

This was not so, however, in any contact with the Arameans, a large, rich, well-established nation whose technological and strategic know-how was comparable to that of the Philistines. With a much larger population than the latter, the Arameans occupied the area now called the Golan Heights, a position that commanded the approaches to the Israelite kingdom, much in the same way that the latter commanded the approaches to Philistia. Even if we take the numbers quoted by the biblical sources as largely exaggerated, the Aramean strength in chariotry, not to speak of infantry, remains formidable.[8]

According to the biblical chronology, the first encounter between the Israelites and the Arameans had already taken place after David's conquest of Moab, 'when he went to establish his dominion by the river Euphrates' (1 Chr. 18:3). The only plausible interpretation of this otherwise inconceivable statement is that with the easing of the Moabite pressure, which had been especially hard on the Israelite districts of Trans-Jordan, David felt free to use his bases in north-eastern Gilead to develop his trade with the Euphrates region. Quite possibly, Solomon's trade-post in Tadmor (Palmyra) was anticipated by David on this occasion.

Whatever the final outcome of these first clashes, David's conquests and trade ventures combined to upset the Arameans, and they readily seized the opportunity to come to the assistance of the Ammonites with the hope of damming the danger of the rising Israelite tide. By the way, we have here an example of the rule of strategic geography that points to one's 'neighbour's neighbour' as a frequent natural ally.[9] The Israelites were fortunate in that the Arameans had split into many small and often mutually hostile kingdoms. Still, when the rulers of Zobah, Rehob, Maacah and Tob sent their armies to oppose David at the bidding of the Ammonites, the combined allied forces must have numbered about 40,000 men or more.

The Aramean allies succeeded in luring the Israelite forces under Joab into a trap, when the Ammonites pinned them down during the siege of the strong fortress of Medeba. But their plan to use Medeba as an anvil on which to pound the Israelite army, with a general enveloping attack by the Arameans from the rear, did not succeed. Fortunately, Joab had taken the precaution of protecting his rear by means of a screening force that was spread out in considerable depth. Alerted by his screen, Joab kept a cool head and quickly arrived at the following decisions: (1) to divide his forces in two, deployed back-to-back; (2) to have the smaller force, under his brother Abishai, contain the Ammonites; and (3) to attack the oncoming Arameans with the best men of his army. Joab's orders to his brother were laconic: 'If the Syrians [Arameans] be too strong for me, then thou shalt help me: but if the children of Ammon be too strong for thee, then I will come and help thee' (2 Sam. 10:11).

The stratagem succeeded, and the enemy was beaten off in both directions. Although no decisive victory was achieved, any soldier with combat experience will agree that repulsing an enemy while being attacked in both front and rear is in itself no mean achievement. British readers may recall that one of their famous regiments, the 28th Regiment (the Gloucesters), was accorded the privilege of wearing two badges on their headgear in honour of a similar feat in 1801, during their Egyptian campaign. This privilege was reconfirmed when the Gloucesters repeated their feat during World War Two.[10]

Although the Arameans had suffered only a stalemate, they sensed that their reputation was at stake, and that if they could not wipe out this blot on their military renown by a quick, decisive victory, their role as a leading power in southern Syria might be played out. Consequently Hadadezer, king of Zobah, who was foremost of the Aramean rulers, brought in Aramean conscripts from as far away as Mesopotamia. His forces included one thousand chariots and possibly cavalry as well.

David rushed his army to meet his foe in the Edrei gap, some twelve miles of traversable ground between the deep gorge of the Yarmuk River and the natural barrier of the Trachona (Ledja, in present-day Arabic), a vast area of petrified lava blocks. Here the Byzantines withstood the Muslim armies between AD 334 and 336 and it was through this area that the British moved against the Vichy French in 1941.[11] The armies clashed at Helam (present-day Aalma in southern Syria). The Israelite victory was complete, and all the Aramean kingdoms from Zobah southwards accepted Israelite domination. Even the king of Hamath hurried to appease David by paying a sizeable tribute (1 Sam. 10:15–19; 1 Chr. 19:16–19). After these events, David was able to pursue his reduction of Ammon unhindered, which he completed

The subjection of the Arameans

by capturing Rabbath-bene-ammon after Joab succeeded in cutting off the city's water supply.

If we try to reconstruct the strategic concept behind David's conquests, we may conclude that David was the first ruler of the Palestinian land-bridge who firmly grasped the fact that complete and secure mastery of the area – and consequently reasonably secure existence in it – required command over all the three major routes that connected Egypt with Asia Minor and Mesopotamia: the Via Maris, the watershed road and the King's Highway. Secondary routes, such as the Jordan Valley road, were, of course, included in the Davidic dominion; and, most important, at least stretches of the desert-fringe road that skirts the portion of the Trans-Jordan plateau inhabited by a sedentary population were also under his sway. David's empire thus extended between the Mediterranean on the west and the desert on the east, while he was free to move his forces on interior lines along the above-mentioned parallel routes to meet any external threat from either north or south.[12]

As to his Mediterranean flank, David's defence policy can be understood by correctly interpreting his abstention from subduing both the Tyrians and the Philistines. Although David had captured the shore and the fortress opposite the peninsula of Tyre and all the Phoenician hinterland as far north as Sidon, he never attempted any military action against these towns and their dependencies proper. The same strange restraint was exercised in his dealings with the Philistines, in spite of their apparent unreliability. The explanation lies in the fact that the Israelites were at that time very much a nation of 'landlubbers' and sorely lacked a sufficient naval tradition or sea-faring knowledge. They were thus unable to deal with their long coastline, either from the point of view of defence or to exploit their position for purposes of trade and commerce. David therefore took what seemed to be a reasonably calculated risk in keeping the seafaring people on the Mediterranean shores intact in order to make the most out of the transit trade that went through his dominions, not only from north to south and vice versa, but between east and west, thus increasing the revenues required for the upkeep of his administration and army.[13]

The organization of the armed forces

The Israelite army underwent great change and development during David's reign. Taken together with the Solomonic army reforms, the new model served as a basis of the organization of the armed forces in the Divided Monarchy; and whatever diversions from this pattern were later discernible must frequently be ascribed to a lack of adequate resources, rather than to basic changes in doctrine. The basic rule of compulsory national military service for every able-bodied male in the tribal period was adopted by the royal charter that the Bible ascribes to Samuel, or that was accepted with his sanction upon Saul's accession: 'He [the king] will take your sons and appoint them for himself, for his chariots, and to be his horsemen; and some shall run before his chariots [foot-soldiers] . . . And he will take . . . your goodliest young men . . . and put them to his work' (1 Sam. 8:11–16).

The technical term for the national army, the people in arms, was in short 'the people'. For tactical purposes they were organized in divisions of thousands sub-divided into units of hundreds and sub-units of fifty and ten – the latter, much akin to our present-day 'section', forming the smallest tactical division to have a permanent commander, the 'captain of ten' (corporal, in modern terms). Whether the 'thousands', 'hundreds' and so forth actually comprised the full complement of soldiers indicated by their name, or whether by David's time they had become a mere designation for a tactical unit of smaller strength, much like the Roman *centuria* (hundred) which in practice numbered between sixty and eighty men, one cannot say.

This conscript army was, like most of the Davidic forces, exclusively an infantry force. But within this general designation there was a great variety of armament, which permitted the formation of task forces of combined arms constructed to meet the needs of the tactical mission in hand. The variety of armament and of its application, so necessary for any balanced war effort, was achieved in antiquity by fostering regional and tribal peculiarities and traditions in military matters. Egyptian wall paintings, the list given by Arianus of the Persian Order of Battle opposing Alexander the Great, and the organization of the Roman army in legions and tribal auxiliaries all serve as evidence of this practice.[14]

The Bible has preserved some details of the tribes' special military proficiencies that enabled David to build his diversified army. The Benjaminites 'were armed with bows'. Their special prowess was their ambidexterity: '[they] could use both the right hand and the left in hurling stones and shooting arrows out of a bow' (1 Chr. 12:2). 'The Gadites . . . could handle shield and buckler . . . and were as swift as the roes upon the mountains' (ibid., v. 8). 'The children of Judah . . . bore shield and spear' (ibid., v. 24). 'And of Naphtali . . . with shield and spear' (ibid., v. 34). The Zebulunites, however, were 'expert in war, with all instruments of war . . . which could keep rank' (ibid., v. 33). Similarly dextrous and equipped were the tribes to the east of the Jordan. The tribe of Issachar seem to have specialized in intelligence missions, since their military proclivity is explained as 'understanding of the times, to know what Israel ought to do' (ibid., v. 32).

In short, David could draw upon the tribal contingents to furnish bowmen and slingers, light and heavy lancers – the former good at fighting in individual combat in difficult terrain, the latter (the children of Judah) forming the closely arrayed heavy phalanx. These were assisted by spearmen, who would hurl their spears before charging the foe with drawn swords. Other tribes were less specialized as far as weaponry was concerned, but were trained to fight in rank and file, while the Issacharians had developed a special flair for scouting and the like.

The great danger of basing armament upon tribal monopolies lay in fostering the recently overcome tribal particularism and thereby counteracting the king's unifying endeavours. To overcome this tendency, David installed a double administrative framework for the people in arms. The tribal chiefs continued to train the young in the use of arms special to their clan, as well as in the maintenance of personal weapons. Another of their duties was the provision of the quota of fighting men required of their tribe.

Alongside this force, twelve monthly, non-tribal and non-territorial divisions were created:

Now the children of Israel after their number, to wit, the chief fathers and captains of thousands and hundreds, and their officers that served the king in any matter of the courses, which came in and went out month by month throughout all the months of the year, of every course were twenty and four thousand. (1 Chr. 27:1)

This organization, which drew its troops from the tribal levies and drafted them into the tactical formations and units of thousands, hundreds and so forth, furnished the king with a large, permanently available army of soldiers on one-month active reserve duty every year. Since their cadres were permanent, and their officers, according to the above, were probably regulars, the other eleven divisions could be called up and mobilized in the shortest time possible.[15] Quick mobilization has always been a necessity for safeguarding national sovereignty and independence in the Palestinian land-bridge, as geopolitical conditions always limited manpower reserves while the strategic importance of the area brought nearly permanent concentric pressure to bear on the bridge state both from the neighbouring states and from the Great Powers of the day. In his military organization David had therefore found the key to having a force immediately at his command and being able to mobilize the entire people quickly, without doing away with the positive tribal traditions.

The general commander of the national levy was Amasa ben Jeter. His clashes with Joab, the ranking chief of the regulars, and the undoubtedly insufficiently defined sphere of authority between them, are a fair prototype of the problems that have bedevilled the co-operation and relationship between regular and reserve forces to the present.

The drawback of the general national levy was, of course, the negative influence upon the economy. The selfsame farmer who served in the ranks of the army was needed to produce the surplus yield to keep the war effort going. The longer he was kept under arms, the greater the danger of his private economic ruin and the collective influence on the economic health of the nation as a whole. All forms of society and government have grappled with this problem. In the eighteenth century rulers used to kidnap their neighbours' citizens, to avoid having to call up their own subjects for military service. It is impossible to say that the question has been settled satisfactorily even today.

In Davidic times, one way of easing the economic pressure was to plan the campaigns for the easier agricultural seasons, such as early summer. The Bible refers to this season in a matter-of-fact way as the 'time that the kings go out to battle'. The enemy, however, was not always so obliging as to give battle or to surrender within the limits of this season; nor was the reserve service sufficient to bring the troops to the highest pitch of perfection. David therefore followed the common practice and established a standing, regular army of career soldiers who were able to serve for long periods and could be trained intensively in times of peace.

David's regular army had two corps, the *gibborim* ('mighty men' of the King James Bible) and the foreign mercenaries. The *gibborim* comprised two regiments that were built around the nuclei of the first and the second 'Thirty'. The first 'Thirty' was the band of loyal followers and retainers that had formed around David in his exile, and each of them had proved his mettle by prodigies of valour, which served as the theme for tales and ballads sung all over Israel. The second 'Thirty' was a similar troop that had formed when David attained the crown of Judah. They were recruited from among the Trans-Jordanians, though probably before David's election by the rest of the people.[16]

These two groups were bound to the king by bonds of common exploits and shared much the same experience in unorthodox warfare as a means of neutralizing the superior armament and technical skill of hostile armies. In making the 'Thirties' the nuclei of his standing army and the spearheads of his campaigns, David imbued his regular forces with much of the spirit and traditions of the days of pre-regular warfare. (It is commonly held that the modern parallel of having built the Israel Defence Forces largely around the pre-state underground, the Haganah, and especially its shock troops, the Palmach, goes a long way to explain the unorthodox approach that typifies the Israeli soldier today.) The 'Thirty' also furnished the king's bodyguard, and many of the high civil and military dignitaries were chosen from among their ranks. We may therefore liken them to the *hetairoi* of Alexander the Great, or the *schara* of Charlemagne, who performed similar tasks.

The second corps of David's regular army was made up of the mercenaries. While the general host was commanded by Joab, the foreign mercenaries came under the command of Benaiah ben Jehoiada. The ranking foreign officer was Ittai, the Gittite, who came from the Philistine town of Gath. The other troops, the 'Cheretites and Pelethites', also came, as their name implies, partly from among the Philistines. (Pelethites might, however, indicate another extraction, such as Crete, the original home of many of the Sea Peoples.) These mercenaries were undoubtedly good fighters. Their armament was heavier than most of the Israelites', and some of them may eventually have become mounted. Their loyalty to the king was proved beyond doubt when, having been released by the latter from their oath of fidelity at the nadir of David's reign (the outset of Absalom's revolt), they refused to abandon their royal master and were instrumental in his restoration. There are allusions to the fact that the nucleus of these foreigners was already included alongside the *gibborim* in David's corps troop when he himself did mercenary service to Achish, the king of Gath. They could well have provided a unit of special (heavy?) archers.[17]

One more Davidic innovation deserves mention. The Levite settlements enumerated in Joshua, 21 and 1 Chronicles, 6 were all located in districts that had permanent security problems: either border districts or newly acquired lands of major strategic importance, such as the Carmel ridge (the main barrier of the Via Maris) or areas that had a strong admixture of foreign inhabitants (such as south-eastern Galilee or the territory of Dan, which faced the Philistines). The Levites, with their special religious zeal and knowledge, combined their moral and religious strength with military prowess in providing a permanent guard against unwanted spiritual as well as physical infiltrations from across the borders. In times of stress, they made an especially reliable home guard in militarily unstable districts.[18]

Almost no direct information has survived on the tactical division of the Davidic and later Israelite armies. In practice, the desire to marshal as many forces as possible has always been checked by the limits of the actual capacity to upkeep and move them. It would seem hardly possible that at any given time the Israelite kingdoms were capable of keeping in the field for any length of time troops surpassing 50,000, not counting the considerable 'home guard' that manned the fortress towns throughout the country.

The breakdown of the forces into combat formations in all armies has been governed by the emphasis put upon the shock effect of massed troops on one side and the wish for maximum flexibility and manœuvrability on the other. The kind of compromise reached between these tendencies has always been one of the major characteristics differentiating existing armies. The tribal skills referred to above enabled David to work out the compromise best suited to his time. While the archers, slingers, and javelin-throwers provided the material for his light troops, the heavily armoured pikemen provided the massed shock force.

Thus one can explain David's capability to withstand both the Canaanite and Aramean phalanx, that went back to much older Mesopotamian and Egyptian prototypes, as well as the shock of their massed chariots.[19] To achieve the latter, history has recorded two basic stratagems. The first entailed the harassment and slowing down of the hostile shock by light troops, its complete arrest by the heavy infantry in close array, and the closing in of the light troops for the kill. The other stratagem employed was to open the ranks of the massed heavy infantry so as to let the enemy, charging along a massed front, pass through the empty space, or to deflect him into these empty passages. Then when veering around and trying to regroup for a renewed attack, he would be engaged by the defending forces. The latter stratagem was used by the Romans against Hannibal at Zama (202 BC) and by Gustav Adolphus against the Habsburg marshal Tilly at Breitenfeld in 1631.

The actual combat formation employed by the Israelite armies seems to have been subdivided into four or three. This can be deduced from the actual numbers of troops quoted in various biblical passages.[20] Both systems have survived until today. The division of three has been found necessary even by relatively unsophisticated armies such as the Greeks before Troia and the medieval Swiss, to assure a staged and mutually supporting attack as well as to exploit success or to avert defeat by being able to shift troops, and even to hold back a part for employment on just these occasions.

We do know of one Israelite campaign where under different conditions a division into four and then into three was adopted. When Abimelech besieged Shechem 'all the people were with him . . . laid wait against Shechem in four companies' (Judg. 9:34). Yet next time 'he took the people and divided them into three companies' (ibid., v. 43). Gideon divided his force into three, as did David for the showdown with his rebellious son Absalom (2 Sam. 18:1). Against this the twelve tribes are described by the later generations as camping and marching in four major divisions subdivided into three (Num. 2:10, 14f.). It seems probable that different echelons had different compositions and that, according to the tactical contingencies, differently composed battle formations were established; although divisions into either three or four were the usual standard.

It has been suggested that the recurrence of the number 600 in the Bible could indicate that it was the strength of the standard Israelite combat force.[21] This could well have been so. The number was divisible both into three sub-units of 200 men and four of 150 each. These 'battalions' would be divided into the traditional 'hundreds', 'fifties' and 'tens', much like modern companies, platoons and sections. The sub-unit of the six hundred would therefore be composed of either two 'hundreds' or of one reinforced 'hundred'.

The thousands might have existed as larger formations, especially for the general levy of the people in arms, or could have served much like the old British regiments as mother formations from which battalions were detached to combat brigades.

Solomon's fortification activities

After David had established the Israelite empire on the main strategic thoroughfare of the ancient eastern Mediterranean, while the Great Powers of the day were temporarily exhausted, it was Solomon's task to guard his possessions against any foreseeable attempts by Egypt or the northern powers to regain dominant influence on the Palestinian land-bridge.

There exist two basic incentives for the permanent fortification of any given realm. The first is the wish to preserve the *status quo* after having attained the desired territorial gains and economic security; the second is the need to strengthen one's defences to meet the threat of impending aggression from without (usually in times of relative weakness). King Solomon's fortification activities can be ascribed to the first category (in contrast to those of King Rehoboam of Judah, for example, which will be discussed in chapter 9).[22]

Nonetheless, if we accept the twenty-fourth year of Solomon's reign (which is explicitly quoted by 1 Kings 9:10 as a date after which he initiated his concerted efforts at fortification), we arrive at a period when the first signs of re-emergent foreign threats were already evident. In Egypt, Shishak I had replaced Pharaoh Pesibkhenno II, who had not only acquiesced in the

A Phoenician portrait mask.

existence of the Israelite empire but had officially transferred his last strong-hold in Palestine, the fortress of Gezer, into Israelite hands when one of his daughters married Solomon. The new Pharaoh's change of attitude became apparent in his harbouring and encouraging of political exiles, such as Hadad, scion of the dethroned royal house of Edom, and Rehoboam, who had attempted to persuade the northern tribes to revolt against Solomon when the latter began building the Temple, the central national sanctuary, in Judean territory.

In one instance, the border with the Tyrians, Solomon was compelled to return to Hiram, king of Tyre, the district of Cabul. This clearly was a far-sighted political move destined to preserve mutually beneficial rela-tions. But it also demonstrates that the Israelite land power had already opted for political alternatives to war, namely, the making of pacts.[23] Worse still, Damascus, which had been governed by an Israelite bailiff since its capture by David, successfully revolted, and Solomon was not able to dis-lodge its new ruler, Rezon. Only a punitive expedition against Aram, Hamath and Zobah (which proves that the other Aramean dependencies had followed Damascus' example) averted the loss of all the northern dominions.

Against this background, we cite 1 Kings 9:15–19:

And this is the reason of the levy which king Solomon raised; for to build the house of the Lord, . . . and Hazor, and Megiddo, and Gezer . . . and Beth-horon the nether. And Baalath, and Tadmor in the wilderness, in the land, and all the cities of store that Solomon had, and cities for his chariots, and cities for his horsemen. . . .

Even before locating these cities on the map, we must recognize that those few mentioned by name clearly did not form a continuous line of defence, much less a border zone defended in depth. Locating them on the map, we find them to be links in a definite, meticulously chosen network of strong-points that served simultaneously as pivots of offence and defence. All this makes sense once we recall that King Solomon's great reform in reshaping the Davidic army was the addition, as a main offensive arm, of the corps of chariots: 'And Solomon gathered together chariots and horsemen [read charioteers]: and he had a thousand and four hundred chariots and twelve thousand horsemen [charioteers], whom he bestowed in the cities for chariots and with the king at Jerusalem' (1 Kgs. 10:26).

Solomon's chariots

The origin of the war chariot, the forefather of our modern motorized forces in general and armour in particular, can be traced back to Sumer in the third millennium BC.[24] The ancient Sumerians had already developed a heavy four-wheeled and a light two-wheeled type of fighting vehicle. Since then four factors – protection, firepower, speed (including manœuvrability) and cross-country performance – have influenced the development of the fighting vehicle throughout history, no less when it was still a horse-drawn chariot than today. Mention has already been made of the Canaanite chariots. The Canaanites had made their acquaintance with the war chariot

in the Hyksos period (eighteenth century BC), when much of Palestine became part of the Hyksos empire, since the Hyksos had made prominent use of the chariot. The Egyptians must have introduced chariots under the influence of the Hyksos and developed them in their wars in Canaan (sixteenth-fourteenth centuries BC) and against the rival Hittite empire of Asia Minor and other northern neighbours.

Summing up the graphic evidence from wall paintings and the plastic arts in all the countries concerned, as well as the contents of whatever written records exist, we can distinguish between a northern (Anatolian–Mesopotamian) and a southern (Egyptian) trend in chariot design. The northerners tended to develop heavier vehicles with possibly greater fire-power and shock effect. The southern tradition was to construct lighter types, with consequent maximum mobility and manœuvrability. Both traditions met on the Palestinian land-bridge, and we consequently cannot attribute to the Solomonic corps any specific type of chariot.[25]

The number of 12,000 charioteers allows for the possibility that not only did each chariot have a double crew of trained men to relieve each other,

A model of Megiddo as it looked at the time of Solomon.

(*Opposite*) The ruins of Hazor
and, in the distance, the
snow-capped peak of Mount
Hermon.

but that at least some of the chariots had a crew of three men: the driver,
or charioteer in the narrow sense of the word; a bowman; and a third man
armed with shield and lance or spear. The lighter chariots were manned
by a crew of two (the charioteer and a fighting man, either archer or spear-
man), while the lance was carried (in line with the northern tradition), as
additional armament by some or all. Biblical sources call the Canaanite
vehicles 'chariots of iron'. Iron-clad war chariots have been identified on
a relief from Carchemish in Syria, but whether Solomon adopted armour
for some of his chariots is another question.[26]

The number of 1,400 chariots also denoted considerable strength in this
period, especially when compared with the 2,500 chariots of the Hittites
at their zenith, the 924 chariots that comprised the contingents of all Syria
and Canaan in the allied campaign against Thutmose III or the 720
chariots that made up the entire complement taken by Amenhotep II from
the whole of Canaan in 1431 BC.[27] Taken together with the general siting
of his main bases, it seems that Solomon had grasped the principle that the
best defensive strategy does not lie in pinning down the majority of one's
forces to a rigid or even continuous line of fortifications and obstacles, but
rather in creating a strong, flexible and highly manœuvrable offensive arm
that could attack any invader from one or more of its strategically sited bases,
which were organized to sustain the basic administrative and logistic effort
involved. The main strategic arm of the Solomonic defence forces was his
charioteers. From external evidence, as well as biblical allusions, we gather
that these were not only trained in co-operation and combined action with
the infantry, but that there existed specially picked foot-men, the biblical
'runners', who were permanently grouped and employed to support the
chariots and exploit their successes when infantry action was needed. In
this way, they were very much like today's motorized and armoured
infantry.

The foresight and vision of Solomon may be gauged correctly if we recall
that only a few decades ago, the official French military doctrine held –
against a few 'visionaries', like Charles de Gaulle – to a purely passive deployment of a force in the Chinese-wall-type Maginot Line. As far as the
ancient Israelites were concerned, the great advance was in Solomon's ability
to create within a generation the complete sophisticated sub- and infrastructure needed to sustain services and maintain charioteers in strength. It is
possible that the foundation for war chariotry had already been laid by
David. The biblical passage hinting at this – 'And David took from him
[Hadadezer] a thousand chariots ... and ... houghed all the chariot horses,
but reserved of them for a hundred chariots' (2 Sam. 8:4) – makes it clear
that his was a modest beginning. Out of these Solomon built a large regular
force that required long and complicated training and the workshops, stores,
training establishments, barracks, sheds, veterinary and other auxiliary services without which it could not operate. All these come under the heading
of 'store and chariot cities' mentioned in the Bible.

The fortification network

The offensive-defensive character, both on the strategic and the tactical level, of the main Solomonic fortifications, is borne out by an examination of their locations.[28] Hazor guarded the major highway from Israel into Syria, the Via Maris, near the point where it branched off into two roads, one along the Jordan Valley past Ijon and on to Hamath or Damascus, the other ascending the Syrian plateau (the Golan Heights) straight to Damascus.

Megiddo commanded the main west-east axis of Palestine, the sector of the Via Maris that branched off from the coastline and passed through the Jezreel Valley, either to Hazor or to Beth-shean and Gilead, where it met the road joining it to the highway coming from Haifa Bay. Its location also permitted the effective blocking of the Iyron Pass, the main traverse of the Carmel ridge.

Tamar, whether identified at Hazeva (Arabic Ain Husub), as some scholars maintain, or in the area of Mezad Tamar–En Tamar (Arabic Ain Arus) or elsewhere, commanded the southern approaches of the realm through the Arabah Valley.

Gezer was located in the centre of the piedmont that served as the first natural barrier against anyone who attempted to penetrate the hill country in the direction of Jerusalem from the central coastal sector. It formed the advance guard for all approaches to the capital from the Jabneh–Jaffa–Lod triangle.

Solomon's four-entry city gate at Hazor. The fortress guarded the Israel–Syria highway, the Via Maris.

Baalath (Mughar or another *tell* in the vicinity of modern Gedera) was sited in the plain to the south-west of the Judean highlands, on the direct line of the most likely approach from Egypt or the Philistine coastal cities. It guarded the lower Sorek Valley, which led up to that of Elah and Rephaim and served as an avenue of invasion for armies coming from Egypt in many periods, such as that of Shishak and Necho (in 924 and 605 BC, respectively); the Ptolemaic forces in the fourth-third century BC; and, in their turn, Fatimids and Mameluks, down to Allenby's columns after his breakthrough at Beersheva in 1917.

Lower Beth-horon blocked the Beth-horon pass, one of the main ascents to the central mountain plateau. As a main artery of war, it is known to us from the wars of Joshua onwards, down to the Six Day War.

All the fortresses above have the following tactical features in common: their position was easily defended, often on a steep hill, and amply provided with water, but they were in terrain that permitted the swift marshalling and deployment of chariots. This explains the choice of Lower Beth-horon in preference to Upper Beth-horon, its naturally much better-sited twin further inland. Upper Beth-horon was singularly unsuited to the deployment of chariots. Another trait common to all these fortresses was their flanking, rather than blocking, position. This enabled the forces based upon, or convening upon, any of them to attack a foe who did not heed the threat to his flank, or to attack in their own time, and under no less favourable conditions, all those enemies who were aware of the danger to their flank and rear and had become pinned down in a siege of one of the major fortresses.

One more fortress is mentioned in the parallel list to the above, in 2 Chronicles 8: Tadmor (later called Palmyra). This one, however, belongs to a category apart. Tadmor was the key to the great and rich trade route that passed through the Syrian desert from Damascus to Mesopotamia. From its halfway point, the desert was policed, Israelite control was exercised and the caravans were furnished or refurbished with all necessary tools, equipment and victuals. When Rezon succeeded in establishing himself in Damascus, towards the end of Solomon's reign, he was able to harass the communications between Tadmor and the Israelite territory and thus upset the general flow of trade.

The general reserve of Solomon's army was kept in Jerusalem. The Bible explicitly states that it included the strategic reserve of chariots. This statement implies the existence of well-guarded roads on which to move the chariots quickly and the exploitation of the interior lines both for offensive action outside the belt of fortified bases and to sustain forces that were engaged in action around any of the fortified bases. While the infrastructure of roads was certainly not yet paved, these highways were obviously well levelled, sign-posted and graded, to make wheeled traffic possible. Because of the very absence of a continuous, permanent pavement (unheard-of in this country until Herodian times), there must have been a regular service

The road network

for road maintenance, with the most frequent need in wadi and mountain passages. A service like that was what the prophet Isaiah had in mind when he wrote: 'prepare ye the way of the Lord, make straight in the desert a highway for our God' (Isa. 40:3) or '... go through the gates: prepare ye the way of the people; cast up, cast up the highway; gather out the stones; lift up a standard for the people' (ibid., 62:10).

This infrastructure must, of course, have been completed with a host of road stations, workshops and stores that were constructed, whenever possible, in or near existing settlements. Similarly, the fortified towns of the Israelite kingdom were an additional network of defence, complementary to the above-mentioned main strategic bases.

Logistic organization   The maintenance of provision for the king and the administration, as well as the army, was based on a territorial schedule that may well go back to Davidic times:

And Solomon had twelve officers all over Israel, which provided victuals for the king and his household: each man his month in a year made provision. And those officers provided victual for king Solomon, and for all that came unto king Solomon's table, every man in his month: they lacked nothing. Barley also and straw for the horses and dromedaries brought they unto the place where the officers were, every man according to his charge. (1 Kgs. 4:7, 27-8)

We prefer to read for *rehesh* (which in the King James version has been translated 'dromedaries'), *rehev* (which is the rendering of this word according to the Septuagint, and means 'chariots'). The rendering of the original Hebrew text by the King James version as 'the place where the officers were' is likewise debatable. The most straightforward translation-interpretation would be: 'the place allocated to them'.

With these remarks in mind, the logistic organization of Solomon's armed forces becomes clear.[29] Each district governor, who seems to have combined the offices of civil and military governor, was responsible for the upkeep of the army for one month during any one year. This was achieved by supplying the royal 'store cities' with the amount of victuals specified for them. The current needs of the troops stationed in Judah, or the special needs of those who formed the general and strategic reserve, were covered by the thirteenth governor, a special commissary for Judah. The special importance of two of the districts is emphasized by the fact that their governors were sons-in-law of the king: the district of Dor, the main Israelite naval base on the Mediterranean, and the district of Naphtali, which included the slopes of the Golan Heights, ever vital for the security of northern Cis-Jordan and eventually the border with hostile Damascus.

It is astonishing to compare the elaborate logistic substructure of Solomon's army with that of Saul's, only two reigns removed from his. When Saul was fighting the Philistines in the Valley of Elah, David was despatched by his father to replenish the dwindling provisions of his brothers, who were in the army – little knowing, of course, that this mission would lead to his

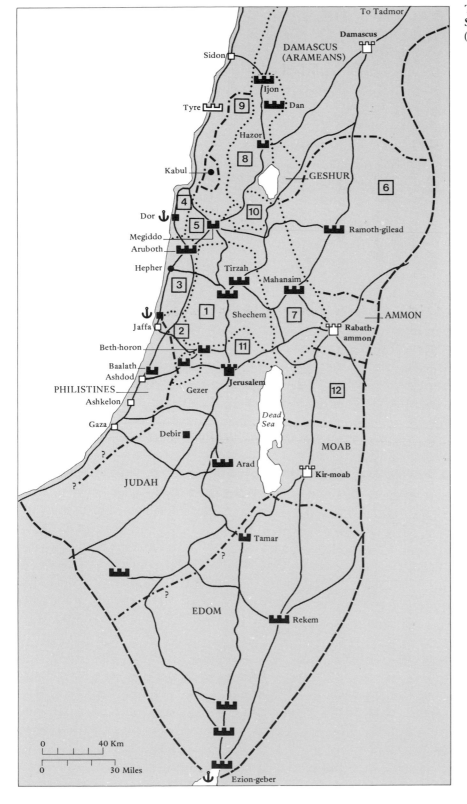

The Infrastructure of the Solomonic Realm
(Numbers denote districts)

To Tadmor

Damascus

DAMASCUS
(ARAMEANS)

Sidon

Ijon

Tyre

9

Dan

Hazor

8

GESHUR

Kabul

6

4

10

Dor

5

Ramoth-gilead

Megiddo

Aruboth

Hepher

Tirzah

Mahanaim

3

1

Shechem

7

AMMON

Jaffa

2

Rabath-
ammon

Beth-horon

11

Baalath

Ashdod

Gezer

Jerusalem

12

PHILISTINES

Ashkelon

Dead
Sea

Gaza

Debir

MOAB

?

Arad

Kir-moab

?

JUDAH

?

Tamar

?

?

EDOM

Rekem

0   40 Km

0   30 Miles

Ezion-geber

encounter with Goliath. In Saul's day, each individual thus had to provide his own upkeep, not to mention his own equipment. The Solomonic system had its counterparts, and probable antecedents, in the similar arrangements of the other eastern empires. How advanced these arrangements were can be better understood if we remember that in the Carolingian Empire, nearly two thousand years later, Charlemagne travelled each month, with his court and army, from one district to another, so as to be fed and furnished with the necessary provisions.

(*Opposite*) The Gulf of Eilat: Eilat is believed to be the site of Ezion-geber, the southern port built by Solomon.

6 THE EARLY DAYS OF ISRAEL

Rehoboam's succession

King Solomon's reign has always been regarded as the most brilliant and magnificent in Jewish history – and rightly so. At the same time, it was also one that taxed national resources and economic effort to the utmost. A staggering financial burden was involved in creating, and no less in maintaining, the imperial army and administration, their necessary infrastructure and all the trappings of empire. To these we must add all the other Solomonic development and building activities and, above all, the erection and endowment of the great Temple in Jerusalem.

To alleviate these almost overwhelming commitments, King Solomon had foresightedly and rigorously developed trade and commerce, making full use of the strategic location of his kingdom, as a bridge between both Asia and Africa and the Mediterranean and the Indian Ocean. The establishment of ties with the queen of Sheba (present-day Yemen), the maintenance of a garrison at Tadmor (Palmyra), the building of a naval base at Ezion-geber (near today's Eilat), as well as the league with King Hiram of Tyre and the preservation of the Philistines as commercial and seafaring agents on the south-western shores, all fall within the scope of Solomon's economic endeavours. None of these, however, could ease the strain on the limited resources of Israelite manpower. On the contrary, they must have added their share to the drain of human resources from private enterprise to short- or long-term royal commissions and errands.

This was the background to the people's demand for an easing of the yoke, voiced when the people of Israel convened at Shechem on Solomon's death to confirm Rehoboam, his son, as king: 'Thy father made our yoke grievous: now therefore make thou the grievous service of thy father, and his heavy yoke which he put upon us, lighter, and we will serve thee' (1 Kgs. 12:4). These demands came at a singularly inopportune moment, since external pressure was mounting, and Damascene, as well as Egyptian, activities must have encroached considerably by then on the temporary monopoly in trade exercised by Solomon along the Red Sea and the approaches from the Syrian desert.

Rehoboam disregarded the advice of his father's counsellors to appease the people by false promises and decided to respond truthfully, telling them that no easing of the burden was to be expected. If we are to believe the biblical chronicler, Rehoboam was urged by his personal entourage, 'the young men that were grown up with him', to word his answer in a harsh, authoritative manner, so as to assert once and for all his royal authority:

And the king answered the people roughly, and forsook the old men's counsel that they gave him; and spake to them after the counsel of the young men, saying, My father made your yoke heavy, and I will add to your yoke: my father also chastised you with whips, but I will chastise you with scorpions. (1 Kgs. 12:13–14)

The division of the kingdom

This attitude made the tribes other than Judah easy prey to any particularist agitators who had not yet lived down the slight to their tribal honour of having to bow to a king residing in Judah: 'So when all Israel saw that the king hearkened not unto them, the people answered the king, saying, What portion have we in David? neither have we inheritance in the son of Jesse: to your tents, O Israel: now we see to thine own house, David' (1 Kgs. 12:16). Thus the Jewish kingdom was divided into two parts: the north, 'Israel' (in the narrow sense of the word) and the south, 'Judah', comprising the tribal territories of Judah, Benjamin, the Negev, and at times Edom as a main dependency.

One of the major instigators of the defection of the northern tribes from the House of David was Pharaoh Shishak I of Egypt. Too weak to attack the United Monarchy openly, he set about disrupting it by subversive action from within. Having harboured the fugitive Jeroboam for just this reason, Shishak had him despatched to Israel prior to the investiture of Rehoboam and, with the connivance of his agents, he put Jeroboam forward as a candidate for the crown of Israel, to which he was duly elected.

Biding his time for the ensuing internecine struggle between Judah and Israel to weaken and exhaust the Israelite kingdoms, Shishak launched a major invasion in 924 BC with all the forces at his disposal. It was not aimed at regaining the Palestinian land-bridge, an enterprise which the Pharaoh seems to have judged still beyond his capability. His goal was to weaken his dangerous (from the Egyptian viewpoint) neighbour to the north. A strong and united Israel was a check on Egypt's reborn desire for political and economic expansion northwards. Worse, the Tyro-Israelite alliance, which had successfully challenged Egypt's naval exclusivity and trade in the Red Sea, had dealt a most severe blow to Egypt's economic independence.

To avert a state of national emergency, Shishak planned and executed his invasion, which was built around a striking force of 1,200 chariots and the Lybian and Nubian infantry, which has often figured in the forefront of the Egyptian armed forces up to recent times. The names of localities captured during Shishak's campaign have been preserved in a list inscribed on the south entrance to the sanctuary of Amon in Karnak. Following Professor Benjamin Mazar's decipherment and interpretation of the Karnak inscription, we can reconstruct two Egyptian task forces, or possibly two major phases of action by the united invasion army.[1]

Force one, or one of the two phases, was directed at disrupting and pulverizing the intricate infrastructure of trade-posts and stations in the Negev between Ezion-geber on the Gulf of Eilat and central Judah (or the Mediterranean coast). Archaeological evidence for the destruction of the fortress of Ezion-geber has been revealed by Nelson Glueck's excavation of the site.[2] In restrospect, one can generalize and say that the power in Egypt has always reacted as strongly as possible to any attempt at dominating her 'private sea', which has always been considered as her soft underbelly. The violent reaction of Saladin to the Crusader threat on the Red Sea, which culminated in the Frankish débâcle at Hattin in AD 1187, or the British reaction to the Turkish occupation of Aqaba in 1903, which nearly triggered off a major war, are two other good examples of the sensitivity of the area. Part of the Egyptian–Israeli conflict since 1948 is undoubtedly to be viewed in the same geopolitical perspective. Similarly, Shishak gave primary attention to the Gulf of Eilat sector and its approaches.

The second task force (or operational phase of the united Egyptian army) was given the mission of an immense spoiling attack, to ravage with fire and sword as much of the Israelite kingdom and its war potential as possible, so as to achieve a lasting weakening of this neighbour. We may compare the mission of these forces to that of a modern strategic bombing campaign, aimed in the first instance not at conquest, but at forcing an enemy to his knees by smashing his capacity to hit back effectively.

The naturally more difficult to traverse, and easier to defend, territory of the Judean highlands made Shishak content himself with a heavy tribute from King Rehoboam of Judah and launch his major offensive against his former protégé, Jeroboam. Hoping to weaken Israel's hold in Trans-Jordan as well, Shishak dared to cross the Jordan and successfully ravaged the Succoth region, the major crossroads of communications between Gilead and the mountains of Samaria.

The Egyptians retreated as swiftly as they came and left a much weakened Israel behind. However, as has been proved even in the most recent wars, destruction without permanent occupation cannot break a reasonably vigorous people. The foundations laid by Saul and David and strengthened by Solomon were solid enough to permit a quick recuperation. Unfortunately for both Israel and Judah, however, both kingdoms continued to waste considerable effort on armed contests with each other; and only eventually (and even then not permanently) did their rulers learn the lesson that only through a close alliance between the two sister kingdoms could sufficient strength be gained and enough forces be marshalled to achieve peace, security and prosperity on the Palestinian land-bridge.

Aram, Trans-Jordan and the Philistines

Israel's main enemy and challenger to its supremacy as a major power in the south Syrian, Greater Palestinian area was to become the Aramean kingdom of Damascus.[3] At first, however, the Arameans thought it opportune to treat and ally themselves with Israel, so as to consolidate their rule in Syria. Weakened by the invasion of Shishak and the inter-kingdom wars, Israel lost some of its towns and villages on the Golan Heights to the Damascenes, without Jeroboam being able to do much about it. Likewise, he must have acquiesced in the complete or partial rebellion of Ammon and Moab. Those two kingdoms were later to become a second focus of Israelite military activity. The measure of their submission to Israel was in direct relation to the latter's military strength at any given time, which in turn was more often than not decisively influenced by the constant trial of strength between Israel and Damascus.

To a lesser degree, and especially in the first decades of Israel's existence, Philistia formed a third focus of military activity for the Israelites. Both Nadab, son of Jeroboam, and Elah, in *c.* 906 and 882 BC respectively, found it expedient to direct the first recorded Israelite offensive efforts (other than fighting Judah) against the Philistines. Their primary aim was to capture the Gibbethon bulge (which commanded the ascents to the mountains of Samaria from the Philistine plain) and to shut off the rear of Jaffa.[4] Gibbethon had once been in Israelite territory, and the fact that it became a major Philistine bulwark proves that the Philistines also profited from the general weakening caused by the division of the kingdom and Shishak's invasion. Both these campaigns, however, were broken off before they attained their goal. In the first instance, Nadab was killed while personally conducting the siege of Gibbethon; in the second one, Elah was assassinated in the royal palace of Tirzah, while the commander-in-chief of his army, Omri, was directing the operations.

Lacking the charisma of scions of the blessed House of David, and the prestige of the guardians of the great and awe-inspiring Temple in Jerusalem, the kings of Israel also lacked the valuable and wholehearted support given to the kings of Judah by the priestly tribe of Levi. Hence they were vulnerable to the violent reaction of popular displeasure, whatever its source and justification. This state of affairs was another reason for the weakness of the northern kingdom, as demonstrated by the two anti-Philistine campaigns. However, this makes even more admirable the many achievements the kings of Israel attained under these adverse conditions.

The very concise Bible narrative about the Philistine campaigns (1 Kgs. 15:27; 16:8–17) includes some valuable hints about the composition of the Israelite forces. Omri was commander of the general national levy (the people in arms) which was called up whenever necessary. Zimri, Elah's assassin, was 'captain of half his [Elah's] chariots' and was stationed with his corps (which comprised the strategic reserve) close to the king at his capital, the fortress town of Tirzah.[5] Tirzah had easy access to roads in all directions and was sited at the head of the Tirzah gorge (Wadi Farah), the main strategic artery between Samaria, the Jordan Valley and Gilead throughout the ages. The rest of the chariots were probably garrisoned in suitable 'chariot towns' throughout the kingdom. It seems feasible that at least part of these forces had been deployed in the plain around Gibbethon

The Israelite army

to screen off the siege operations from hostile interference and for subsequent exploitation of the hoped-for capture of the city.

The Israelite army seems thus to have carried on the Solomonic tradition in all its branches, and one may safely assume that its logistic pattern also followed the Solomonic model. The charioteers being regulars, it is natural to assume a modicum of rivalry and friction between them, especially between the household troops stationed at the capital and the general levy. It certainly seems likely that one aspect of the confrontation between the commanders of the former and the latter, following Elah's assassination, can be ascribed to the easily inflammable relationship typical between regulars and reservists.

Israelite fortifications

One field of action in which the first kings of Israel had to change the Solomonic model was in the concept of the role of permanent fortifications in the general national defence. Although we have no lists like those of the Solomonic or the Rehoboamite fortresses, we may deduce, from the enumeration of fortresses attacked by Ben-hadad I of Damascus in 885 BC, the existence of a strong line of closely placed fortresses, the 'Naphtali line', that fulfilled a fourfold purpose: (1) to block the descent from the Syrian plateau (the Golan Heights); (2) to prevent the ascent into Galilee from its eastern approaches; (3) to arrest hostile movement along the Upper Jordan Valley; (4) to serve as permanent bases for offensive action against the Golan and the Biqa (the great valley between the Hermon and the Lebanon massifs, known as Coele-Syria in the Second Temple period).

The passage about Ben-hadad's conquest mentions 'Ijon and Dan, and Abel-beth-maachah and all Cinneroth, with all the land of Naphtali' (1 Kgs. 15:20). A similar list from the time of the Assyrian invasion of Tiglath-pileser III (2 Kgs. 15:29), about 150 years later, mentions among the fortifications of the 'Naphtali line' (in addition to the above) Kedesh and Hazor. Since the destruction of Hazor after Solomon and its subsequent rebuilding under Omri or Ahab has been established by Professor Yigael Yadin's excavations,[6] one may assign its destruction to the conquest by Ben-hadad I and include it in the 'Naphtali line' from its inception. The inclusion of Hazor makes us allocate it to the last portion of the 1 Kings passage, which completes the list of fortresses mentioned by name with a general description: 'all the land of Naphtali'. Under pressure of military necessity, as well as the analogy of Hazor, one is tempted to add Kedesh to the original line and include among it the sites unnamed above. Surface finds on top of this still unexcavated site strengthen this hypothesis.[7]

The fortress of Cinneroth guarded the Via Maris, as well as the road around the Sea of Galilee, on top of a steep traverse, just north of the Genossar Valley, squeezed between the fortress hill and the sea into a defile a few yards wide.

Hazor's strategic role has been described on page 94.

Kedesh commands the only descent from the central highlands of Naphtali into the Upper Jordan Valley, opposite Lake Huleh. A modern asphalt-covered road was constructed there by the British for strategic purposes in their fight against Arab marauders in 1938. It was guarded by the police station of Nebi Yusha, which assumed the role of biblical Kedesh. True to its strategic importance and tactical qualities, this stronghold figured prominently in the heavy fighting for Galilee in the 1947–8 war for Israel's independence.

Abel-beth-maachah is in the centre, near the head of the Jordan Valley, where the road coming from the Biqa splits into two branches that pass to the west and east of it and descend from the Metulah ridge into the Huleh Valley.

Dan occupied a blocking position on the lowest spur of the Hermon massif, along the road that leads via Banias (classical Panias) to the top of the Syrian plateau. Crusaders, Saracens, Turks, British, Arabs and Israelis have subsequently fought for its possession. Typically, the kibbutz called Dan, built near the ancient city mound, has served both as a blocking position against Syrian attempts to gain the Jordan Valley and as a staging area for the conquest of the northern Golan during the Six Day War.

Ijon (Tell el-Dibbin) was the most northerly and advanced position. It was sited in the heart of the Biqa and reminds us, by its location, of the Solomonic strongholds. If it was not sustained by a number of secondary fortifications, it must have commanded this fertile valley and international highway by a detachment of chariots, for which it also served as a base.[8]

The ruins of the Israelite gateway of Dan.

The strongest belt of fortifications, however, must depend on the alertness of its defenders. When Baasha, king of Israel, attempted to push his borders on the central mountain plateau to a point some five miles from Jerusalem, and, after initial success, started to build the fortress of Ramah as a permanent menace to the Judean capital, Asa, king of Judah, took the fateful step of proposing to Ben-hadad an offensive alliance against Israel. This was the opportunity Ben-hadad was waiting for, only his armaments were not yet strong enough to wage a war of conquest. Thus he embarked upon a campaign with arms similar to those of Shishak. While Baasha's attention was firmly focused upon Judah (especially since he believed his rear was secured by his alliance with Damascus), the Aramcans swiftly moved down, and 'smote' the towns of the 'Naphtali line'.

Baasha was forced to break off his construction of Ramah, and Asa could use the respite to turn the tables on Israel: '... And they took away the stones of Ramah, and the timber thereof ... and king Asa built with them Geba of Benjamin, and Mizpah [as border fortresses against further Israelite aggression]' (1 Kgs. 15:22). Judah was saved, but the dangerous precedent of entering into a pact with an external power against the sister kingdom had been created, and a way had been pointed out to future aggressors.

7 ISRAEL UNDER OMRI AND AHAB

Omri was the king who succeeded in re-establishing Israel, in close coalition with Judah, as the major power in southern Syria and Greater Palestine. Surprisingly enough, however, nothing of his deeds has been preserved in the biblical records. A Jewish king who did not bow to the crown of David and did not accept the uniqueness of the Temple of Jerusalem – which means any of the kings of the Northern Kingdom – was mentioned by the biblical chronicler only insofar as he felt the matter was relevant to his own representation of the history of Judah.

It is from an extra-biblical source – the inscription upon the stele of Mesha, king of Moab – that we learn that Omri had conquered Moab again, from which we may infer that Ammon, too, must have come under his sway.[1] The Bible mentions in passing the foundation of Omri's new capital, Samaria, after which all of the Northern Kingdom came to be called the Kingdom of Samaria. Archaeological excavations have uncovered sizeable portions of the Israelite capital; strong and intricate fortifications, a sumptuous palace quarter, store houses and sundry administrative installations. We are left with an impression of might and prosperity.[2]

One of the main sources of Omri's economic strength was his intensification of the traditional alliance with the Phoenicians. The closeness of this alliance is inferred from the fact that it was cemented by the marriage of Ahab, Omri's heir apparent, to Jezebel, daughter of the king of Tyre. The alliance with Tyre is in itself a sign of military and political ascendancy. The political and economic survival of the Phoenician seafaring coastal states depended on securing their food-producing hinterland and the trade routes leading to their coastal dominions. This was generally achieved by entering into a pact with the most suitable (usually the strongest) of their neighbours.

The invasion of Ben-hadad II

The re-emergence of Israel was viewed with great concern by the Damascenes, and in the days of Ahab, who succeeded Omri *c.* 870 BC, Ben-hadad II decided to launch a preventive war before Israel could grow too strong and possibly launch a war of its own to regain the former Solomonic possessions on the Golan Heights and further north and east: 'And Ben-hadad the king of Syria gathered all his host together: and there were thirty and two kings with him, and horses, and chariots: and he went up and besieged

Samaria, and warred against it' (1 Kgs. 20:1).

Ben-hadad thus led a coalition of all the Aramean rulers who had become alarmed by Israel's regained strength. In the initial stage of his campaign, he succeeded in out-manœuvring the Israelite king. Ahab was still closeted with the 'elders' and the 'district governors' in Samaria deciding what strategy to choose when Ben-hadad appeared before the walls and laid siege to the city.[3] Cut off from the major part of his regular army, which was either still in its garrisons or had been cleverly evaded by Ben-hadad in his approach, Ahab had with him (for consultation) the functionaries and commanders of the reserves (the national levy). The national levy had therefore either not yet been called up or had not yet been deployed, and anyhow it was cut off from its leaders and chief staff officers. The situation of the Israelite forces may be compared to that of the British forces in North Africa when, during the initial stages of the German surprise attack on 31 March 1941, their commanding officers, Generals O'Connor and Neame, and their companions, walked into a German patrol and were taken prisoner.

Ahab's situation seemed desperate – and Ben-hadad certainly thought so.

(*Opposite*) An ivory sphinx from Ahab's palace at Samaria.

Samaria from the air: Omri's acropolis lies on the plateau behind the modern village of Sebastia, and the presumed site of Ben-hadad's camp is the valley at the top left of the picture.

To gain time and avert the worst, Ahab was prepared to accept Ben-hadad's terms, humiliating as they were. But Ben-hadad, judging Ahab's will to resist as broken, increased his terms to mean complete and humiliating prostration. It seems that this was exactly the development Ahab had waited for, as he used the degrading terms offered by the Damascenes to rouse the indignation of his counsellors and any flagging spirits among the elders and, backed by their support, rejected the Aramean offer.

Ben-hadad did not take Ahab's refusal as a major calamity. He believed Samaria's fall was a foregone conclusion. He had settled down to a hermetic but leisurely siege, well screened by his chariots from any possible outside interference and secure in his superiority. The Bible records the number of troops with Ahab in Samaria as no more than 8,000. Ben-hadad's confidence may be gathered from his reaction to Ahab's refusal to submit: 'The gods do so unto me, and more also, if the dust of Samaria shall suffice for handfuls for all the people that follow me' (1 Kgs. 20:10). Ahab's proverbial answer is still used in Hebrew to this very day: 'Tell him, Let not him that girdeth on his harness boast himself as he that putteth it off' (ibid., v. 11), upon which Ben-hadad ordered the preparation for the general assault. But his assault was anticipated by Ahab's.

The Israelite forces formed two divisions. The first, a small force of 232 men, was made up of the *ne'arim*, picked soldiers who formed the body-guards of the provincial governors (whom they had accompanied to the great council convened by Ahab at Samaria).[4] When Ben-hadad, who was drinking with his allies in the huts which had been erected for them outside the city, learned of the small number of assailants, he was in two minds about their purpose. Mellowed by wine, he treated the matter as a joke, saying: 'If they come out for peace, seize them alive; and if they come out for war, alive I want them seized' (author's translation, 1 Kgs. 20:18; the joke is based on a pun in the Hebrew original).

What followed next is largely conjecture, for the laconic biblical rendition simply states:

> So these young men of the princes of the provinces [provincial governors] came out of the city, and the army which followed them. And they slew every one his man: and the Syrians fled; and Israel pursued them: and Ben-hadad the king of Syria escaped on a horse with the horsemen. And the king of Israel went out, and smote the horses and chariots, and slew the Syrians with a great slaughter. (1 Kgs. 20:19–22)

It would appear that the Arameans treated the small Jewish force that made its way out of the city in the early afternoon, marching down the slope of the hill on which Samaria was built and in full sight of the enemy, like so much prey to be taken alive and paraded before their overlord to gratify his whim. But the *ne'arim* served as a decoy. While the general attention was focused upon them, the rest of the forces in Samaria pushed out and overran some of the Aramean regiments. The Israelite force must have included the household chariots which were quartered in Samaria and other élite units that formed the king's guard. The astonished Arameans wavered; and since their leaders were not with the troops, but drinking in Ben-hadad's company, their ranks broke and a general flight ensued, in which Ben-hadad and his companions were caught up. So sudden was Ben-hadad's flight that his royal chariot could not be made ready, and he had to jump on a horse to escape with a troop of fugitive horsemen. We note in passing here that cavalry makes its début on the Palestinian battlefield.

The fleeing Arameans were forced to pass within striking distance of one or more of the Israelite army bases, such as Shechem, Tirzah, Penuel, Megiddo or even Hazor. A considerable part of their flight took them through mountainous territory and defiles like the Tebez–Bezek or Wadi Tirzah road, which were deathtraps to retreating army units as late as 1918.[5] The alerted Israelite garrisons, as well as the spontaneous turn-out of people

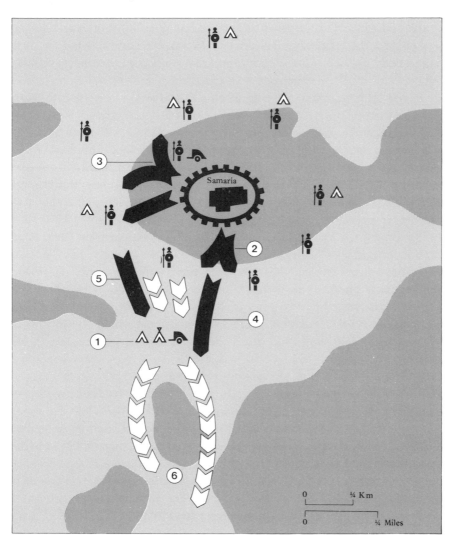

Ben-hadad's Siege of Samaria

1 Ben-hadad's camp during the siege.
2 The *ne'arim* distract the attention of the besieging Aramean forces.
3 The main Israelite army attacks the besiegers.
4 The unsupervised Aramean troops panic and retreat.
5 The Israelites press on to the Aramean base camp.
6 The Aramean base camp is routed, and they flee in disorder.

in arms, may have inflicted more damage on the fugitives than they had
suffered in actual combat.

The Samarian débâcle was closely scrutinized by Ben-hadad and his
aides:

And the servants of the king of Syria said unto him, Their gods are gods of
the hills; therefore they were stronger than we; but let us fight against them in
the plain, and surely we shall be stronger than they. And do this thing, Take the
kings away, every man out of his place, and put captains [governors] in their rooms:
and number thee an army, like the army thou hast lost, horse for horse, and chariot
for chariot. . . . And he harkened unto their voice, and did so. (1 Kgs. 20:23–5)

Were we to translate the causes found by the Damascene council for the
dies acer at Samaria into modern military jargon we would come up with
the following: (1) entanglement in terrain unsuitable for the deployment
and operation of the Aramean wheeled and mounted shock troops; (2)
decentralization of command and all other drawbacks endemic in a coalition
of many partners. The remedy proposed and accepted was: (1) manœuvring
so as to force the Israelites to fight in terrain congenial to the Aramean arms
and tactics; (2) prior to that, setting the Aramean house in order, by reshaping the Damascene state from a feudal confederacy into a single, centralized
state; and (3) rebuilding and re-equipping the Aramean army to a strength
equal to that before its rout.

The Damascene programme, especially points 2 and 3, necessitated a considerable amount of time for preparation and execution. This gave Ahab
years of peace from his north-eastern neighbour but, once bitten, twice shy,
he kept a constant watch over its military movements and preparations. So
he was forewarned when Ben-hadad's preparations had matured and he was
planning a second invasion.[6]

Ahab in the Golan Heights

This time Ahab was fully prepared, and he decided to prevent Ben-hadad
from launching his offensive and reaching Israelite territory. The Israelite
army attacked, but although it succeeded in gaining the Golan plateau before
the Arameans could halt its momentum, Ben-hadad was in time to lock the
narrow defile created by two parallel river gorges, leaving only a steep and
narrow ridge on the approach to the town of Aphek, which served him as
a rear base. In following Professor Yadin's placement of the armies in his
reconstruction of the battle,[7] we can imagine the two armies arrayed opposite
each other at the two ends of the defile for eight days. Then Ahab attacked
and routed his enemy. The Bible gives no hint of how the Israelite victory
was achieved. The Aphek defile is no more than 330 feet wide for about
440 yards and no frontal charge could succeed against a resolute defender.
There do exist, however, two flanking approaches: it was possible to make
a detour of the Aramean army on the east side of the defile by climbing
up to the rear from the north and south. The northern approach passes over
the Susita (Hippus) ridge, and the southern one, or rather ones, consist of
three or four steep foot-paths that lead up the northern slope of the Wadi
Barbara gorge.[8]

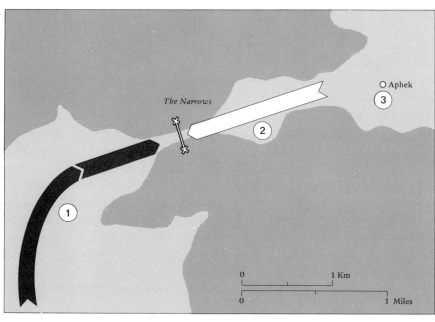

The Narrows

O Aphek

③

①

②

0   1 Km

0   1 Miles

**Ahab's Bid for the Golan
Heights** (phase one)

1 Ahab leads his troops to
prevent the new Syrian
invasion.
2 Ben-hadad blocks the
Israelite advance at the
Narrows.
3 The Aramean base camp at
Aphek.

Ahab's Bid for the Golan Heights (phase two)

By using the two flanking approaches, Ahab attacks the Arameans from all sides and succeeds in breaking their blocking position. The fleeing troops create chaos at Aphek, and Ben-hadad is forced to plead for mercy from Ahab.

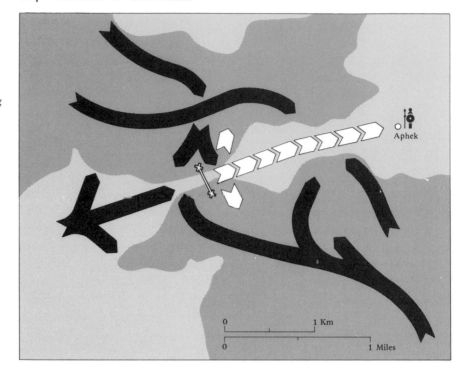

During the eight days of watching his enemy, Ahab had ample time to reconnoitre those outflanking approaches and to make up the assault parties that could turn the Damascene flank. It could be that Ahab had perfected his plans earlier but waited for over a week in order to exert psychological pressure on the Aramean soldiers, who, keyed up the whole time to counter any suspicious move through the defile, must have become jumpy or less alert by the end of the week. So when the Israelites appeared in their rear, and possibly unleashed a concerted frontal attack through the defile as well, the Aramean front broke and the fugitives made for nearby Aphek, whose defences literally crumbled under the press of people seeking refuge within its walls. Famous battles of more recent history, such as Blenheim (fought by the Duke of Marlborough in 1704) or Leuthen (fought by Frederick II of Prussia in 1757), have proved that even in a more controlled withdrawal the overflow of retreating troops makes the defence of a town of refuge impossible. Their sheer mass impedes the movement in the narrow space and makes their tactical employment an illusion.[9]

This fact was recognized by Ben-hadad, who decided to give himself up and throw himself at Ahab's feet in a passionate appeal for mercy. Much to the disgust of many an Israelite, Ahab showed great mildness and restraint towards his vanquished foe. In return for a pledge to renounce any claim on the former Israelite towns that had been captured by the Arameans, and his consent to the establishment of extra-territorial and otherwise privileged Israelite trade facilities in Damascus, Ben-hadad was released with honour and given safe-conduct home.

Ahab's gesture was more than simply magnanimous, although it was in character with his chivalrous nature, for he was also a far-sighted ruler. For once he hoped that by magnanimity towards his almost hereditary foe he might break the vicious circle of continuous wars. He therefore refrained from making the terms and form of victory too humiliating for the Arameans, whom he knew he had no power to control effectively in the long run and with whom he simply had to live. Furthermore, Ahab was most probably aware of the re-emergence of Assyria as a great expansionist power and envisaged the need to preserve the available resources and forces of Syria and Palestine for a major united effort to stem the Assyrian tide.

Indeed, it took only about two years for matters to come to a head and for the Assyrian invasion to materialize.[10] In the sixth year of his reign, Shalmanezer III (858–824 BC) began his great war of conquest to subdue the lands west of the Euphrates, after those east of the river had been subjugated. The strength of the Assyrian war machine can only be guessed, but it was undoubtedly the most sophisticated and complex the ancient world had known to date. This fact becomes apparent from studying the reliefs on the bronze gates at Balawat in ancient Iraq, on which some of Shalmanezer's campaigns are depicted.[11] They show variously armed corps of infantry fighting alongside chariots with a crew of three and cavalry armed with lance, spear or bow. Some of the troops are cased in heavy armour, others seem to wear no body armour at all. The siege train included, besides the well-known breaching tools and scaling ladders, modile four- and six-wheeled rams covered with sheet metal and/or hides. Boats, rafts and inflated animal skins served the first line as river-crossing equipment, and schematically laid-out fortified camps serviced the troops on their march.

The Assyrian cavalry appears here already at its fullest development. Its tactical employment was often in mixed units, either with infantry or

Meeting the Assyrian threat

Assyrian war chariots, a detail of the bronze gates of Balawat from the reign of Shalmanezer III.

variously armed horsemen. Experiments in minor tactics included the combat group of two troopers, one an archer and the other differently armed and shielding the archer when shooting his bow, much like the heavy foot-archers who were covered by a shield-bearing comrade.

Mounted troops were introduced to some extent in the Israelite armed forces as well, though they never attained the prominence that chariots retained throughout the existence of the Northern Kingdom. The independent cavalry arm may have evolved here, as elsewhere, out of the outrider who accompanied the chariots. On some Assyrian reliefs, these appear as couples teamed up with the chariots. Jehu's words to his lieutenant, Bidkar – 'when I and thou rode after Ahab' – have been quoted as proof that in Israel, too, mounted troops may initially have been used as couples fighting in support of one chariot each.[12]

The Assyrian army reached the Upper Orontes Valley but moving southwards found its way blocked by the Syro-Palestinian allied armies, which had drawn up in full battle array on the marches of Qarqar. Shalmanezer's annals have preserved the order of battle of forces allied against him: 'Hadadezer [Ben-hadad II] of Damascus: 1,200 chariots, 1,200 cavalrymen,

Assyrian archers, from an eighth-century BC relief.

(*Above*) Assyrian stone-slingers.

Assyrian pikemen, from a relief in the palace of Ashurbanipal at Nineveh.

A horse bit.

10,000 foot-soldiers; Irhuleni of Hamath: 700 chariots, 700 cavalrymen, 10,000 foot-soldiers; Ahab the Israelite: 2,000 chariots, 10,000 foot-soldiers; Que: 500 foot-soldiers; 1,000 soldiers from Musri [either a Syrian state or Egypt]; Arqad: 10 chariots, 10,000 soldiers; Arvad: 200 soldiers; Usanata [Usnu]: 200 soldiers; Shian: 30 chariots, 10,000 foot-soldiers; 1,000 (?) soldiers from Ammon; Gindibu the Arab: 1,000 camel riders.' In total, the allies mustered 3,940 chariots, 1,900 horsemen, 1,000 camel riders, and 52,900 foot-soldiers.[13]

This list is one of the most illuminating documents on the military history of the period. The Assyrian annalist cannot be suspected of having purposely decreased the size of the enemy's forces. The relatively modest number of each participant's contribution to the coalition army must therefore be taken at face value. Of course, these figures do not represent the complete strength of the respective armies, but they serve as a good yardstick as far as the size of the forces engaged in major campaigns is concerned. Incidentally, these numbers compare very well with the actual strength of forces on European battlefields. As far as individual battles are concerned, only nineteenth-century armies were able to deploy larger forces for a concerted effort. Those of the Middle Ages were all smaller.

Another interesting point is the meagre contribution of the Phoenician maritime cities, such as Arvad, and the absence of any mention of others, such as Tyre. As they were chiefly naval powers, they must have alerted their fleets to provide whatever naval support necessary, while their contribution to the warfare on land would have been confined to token forces and monetary contributions to the war effort, like the maritime powers of later ages (such as Venice, or Britain during much of her history).

Ahab, though third on the Assyrian list (which was more familiar with Assyria's more immediate neighbours), must have been among the prime movers, if not the central figure, of the coalition. Ben-hadad could not have assumed this position so shortly after his crushing defeat by the Israelite king. Although Ahab's cavalry force, if present, was so small as not to have deserved mention, his was by far the largest chariot contingent. The Israelite chariot corps was 800 chariots stronger than Ben-hadad's, the next strongest on the list. Interestingly enough, the strength of Ahab's vehicle force was also 800 chariots larger than that of Solomon, who had the resources of the

The terracotta bust of a horse, found at Achziv in western Galilee.

United Monarchy at his command. Moreover, the capacity of the stables at Megiddo has been calculated at 492 horses, which means that to maintain a corps of 2,000 chariots, twelve other bases with stables of similar capacity were required. Ahab's alliance with Tyre may explain part of his capacity to finance this expensive force. Another possibility is that part or all of his additional strength should be explained by the inclusion of the Judean chariots in the Israelite ranks, on the basis of the alliance of mutual assistance – defensive as well as offensive – that existed between Judah and Israel at that time.

The relatively small number of Israelite foot-soldiers is easily explained by Ahab's reluctance to denude his country of all armed forces, leaving them to fight another day if the expedition into northern Syria proved a failure. Besides, he had to leave sufficient forces behind to keep Moab at bay and to guard his borders against the Philistines in the west and tribal incursions from the east. Furthermore, for a campaign of a predictably considerable extent and a complicated logistic nature, Ahab would have used only regular troops.

The logistic effort involved in moving, feeding and maintaining an army of no less than 15,000 men and its train over roughly 300 miles was formidable. Comparison with early twentieth-century staff tables proves that, taking the Boer War as an example, a march of this extent took about thirty days.[14] This calculation, however, does not include bullock carts or camel trains, which move at a speed of about two miles per hour and slow up marching columns considerably. The sheer length of the Israelite marching columns comprising the expeditionary force is to be reckoned as about six miles, which necessitated a high standard of discipline with limited means of communication (visual, oral, runner and rider) at the command and staff's disposal. Each horse had to have about four pounds of fodder, if green fodder could not be provided, and each bullock would have consumed about three pounds of fodder for every twenty pounds of its own weight. The Israelite army's daily consumption of water amounted to an all-purpose average of 110,000 gallons. Although most of the marching was done through friendly terrain, and most of the supplies might have been provided by bases that were established near the march route, the methods and routine employed to safeguard the necessary supply at the right time from the right points, depots and bases meant a high degree of staff routine, the more so as we are dealing with a multi-national and multi-lingual alliance.

In spite of all these handicaps, the allied forces arrived at Qarqar in good order and, whatever their deficiencies in the latest weapons and equipment, they succeeded not only in beating off the Assyrian army, but mauled it so severely that for the time being Shalmanezer gave up any further military designs on Syria and the Palestinian land-bridge. No mention is made of the Qarqar campaign in the Bible, and it is to the credit of archaeological spadework that the Assyrian annals, chiselled in stone and bearing the story of this event, have come to light and to our attention.[15]

The Bible, for reasons of its own, takes up the thread of history some time after Ahab's return to Israel, when he was at the zenith of his might and prestige:

And it came to pass that Jehoshaphat the king of Judah came down to the king of Israel. And the king of Israel said unto his servants, Know ye that Ramoth in Gilead is ours, and we be still, and take it not out of the hand of the king of Syria? And he said unto Jehoshaphat, Wilt thou go with me to battle to Ramoth-gilead? And Jehoshaphat said to the king of Israel, I am as thou art, my people as thy people, my horses as thy horses. (1 Kgs. 22:2–4)

The historical setting and circumstances are clear. Jehoshaphat arrived at Samaria for one of the periodic consultations between the royal partners that had been going on since the conclusion of the treaty of alliance between the two kingdoms during the reign of Omri (?). Since Ben-hadad had not kept the promise given after his defeat at Aphek to restore all the former

Israelite towns, and he held on to the northern fringe of Gilead, Ahab proposed to his ally a common effort to retrieve by force what was his by right. Jehoshaphat's immediate and unreserved declaration of complete co-operation was prompted by three considerations: (1) his confidence in Ahab's military leadership; (2) his understanding of the importance of regaining the Yarmuk River as a border for the security of both kingdoms; and (3) his appreciation of the strategic and economic advantages of holding Ramoth-gilead, which straddled the King's Highway and the gateway to the rich grain-bearing regions west of the Hauran Mountains and the grazing

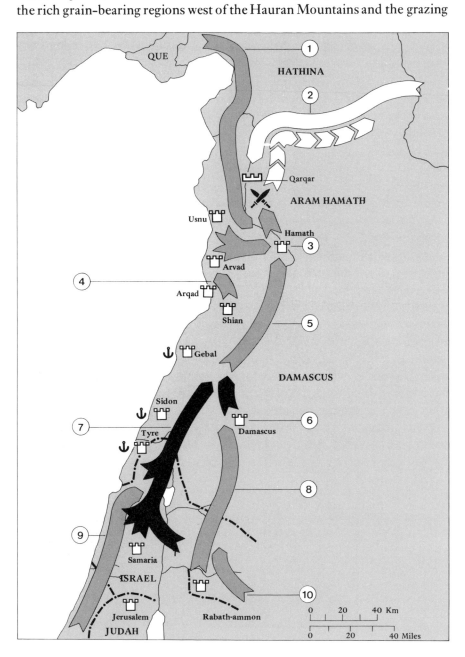

The March to Qarqar Against the Assyrians

1 The Queans: 500 foot-soldiers.
2 The huge Assyrian army.
3 The Emesians from Hamath: 700 chariots, 700 cavalry, 10,000 foot-soldiers.
4 The Phoenicians (from Arvad, Arqad, Shian and Usnu): 40 chariots, 20,200 foot-soldiers.
5 The combined forces of the southern allies.
6 The Damascenes: 1,200 chariots, 1,200 cavalry, 10,000 foot-soldiers.
7 The Israelites: 2,000 chariots, 10,000 foot-soldiers.
8 The Ammonites: 1,000 foot-soldiers.
9 The Egyptians (from Musri): 1,000 foot-soldiers.
10 The Arabs: 1,000 camels.

areas beyond, where the Jewish settlers were always hard pressed by sundry tribes and peoples.[16]

On the eve of the decisive encounter at Ramoth-gilead, which had been occupied by the Damascenes, Ben-hadad had some anxious hours contemplating his past defeats at the hand of Ahab. In briefing his officers, he betrayed his awe of Ahab's superior military leadership, for he judged him more dangerous than many a troop of soldiers: 'But the king of Syria commanded his thirty and two captains that had rule over his chariots, saying, Fight neither with small nor great, save only with the King of Israel' (1 Kgs. 22:31).

When the armies clashed on the following day, therefore, picked chariot troops attacked with the sole mission of hunting down Ahab and killing him. When one of these units attacked Jehoshaphat by mistake, it immediately broke contact when the king of Judah was properly identified. Ahab had been in the forefront of the mêlée from the start. By chance he had escaped the attention of the units of charioteers sent to trap him. But, while the battle was raging, a stray arrow struck between the joints of his armour and entered deep into his body. Seriously wounded, he was unable to carry on the assault personally. At the same time, however, the Aramean opposition was so strong and resolute that Ahab was afraid of leaving the battlefield even for a short time to dress his wound, in case his action was misinterpreted and led to an Israelite retreat. 'And the battle increased that day: howbeit the king of Israel stayed himself up in his chariot against the Syrians until the even: and about the time of the sun going down he died' (2 Chr. 18:34).

By heroically bleeding to death and hiding his mortal wound from the eyes of his troops until evening, and only then collapsing in mortal exhaustion, Ahab had averted defeat. Yet before the armies renewed their struggle on the following morning, the news of Ahab's death had spread among his troops. In the absence of any other outstanding leader to use this news to create anger and a clamour for revenge, consternation was paramount and the dispirited Israelites and Judeans retreated, 'every man to his own city and every man to his own country'.

8 ISRAEL AFTER AHAB

The indecisive outcome of Ahab's campaign against the Arameans, his death on the battlefield of Ramoth-gilead and the subsequent general consternation in Israel and Judah were exploited by Mesha, king of Moab, who rose in revolt to liberate his country from Israelite hegemony. His feats are described in detail on the famous stele he erected after his final victory (which was discovered about a century ago near ancient Dibon in Moab).[1] From this nearly unique source, insofar as it substantiates events mentioned in the Bible, we learn that Mesha did not stop at the borders of his kingdom, but crossed the Arnon River in the north and the Zered River in the south and captured towns and settlements in the Mishor (the lower hill country of Gilead) and, to a lesser degree, in northern Edom.[2]

The campaign against Mesha

King Ahaziah's accidental fall through a palace window left him a sick man for the larger part of his two-year reign, and it was only when his brother Jehoram succeeded (*c.* 850 BC) that Israel regained its equilibrium and the reconquest of Moab was planned.

And he [Jehoram] went and sent to Jehoshaphat the king of Judah, saying, The king of Moab hath rebelled against me: wilt thou go with me against Moab to battle? And he said, I will go up: I am as thou art, my people as thy people, and my horses as thy horses. And he said, Which way shall we go up? And he answered, The way through the wilderness of Edom. So the king of Israel went, and the king of Judah, and the king of Edom: and they fetched a compass of seven days' journey. . . . (2 Kgs. 3:7-9)

The Israelite–Judean alliance was thus still functioning. We know from the Mesha stele that the king of Judah was not only fulfilling his treaty obligation but was very much an interested party, since Mesha had occupied part of Edom, which was a Judean dependency and was ruled by a Judean governor.

The expeditionary force included foot-soldiers as well as chariots, and its senior commander was Jehoram, in spite of his youth. His planning displays imagination and daring. Since the direct approach over the River Jordan at Adam (or another ford) and then into Moab was the obvious route, he decided on an indirect approach, attacking Moab from the south. The Jordan area had always been the scene of border raids and clashes. Mesha made its refortification one of his first concerns and seems to have placed the area in a high state of military preparedness. He did so at the expense of the additional defence of his southern frontier, the approaches to which he knew to be most difficult owing to the severe topographic and climatic conditions.

Jehoram planned upon exactly this neglect of Moab's defences in the south, especially since he knew that the northern approaches to Moab were hardly topographically inviting either. The fate of the raids in World War One against Amman and Es-Salt, where superbly trained British forces were severely mauled by the Turkish defenders, illuminates the difficulties involved in fighting in this terrain. Besides, in Jehoram's time the only major passage over the Arnon River (Wadi Mujib) was effectively blocked against major troop movements by the newly refortified town of Aroer.

Consequently Jehoram chose the calculated risk of a desert match, in spite of his vulnerability to desert raiders and the difficulty of providing water for man and beast alike. We do not know the strength of the combined expeditionary force, but a reasonable estimate is about 35,000 men and some 400 horses. For a 20,000-strong expeditionary force, fourteen days' water supply was carried by 5,000 camels during the Turkish attack on the Suez Canal in January–February 1915, while another 2,500 camels carried the rest of the supplies.[3] The allies in about 849 BC could not have done with less than half of the total amount of camels at the Turks' disposal. These, of course, needed water for themselves, as did the live cattle that were driven behind the army to serve as the supply of fresh food during the desert march.

The extent of the turning movement and the sector where the allies wheeled in a northerly direction and began to penetrate Moabite-held territory can be estimated with the aid of two biblical passages: the first (2 Kgs. 3:9) mentions seven days as the length of the approach march. The second (2 Kgs. 3:16–20) states that on the seventh day, when the allies were in dire straits because of an acute water shortage, they were saved by the sudden flooding of a nearby wadi, caused by rain in the mountains of Edom so far in the distance that neither cloud nor tell-tale signs of rainfall could be seen or felt.

The region that is topographically and climatically most likely to yield a phenomenon of this type is the sloping south-eastern portion of the plateau of Edom. If we reckon an average of fifteen miles per day (commencing at Samaria) for the approach march of the allied army – encumbered with the herds of live cattle, food and water for men, horses and beasts of burden and slaughter – we come up just in this area and close to where the desert-fringe road bypasses the head of the Zered River (Wadi el-Hesa) gorge. Qalat el-Hasa was built here in the Middle Ages to protect this passage. It seems unlikely, though, that Jehoram would have taken all the risks involved in the southern approach only to have it lead him to the natural obstacle of the Zered River and the towns that guarded its banks and hinterland. A deep outflanking movement was thus the only logical solution, the more so since the Edomites were certainly knowledgeable about the water sources available even in these parts.

Whatever the reasons for the lack of water, a 'miraculous' downpour saved the attackers and, after successfully defeating the Moabites, they shut up Mesha in the strong fortress of Kir-hareseth, elsewhere called Kir-moab (present-day Kerak). Kerak's extremely favourable location made it one of the strongest forts of the realm in the Crusader period and later in Mameluk days, and it was famous for the many long sieges that it had withstood successfully. Though beset with many difficulties, the allied siege did make progress. When the crisis approached, Mesha attempted a massive break-out at the head of 700 picked men. For his breakthrough he chose what he justly considered the most vulnerable part of the besiegers' front, the sector held by the king of Edom and his levies. But even there he was beaten back; and in this hour of general disaster and last hope, 'he took his eldest son that should have reigned in his stead, and offered him for a burnt offering upon the wall' (2 Kgs. 3:27), upon which, according to the Bible, the Israelites broke off action and terminated the campaign.

No factual explanation exists for this abrupt end to so costly and so meticulously prepared a campaign, just on the verge of final, complete success. Child sacrifice has been known in the ancient East as an act performed *in extremis*, because of imminent plague. Some scholars have suggested that the plague would have broken out in besieged Kerak and that by this desperate act Mesha hoped to exorcise the evil spirits and stop it from spreading. The allies, afraid of contagion, thought it wisest to disengage as quickly as possible. Another explanation could be that Mesha believed in child sacrifice as a last resort to avert the anger of the gods, but by performing this act he unwittingly gave the impression that the plague had broken out which made the allies decamp.[4]

The precipitate retreat from Moab did much to annul the achievements of the first phases of that war. Mesha succeeded in preserving his independence and eventually regained the strongholds he had lost. Although the retreat from Moab did not in itself impair the sound substructure of ancient Israel's military strength, or the political alliances between the sister kingdoms or those between the sister kingdoms and Tyre, it was a humiliating experience. It is tempting therefore to look for further reasons for the hurried and complete termination of the allied campaign. A full-scale war on more than one front has been shunned, whenever possible, even by the great powers of the ancient East; and it could be that the decision to break off the Moabite campaign was prompted not, or not only, by the menace of contracting the plague from the stricken Moabites, but rather by warlike preparations by the Arameans.

The Bible speaks, for instance, of Damascene raiding parties. One such party captured the little girl who became a servant in the household of Naaman, 'captain of the host of the king of Syria'. Israel's natural strategic advantage was its interior lines. Merely by retracing its steps back from Moab,

The War Against Mesha

1 Mesha, King of Moab, revolts against Israelite hegemony and catures the Israelite garrison towns.

2 Jehoram decides to attack the rebellious Mesha from the south.

3 Jehoram is joined by the forces of Judah led by Jehoshaphat.

4 The Edomites join the Israelites and Judeans.

5 Mesha moves south to encounter the allies.

6 Mesha is defeated and chased to the fortress of Kir-haraseth, where the allies set up a siege.

7 The siege is broken off in mysterious circumstances and the allies retreat.

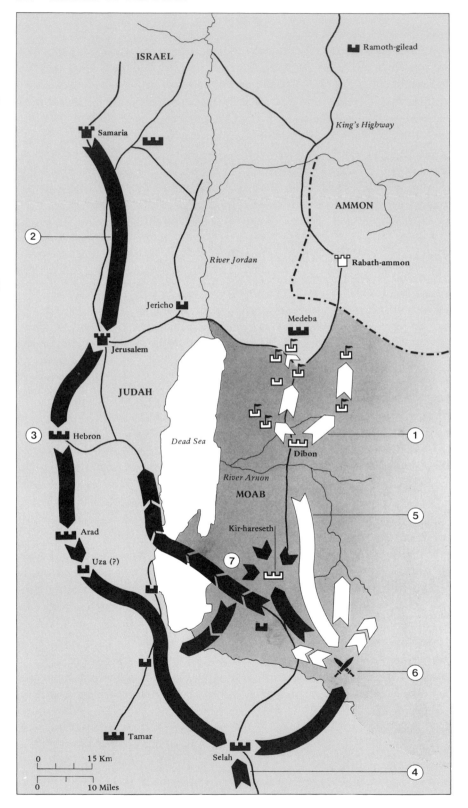

it strengthened the front against Damascus. Yet the Syrians had made good use of the years of respite from Israelite offensive activities, and before they could be stopped they went over to the attack. Famine and death impeded the victualling of the Israelite forces, and a Syrian offensive thrust brought the Damascenes right up to the gates of Samaria – only to beat a hasty retreat because of Jehoram's successful political manœuvring.

Having experienced at first hand the compelling force of a threat to his rear, Jehoram sought, and found, an understanding with his enemy's neighbours – 'the kings of the Hittites'. The tables were now turned on the Damascenes and, just as they had exploited Israel's war with the Moabites, Jehoram now utilized their entanglement with their northern neighbours to mount an attack on the Syrian rear.[5] The kings of Israel and Judah therefore renewed Ahab's struggle for north-eastern Gilead, the region of Ramoth. The preference given to Aram-Damascus over Moab makes good strategic sense. Damascus was a stronger and much more dangerous enemy. Once the Arameans were beaten and the Gileadite border safely established on the Yarmuk River, the field became clear for an attack upon Moab, the reduction of which was a sound assumption in those circumstances. Besides, the previously mentioned economic importance of the Ramoth region certainly was an additional motive for making it a primary objective.

Outwardly, at least, the second allied campaign to take Ramoth-gilead was a sign that the offensive capability of the sister kingdoms had not been permanently curtailed, nor were their spirits flagging. But when Jehoram was wounded (not far from where his father had received his fatal injury) and had to withdraw from the fighting to recuperate at his palace in Jezreel, revolt broke out in the allied camp. Elisha the prophet exploited the king of Judah's absence from camp (to visit his wounded cousin) to fan into open rebellion the long-simmering discontent of those who resented both the autocratic tendencies and the foreign cultural and religious practices that were spreading through the country. These factors were at least partly unavoidable by-products of Israel's international obligations, standing and relations. Yet they were basically alien to the traditionally simple mores of the people. The opposition naturally focused upon the king. To Elisha, the Phoenician alliance – with the religious and cultural influence exercised by the intermarriage between the royal houses of Israel and Tyre – was anathema. This influence was steadily spreading to Judah, as a consequence of the alliance between the two kingdoms, and the more so as Joram of Judah (father of the reigning King Ahaziah) had married Princess Athaliah, Ahab's daughter. So the prophet Elisha chose Jehu, 'captain of the king's host', from among the commanding officers assembled in the camp before Ramoth-gilead, and anointed him king over Israel.

Jehu's subsequent assassination of Jehoram and Ahaziah may be reckoned as the beginning of thirty-five years of decline for both the Jewish kingdoms.[6] By his deed, Jehu broke the traditional alliances with Tyre and Judah. Too weak to withstand the mounting Syrian pressure alone he called

The rise of Aram

upon the assistance of Shalmanezer of Assyria. But this step only increased Jehu's isolation, for we learn from the Assyrian annals that the coalition of the Syrian rulers against Shalmanezer did not break up after the Qarqar campaign and that three more times – in 849, 848 and 845 – Shalmanezer was successfully beaten back by the allied Syrian forces. Although Israel did not participate in these campaigns, or at least not with any force worth mentioning, the strictly neutral attitude of the Israelite king in these conflicts was in itself a contribution to the common cause. It permitted the Syrians to concentrate all their available forces against the Assyrians and served as a strong cover for the allies' rear. In the event of a more direct threat to his realm, Jehu was a major potential partner. But all this was lost once Jehu had openly and of his own free will declared for Assyria. So once the Assyrian tide had for the time being been beaten back, Hazael, the ruler of Damascus, spared no effort to crush the threat to his rear before the Assyrians could renew their attacks.

Hazael was now the central figure among the Syrian leaders, while the Jewish sister kingdoms – true to the saying 'united we stand, divided we fall' – were at the nadir of their power. In a series of campaigns, Israel was

King Jehu, whose assassination of Jehoram and Amaziah weakened Israel and forced him to seek Assyrian protection against Syria, pays homage to the Assyrian monarch, Shalmanezer III.

ravaged, parts of its territory were incorporated in the Damascene kingdom and the rest of the country, and Judah as well, were made tributary to Hazael. Only the Arameans' reluctance to become enmeshed in mountain warfare saved the kingdoms from complete conquest.

Once more the natural mountain redoubt, the mountains of Judah and Ephraim (Samaria), permitted the Jews to bide their time, while in Assyria the preparations for the conquest of the eastern Mediterranean from the Taurus Mountains to the Nile were completed. In a preliminary expedition the Assyrian king, Adadnirari III, crushed Damascus so decisively in 806 BC that it could no longer hinder the sister kingdoms from pushing out of the mountains and embarking on a speedy course of reconquest.

The period of external defeats and danger to the very existence of the Jewish states, even as vassals to their stronger neighbours, had produced a spiritual and moral revival, which was preceded by a period of soul search-ing among priests and laymen. While in the north the fiery Elisha tried to imbue king and country with religious zeal and Jewish consciousness, the High Priesthood of Judah brought about a cultural revolution and revival that was carried on by Jehoash, who reigned for thirty-eight years (836–798 BC). The more complete social revival, which was abetted by Judah's topographically more secure position, enabled Amaziah, son of Jehoash, to take the initiative even before the Israelites. In his war against the Edomites, the latter were once more reduced to vassaldom, and the trade routes from Eilat and Selah (later Petra) through the Negev to the Mediterranean coast were reopened.

This initial ascendancy was the background for a trial of strength between Amaziah and Jehoash of Israel, by the end of which Israel regained its former primacy. With the blessing of the dying Elisha, in about 790 BC Jehoash embarked on the reconquest of the territories lost to the Damascenes. In three campaigns the power of the Arameans was broken. The main focus of the decisive combat was Aphek. From there the Israelites outflanked the traditional routes to Damascus and the ridges that have served as its natural lines of defence down to the Yom Kippur War of 1973 by pushing out to-wards the east and approaching the enemy capital along the desert fringes.

The main base for this move was the town of Karnaim. Its capture was a necessary prerequisite to the approach from the east. The prophet Amos has preserved for us his generation's consciousness of the crucial importance of this achievement for subsequent developments. He mentions Lo-debar as the second crucial point to be taken by the Israelites.[7] Its location in the foothills of north-western Gilead proves that the victory here was the pre-liminary step to the reconquest of the Ramoth region and all the rest of Gilead, which, in turn, may be safely assumed to have paved the way for the reconquest of Ammon and Moab.

How much of the above, after the Aphek victory, was achieved by Jehoash or must be attributed to his son Jeroboam II is open to argument. The com-bined reigns of Jeroboam and Uzziah of Judah are to be considered as the

The Solomonic borders regained

second Golden Age of biblical Israel. Jeroboam occupied Damascus and re-established his border at Lebo-hamath on the Orontes. During the almost forty-five years of his reign, the Israelites, as well as their neighbours, grew accustomed to the idea that Israel was the foremost power in Syria. When Zachariah, the son of Jeroboam II, was murdered in (to us) unknown circumstances, it seemed only natural that Uzziah of Judah would step into his place and become the head of the Syrian rulers, who were burying their hatchets to combine forces against Assyria's renewed preparations for invasion.

The prophet Amos was active during the lifetime of Jeroboam, when Israel was at its zenith. His preaching starkly illuminates the causes of Israel's subsequent downfall. The sudden change from misery and weakness to the position of foremost military power created a false sense of self-reliance and security. The gathering clouds of military threat went unheeded, while the growing social gap between the 'haves' and the 'have nots' sapped the spirit that had contributed so much to the ascendancy of the Israelite host over that of its foes. When Zachariah was murdered by Shallum, the stage was set for a series of palace revolutions. The quick turnover of governments disrupted the continuity and stability of strategic planning and political activities. The prophet Hosea described this situation by calling Israel 'a silly dove without heart: they call to Egypt, they go to Assyria' (Hos. 7:11).

It is possible that this political indecision was the reason why Israel did not join the coalition that had formed under the leadership of Uzziah of Judah. The biblical text being silent on this subject, we have only the severely mutilated Assyrian inscriptions found at Calah on the Euphrates to rely upon. The outcome of the battle (described below) that raged in northern Syria was at best indecisive. Within a year or two, in 738, Tiglath-pileser III (Pul of the Bible) was able to invade the whole of Syria and levy a heavy tribute even from Israel and Judah. Israel's acquiescence in the Assyrian overlordship brought about the revolt of Pekah ben Remaliah, a senior officer, against Pekahiah, the reigning monarch. Pekah was a Gileadite and his ascendancy was typical of the increasing importance Gilead and its men had assumed in the Israelite kingdom. Appealing to the *amour propre* of his countrymen, who were conscious of their historic primacy over the Cis-Jordanians and their economic as well as military importance, Pekah used a company of Gileadites to overthrow and kill his king and master. To strengthen his hold over Israel, he must have moved additional units from their permanent station in Gilead, thus throwing it wide open to agression from Damascus (which had defected from Jewish hegemony some time before).

The fall of Israel

Rezon, king of Damascus, was quick to seize this chance, and his troops charged down as far south as Eilat. Thus Israel's malaise enabled Damascus to gain control over the whole King's Highway for the first time in biblical history. Economic implications aside, the Arameans could now move and

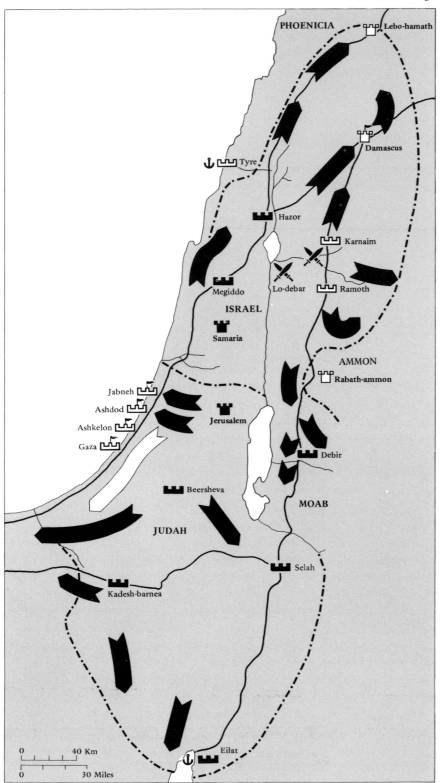

The Expansion of Israel
and Judah under
Jeroboam II and Uzziah

PHOENICIA

Lebo-hamath

Damascus

Tyre

Hazor

Karnaim

Megiddo

Lo-debar

Ramoth

ISRAEL

Samaria

AMMON

Rabath-ammon

Jabneh

Ashdod

Ashkelon

Jerusalem

Gaza

Debir

Beersheva

MOAB

JUDAH

Selah

Kadesh-barnea

Eilat

0   40 Km

0   30 Miles

deploy their forces as they wished all along the eastern borders of both Judah and Israel. While Israel accepted, willy-nilly, the status of a *de facto* Damascene satellite, Judah balked at an enforced alliance with Rezon and Pekah against Assyria. When these two monarchs tried to depose Ahaz of Judah, the latter, in desperation, declared his complete subjugation to Tiglath-pileser, who had in turn used the opportunities offered by Israel's evident dismemberment to launch an offensive along the Syro-Palestinian coast that went as far south as the borders of Egypt (present-day El Arish).

Tiglath-pileser was only too glad to use the pretext of coming to the rescue of his hard-pressed vassal. In a series of campaigns between 734 and 732, the whole of Syria and Palestine were conquered Assyrian reliefs prove that the Assyrian armies were even more diversified than before, and new types of arms and equipment had been added both for attack in the open field and for the siege of fortified places.[8] The defeats suffered by Tiglath-pileser's foes were so crushing and the Assyrian resources so well geared to the national war effort that he decided to turn all the conquered territories into permanent provinces. All Syria east of the tributary Phoenician coast (including Damascus), the Sharon coast, Galilee and Gilead were divided into provinces which became integral parts of the Assyrian empire. Israel was reduced to vassaldom within the confines of the mountains of Samaria. The fate of Judah was similar, while the former dependencies of both

Tiglath-pileser leads his troops in the siege of a city. From a relief in the Central Palace at Nimrod.

kingdoms were made into Assyrian provinces, independent of them. To weaken Israel further, Tiglath-pileser exiled to Assyria 13,500 Israelites from those walks of life essential for any further war effort.

Pekah did not survive this débâcle. He was deposed by Hoshea ben Elah, who began his reign as an Assyrian vassal. But neither king nor country were able to bear the foreign yoke listlessly. The basic urge for independence – that legacy from the tribal period which had never, even under the most autocratic monarch, been erased – reasserted itself once more, and the now tiny Israel, banking on its traditionally high political prestige, secretly began to conspire against Assyria: 'And the king of Assyria found conspiracy in Hoshea: for he had sent messengers to So king of Egypt, and brought no present to the king of Assyria, as he had done year by year: therefore the king of Assyria shut him up, and bound him in prison' (2 Kgs. 17:4). The biblical narrative is either incomplete or inconsistent. If Hoshea had foolishly decided to defy Shalmanezer V, Tiglath-pileser's successor, solely on his own, he cannot have been foolhardy enough to entrust himself, without a struggle, into the hands of the Assyrian authorities. Betrayal is a more plausible explanation – betrayal without sufficient proof, for otherwise Hoshea would have been put to death immediately. Another possibility is that in the hope that his country might be spared the full vengeance of Assyria, Hoshea decided to sacrifice his own person and gave himself up.

Whatever the cause, Samaria was left in its final hour without its king and leader. 'Then the king of Assyria came up throughout all the land, and went up to Samaria, and besieged it three years' (2 Kgs. 17:5). The deeds of valour, the persistence and all the suffering that made up the saga of the three-year siege of Samaria have remained unsung, or, rather, have been lost to posterity. Yet by its length alone, the siege of Samaria ranks with the most famous last stands against overwhelming odds in the annals of antiquity. Nineveh, the capital of Assyria, itself withstood Nabopolassar for less than two years; Carthage fell to the Romans after three years, about the same time as Samaria had held out; Alexander the Great captured Tyre after seven months; and the Roman general Marcellus reduced Syracuse after two years. Among the longest sieges of the modern period was that of Sebastopol in 1854–5, which lasted eleven months, and that of Paris in 1870–1 which lasted 132 days. The actual conquest of Samaria is credited to Sargon II, who entered the town in 722–721 BC. Major portions of the population of 'the ten tribes' were exiled and exchanged with gentile settlers from Syria and Mesopotamia. In this way, Israel was finally subdued.

9 JUDAH'S FORTIFICATIONS UNDER REHOBOAM

King Rehoboam was the architect of a security and defence system in Judah that lasted for generations after the United Monarchy split.[1] The whole subsequent military history of the Southern Kingdom must be understood as an outcome, development and elaboration of the strategic possibilities inherent in the military infrastructure of Judah as conceived by Rehoboam. Like Israel, immediately after the division of the United Kingdom Judah was made conscious of the changed balance of power by Pharaoh Shishak's invasion. Amazingly, after Shishak's move, Judah had enough resources left for Rehoboam to begin creating an all-round defence system:

And Rehoboam dwelt in Jerusalem, and built cities for defence in Judah. He built even Bethlehem, and Etam, and Tekoa, and Beth-zur, and Shoco [Socoh], and Adullam, and Gath, and Mareshah, and Ziph, and Adoraim, and Lachish, and Azekah, and Zorah, and Ajalon, and Hebron, which are in Judah and in Benjamin, fenced cities. (2 Chr. 11:5–10)

It could well be that it was precisely Shishak's invasion which made the Judeans realize the need for further sacrifice in order to prepare themselves against all future contingencies of a similar nature. It seems that, as so often in history, Shishak's terror campaign, aimed at weakening the will to resist, produced the opposite effect of a nationwide upsurge of spirit and a strengthening of the will to hold out against hostile coercion.

Rehoboam's system of defence represents a concept diametrically opposed to that of Solomon. With the limited resources at his disposal, Rehoboam decided to concentrate on the defence of the area primarily essential for the preservation of Judah's independence. His other outstanding consideration was the use of the fortification as a means to block any hostile penetration into that area. The fortifications were to be sited and disposed so as to compel the enemy to besiege as many strongholds as possible on any potential line of approach and to serve as bases for counter-attack once the enemy had exhausted much of his resources and offensive capabilities, or when, for whatever other reason, the hour for counter-offensive was deemed proper. Accordingly, Rehoboam decided to renounce the defence of all territory outside the Judean heartland (i.e. the Judean mountains), the cradle and natural bulwark of the southern tribes.

(*Opposite*) Lachish, one of Rehoboam's fortress towns, from the air.

The siting of Rehoboam's fortifications

Fixing the above-listed fortresses on the map elucidates the operational concept of the defences. Ajalon, Zorah, Socoh, Mareshah and Lachish each block one of the western approaches into the Judean mountain massif: Ajalon guards the Beth-horon ascent and the road over the Gibeonite cities to the plateau north of Jerusalem; Zorah the Sh'ar Hagai road (the modern Latrun–Jerusalem highway); Socoh the Elah Valley; Mareshah the Mareshah–Hebron road; and Lachish the Lachish–Hebron road.

All these fortresses were sited at an entrance to the mountains, where the east–west roads pass from the foothills into the slopes leading up to the central watershed plateau. Nature has marked this line of transition by a valley known in its northern portions as the Valley of Ajalon (discussed earlier in Joshua's pursuit of the Amorites). In this natural division between the piedmont and the steeply mounting slopes, the north–south avenues cut the east–west axes at the point of their entrance into the mountain territory. All the above-mentioned sites are located either directly above these cross-roads or close to them, thus permitting easy communications and the shift of troops from one fortress to the other, as well as creating a constant potential threat to the rear of any besieging force.

To provide more depth and cohesion to this line, one or perhaps two fortresses were erected on the chain of the foothills themselves: Azekah and Gath (Tel Saphit?). Some miles inside the Valley of Elah, an important side road branches off and reaches the plateau north of Hebron. This detour

Ruins at Lachish.

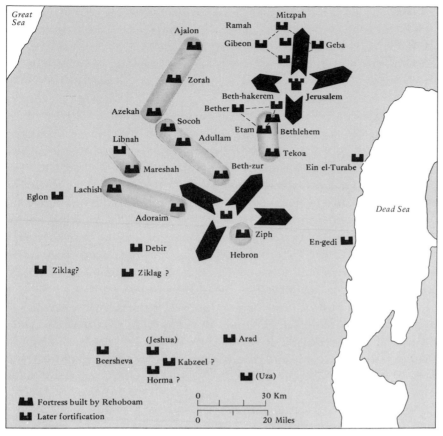

Great
Sea

Mitzpah

Ramah

Ajalon

Gibeon   Geba

Zorah

Beth-hakerem

Bether

Azekah   Jerusalem

Socoh   Etam

Libnah   Adullam   Bethlehem

Mareshah   Beth-zur   Tekoa

Eglon   Lachish   Ein el-Turabe

Adoraim   Dead Sea

Debir   Ziph

Hebron   En-gedi

Ziklag?   Ziklag ?

(Jeshua)   Arad

Beersheva   Kabzeel ?

Horma ?   (Uza)

⌊▄⌋ Fortress built by Rehoboam

⌊▄⌋ Later fortification

0   30 Km

0   20 Miles

was effectively blocked by the fortress of Adullam.

In the south, the topographical features of the terrain change considerably. The central mountain massif splits into two ridges. The western one descends in rather moderate gradients towards the Philistine plain and the Beersheva Valley, while the eastern one descends steeply to the Beersheva Valley and the Judean desert. The effective blocking of the fan-like approaches on the lower slopes of the western ridge necessitates the construction and maintenance of about half a dozen fortresses. The need to economize made Rehoboam abandon this idea, and he based the defence of this sector on the fortification of the nodal point where the fanning-out ascents converged. Adoraim, which fittingly has given its name to the whole of the western ridge, was therefore made the pivotal fortress of the southwestern approaches to the Judean heartland.

Like Adoraim in the west, the town of Ziph has lent its name to the eastern ridge, where it fulfilled the same function of nodal point. A large number of tracks from the Negev and the Dead Sea area converge upon Ziph. As long as the entrances of these tracks into the Judean mountains could not be fortified permanently, Ziph was the point to defend. A further consideration for the recession of the permanent line of defence in this sector was the scantiness of rain and water sources in the more forward, lower region.

Rehoboam's Fortresses in Judah (excluding the Negev)

Conditions along the eastern borders of the Judean mountains were similar to those along the south-eastern ridge, only more severe; so the two eastern fortresses, Tekoa and Etam, like Ziph, were designed as protection against Judah's eastern neighbours and the nomads. They, too, were built not at the entrance to the mountains but at the upper end of the slopes, on the edge of the watershed plateau.

The backbone for the entire defence system was the watershed road, along which troops from the central reserves (stationed at Jerusalem) could be moved quickly on interior lines to aid any threatened sector or to issue forward through any of the defended approaches and wrest the initiative from the enemy by means of a pre-emptive attack, a simultaneous movement or an offensive counter-action. This vital line was guarded by the fortresses of Bethlehem, Beth-zur and Hebron, each of which also straddled one or more of the ascents to the plateau at their junction with the watershed axis. From its location alone, Hebron was predestined to form a southern counter-weight to Jerusalem and to be chosen as a base for part of the strategic reserves kept ready for immediate deployment in the south.

The choice of existing towns as sites for royal fortresses can be explained by the fact that, in the Ancient East, all towns were built with an eye to the natural defensive qualities of their sites. Moreover, they had to control an adequate water supply and be easily connected to the existing road network. Besides, according to custom, the debris of destroyed towns was never

Tell Beersheva: the debris of successive towns built on one site created artificial mounds which afforded extra protection.

completely cleared; rather the existing wreckage was levelled out on top, so that the street levels grew higher and higher, and each successive town was built literally above its predecessor. These artificial additions to an originally elevated site furnished the *tells* (artificial city mounds) with their typically steep slopes, which afforded the towns additional protection. Also, the choice of existing town sites for fortifications permitted the incorporation of the towns' existing defences, or building materials from earlier defences, into the new fortifications.

Last but not least, by turning existing towns into fortresses, the town-dwellers themselves became a permanent addition and reserve to the necessarily limited regular garrison. Whenever these garrisons became depleted, either through withdrawal or by extended siege, the civilian population would be called upon to man the gaps on the battlements or in the breaches. Incidentally, the principle of using the civilian population in the stationary defence of their fortified settlements became one of the basic patterns of early Zionist planning and was incorporated into the overall national defence planning and organization of modern Israel.

If we return once more to our map, we discover, in spite of the substantial list of fortifications, some completely unprotected sectors. Most glaring is the absence of any fortification in the north, where the border was at best some $7\frac{1}{2}$ miles from Jerusalem, the capital, and on easily approachable terrain at that. The answer to this enigma is political. Rehoboam did not want to appear to be acquiescing in the defection of the north by purposely creating a permanent border with Israel. To serve the current needs, he made do with whatever facilities the existing defences of the border towns offered.

It is more difficult, however, to interpret the lack of any direct blocking of the Sorek Valley, the notorious axis of Philistine penetration, even as far as Jerusalem. Applying modern military thinking, with all due reservation one is by force of circumstances reminded of the principle of the 'killing ground' and the 'battlefield of one's own choosing'. Over the centuries, military thinkers have stated that a resolute enemy will usually attack, however strong the defences. But he will nonetheless try to attack at a spot he thinks is to his own best advantage. If confronted with a strong belt of fortifications, the reduction of which is estimated as extremely costly in resources and time, he will try to discover a weak link or detour to effect his breakthrough. Following this common human attitude, as late as World War Two planned area defences left considerable gaps in minefields and obstacles precisely to entice the enemy into directing a major effort along these less difficult approaches. In these presupposed sectors of enemy penetration, many measures were envisaged to meet the expected attack under the best possible conditions and with the highest chances of turning it into a costly and crushing defeat. In just this manner, the Germans were beaten at Alam el-Halfa in 1942 to such an extent that the conditions were created for the great British counter-attack at El Alamein.[2]

It is therefore possible to see in the lack of fortifications in the Sorek Valley

The gaps in the border fortifications

approach the intention of luring any future Shishak into the narrow valley, which could easily have been turned into a vast killing ground for the attacker. A further point indicating the intentional exposure of this route is the disregard of Beth-shemesh as a potential fortress. An existing town between Zorah and Azekah, Beth-shemesh was in a strong position and ideally placed to block the Sorek Valley effectively. This impression is sustained and strengthened by the channelling effect that the fortresses of Socoh and Azekah (to the south) and Zorah (to the north) must have had on any force approaching Jerusalem. Anyone who wished to avoid entanglement with them was automatically deflected towards the more southerly Sorek Valley gap.

The internal organization of the Rehoboamite defences is given by the chronicler as follows: 'And he fortified the strongholds, and put captains in them, and store of victuals, and of oil and wine. And in every several city he put shields and spears, and made them exceedingly strong, having Judah and Benjamin on his side' (2 Chr. 11:11–12). Rehoboam's formula to ensure the loyalty and smooth operation of his fortresses and their governors was rather amusing. His eighteen wives and threescore concubines had borne him twenty-eight sons. From among them, he chose both the commander of his standing army and the governors of his fortress towns: 'And he dealt wisely, and dispersed of all his children throughout all the countries of Judah and Benjamin, unto every fenced city: and he gave them victuals in abundance' (ibid., v. 23).

No belt of fortifications consists of main strongholds alone. Advanced positions, outposts, secondary approaches, detours and water sources all had to be guarded by variously shaped and sized forts, blockhouses and towers that connected the main links of the defensive belt and gave it depth in front and rear. In addition to these, a network of observation posts and signal stations, mostly in the form of towers, formed a vital adjunct to the Judean fortifications. Like any other chain of defence, it was operational only as long as its eyes and ears were functioning. In other words, there had to be a constant watch and a quick means to pass the alarm and the alert, as well as any tactical messages. This was usually done by smoke or fire signals, according to the state of visibility.[3] The Bible recognized the complexity of the defence system by using the phrase 'from the tower of the watchmen [observation post, smallest link of the chain] to the fenced city [the main link]'. The systematic research carried out over the last decade by the Archeological Survey of Israel, an organization created to register all surviving antiquities in the country, has brought to light remains of many minor fortifications that together created a small defence network between the major strongholds.

Of course, in the absence of suitable existing towns, even the major fortifications had to be built on virgin soil and as purely military sites. This was the case especially in the Negev, of which we shall write later. There, too, archaeological surveys and excavations have proved the existence of the above-mentioned lesser fortifications. Unfortunately, we are not able to assign most of the ruins registered so far either to Rehoboam or to any one of his successors. We do know for sure that Rehoboam's heirs constantly added to his fortification network until the fall of Judah, decreasing or expanding them according to the prevailing conditions. Consequently, many other main fortifications must have been added as well. But whatever the extent of the kingdom and its borders, the original belt of bulwarks as conceived by Rehoboam always remained the backbone of the national defence. The best proof of their value and function was the perseverance of Judah, more often than not under strong external pressure for 135 years after the destruction of Samaria. 'Rehoboam's fortifications' were, of course, not the only reason for this, but they were undoubtedly a major contribution.

Three instances have been chosen from those preserved in the biblical sources to show how the Judean defences broke actual invaders. The first is the invasion of Judah by 'Zerah the Ethiopian, with a host of a thousand thousand, and three hundred chariots' (2 Chr. 14:9) in the days of Asa, Rehoboam's grandson. 'Zerah the Ethiopian' was in all probability a local Kushite chieftain who enjoyed the support of the Pharaohs, and possibly even some kind of official standing within the framework of the Egyptian endeavours to gain a permanent foothold at the southern edge of the Palestinian land-bridge following Shishak's invasion.[4] Zerah's residence was at Gerar, which he had evidently temporarily lost to Judah. It is probable that he enjoyed the assistance of the Philistines, who took a step towards gaining their former status with any weakening of the Judeans. Although the number of his 'thousands' is vastly exaggerated, the amount of his chariots makes sense, even as an Egyptian auxiliary force.

Invasion attempts

The course of the Kushite invasion is a good example of the skilful use and exploitation of the Judean defences – or, for that matter, of any similarly conceived zone of defences. In the first phase, the aggressor was forced to brake his initial offensive impetus and finally to besiege one of the blocking fortresses, in this case Mareshah. While Zerah was losing time, supplies and forces on the siege and screening the besieging forces against interference from flanking fortresses, Asa was able to marshal his forces along the main lateral axis of manœuvre in the rear of his fortifications, the watershed road. In the next phase, Asa in his own time took the initiative by launching a counter-attack, which beat his enemy in a headlong flight. Exploitation of the victory enabled Asa to destroy many of the hostile strongholds, which paved the way for the reconquest of the lost territories in the southern plains by Jehoshaphat, his son.

The second instance in which a hostile invasion was broken by the defence belt of Judah is too shrouded in mystery to permit a rational appreciation. Suffice to say that an invasion of Ammonites, Moabites and Midianites, which included a large mass of lightly armed nomad fighters, was stopped and caught in the meshes of the eastern defences of Rehoboam's fortifications in the Tekoa area.

Assyrian helmet crests, found at Lachish.

The third instance in which we witness the successful functioning of the Judean fortress belt was in most severe conditions. In 701 BC Sennacherib, the great Assyrian warrior king, invaded the Palestinian land-bridge, where a coalition headed by Hezekiah, king of Judah, and Zidka, king of Ashkelon, had (with Egyptian aid) raised the standard of revolt against Assyrian domination. Reliefs from Nineveh, as well as the royal Assyrian annals, create a vivid picture of the desperate struggle. After the Egyptian expeditionary force had been defeated in the battle of Eltekeh, Sennacherib wheeled eastwards to attack Judah from the west. Simultaneously, a second army under Tartan, the Assyrian field marshal and royal cupbearer, advanced southwards along the watershed road from the Assyrian province of Samaria to Jerusalem. Sennacherib's plan was to pin down the Jewish king with a maximum of his forces in Jerusalem, thereby impeding his ability to direct the overall national defence effort and to neutralize all the reserves that might be employed for the relief of other sectors by shutting them up in the capital.

The Assyrian plan worked up to a point. Jerusalem was besieged, and King Hezekiah was shut up in his capital. Sennacherib could thus conduct the campaign aimed at the reduction of the strongholds with considerable freedom and little fear of interference. By this success the strategic utility of the Judean defence belt was severely impaired, since it was based largely on the ability of the reserves in Jerusalem to intervene at any given moment in any appropriate spot, as they had done during Zerah's invasion. But luckily for the Judeans, another quality of the Judean fortifications proved its worth, namely the exhaustive property of the fortresses, which had been strong to begin with and had been further strengthened by a succession of kings who were conscious of the necessity to improve the bulwarks of the Judean heartland.

Sennacherib's first major objective was Lachish. From the Assyrian graphic record, as well as from archaeological evidence, we gather that in spite of Hezekiah's inability to direct the Judean defence effort personally, the defensive campaign was waged with full vigour. Lachish did fall in the end, but the Assyrian losses were considerable. Yet even then Sennacherib could not unite his forces, but had to commence the siege of another main fortification, the strong fortress of Libnah. By that time, according to Assyrian sources, Sennacherib had been forced to capture forty-six fortified places in Judah.[5]

Hezekiah tried to placate his still terrible foe by a declaration of submission and payment of heavy tribute. However, Sennacherib felt that as long as Jewish independence was preserved in the vital land-bridge and as long as a rebellion against his hegemony was not punished with complete destruction of the rebel and his country, his hold over Syria and Palestine would not be secure. Accordingly, he doubled his efforts at the reduction of Judah and incurred further losses, which he was not able to make good within a short period. At that moment, the Egyptian Pharaoh Tirhakah culled fresh hope from the intelligence that Sennacherib was wasting his forces in Judah and decided that no better opportunity would be found to fall upon the weakened Assyrian rear and bring about Sennacherib's complete defeat.

When Sennacherib became aware of this imminent danger, he had no choice but to break off contact everywhere and to beat a hasty and ignominious retreat under cover of night. His retreat was so sudden that it seemed a miracle in the eyes of his generation. The modern military critic is reminded of the 'miracle' of Verdun, where in 1916 German obstinacy led to a tremendous sacrifice of men before they retreated out of sheer exhaustion; and, on a smaller scale, of Napoleon's retreat from before Acre because of the Turko–British threat to his Egyptian rear. An important factor in favour of holding out against Sennacherib was certainly the high

The Assyrian siege of Lachish, from a relief at Sennacherib's palace Nineveh.

The Assyrian Conquests

Assyrian commanders were always careful to avoid the Judean mountains, as this map of four important campaigns reveals:
1 Tiglath-pileser III's campaign in 734 BC.
2 Tiglath-pileser's campaign in 733–732 BC.
3 Sargon II's campaign in 721 BC.
4 Sargon's campaign in 720 BC.

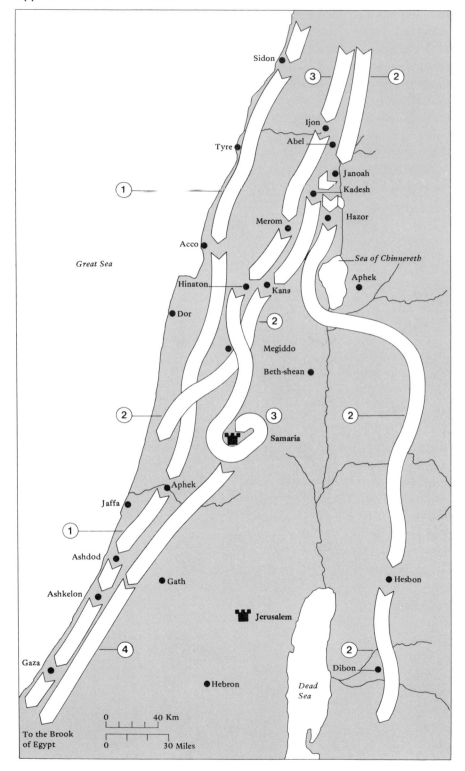

morale of the defenders. We do not wish to deny that belief in divine aid and counsel strengthened the Judeans in their desperate fight for survival, but we do wish to stress the decisive part played by Rehoboam's fortifications in making this miracle possible. Sennacherib's offensive power was severely curtailed, his heirs avoided becoming entangled in a war in the Judean heartland and Judah was able to survive for another 115 years, until its conquest in 587 BC by Nebuchadnezzar.

If we wish to sum up the factors behind Judah's survival after the division of the United Monarchy and its recurrent emergence as a vigorous state that was able to implement offensive strategy, Rehoboam's fortifications are the main material factor to be cited. Judah was like a large porcupine that could turn its bristles in all directions whenever it was threatened. Thus hostile forces operating on the Palestinian land-bridge tried their utmost to avoid entanglement in the Judean mountains, unless they had very particular reasons for doing otherwise.

Shalmanezer III (841 BC) and Tiglath-pileser III (734–732 BC), as well as Sargon II and Esarhaddon, all kept away from the Judean mountains, which curbed their impetus and neutralized much of their sophisticated offensive armament, while exposing them to all the dangers and rigours of one of the most wasteful types of war: that in well-defended mountain terrain. Only thus can we understand the reluctance of Sargon to press home his attack against Judah in his war of 712, when a coalition headed by the king of Ashdod and Hezekiah of Judah, with the active assistance of Shabaka – the vigorous first Pharaoh of the 25th (Ethiopian) Dynasty – threatened his hegemony. Although Azekah was captured after a long-drawn-out siege, conducted under the eyes of the supreme warlord himself, the effort involved in taking this fortress – which, according to the Assyrian description, 'was seated on the back of a mountain ridge, as sharp as sword's blade' – caused Sargon to desist from carrying his offensive further into the mountains.[6]

A similar sentiment was voiced by Pharaoh Necho in 609 BC, when he tried to convince Josiah, king of Judah, not to interfere with his progress along the Via Maris to fight the Assyrians: '. . . He sent ambassadors to him saying, What have I to do with thee, thou king of Judah? I come not against thee this day, but against the house wherewith I have war . . . forbear thee from meddling with God, who is with me . . .' (2 Chr. 35:21). As a matter of fact, it was usually only when Judah interfered with matters along the coastal plain that the armies of the Great Powers saw no alternative to assaulting the Judean mountain redoubt.

Small wonder that whenever resolute defenders occupied Judah in subsequent ages, attackers from the plains shied away from fighting in the mountains whenever possible. The great Napoleon himself expressed this attitude. When pressed by his generals and aides to turn eastwards after the capture of Gaza in 1799, he retorted: 'Oh no! Jerusalem is not in my line of operations. I do not wish to be assaulted by mountaineers in difficult roads . . . I am not ambitious of the fate of Cestius.'[7] Similarly, in 1917

Allenby turned into the mountains only after having conquered the plains as far as Jaffa, the Yarkon River and beyond. Typically, once he had been able to force the Beersheva–Gaza line, it took his troops only twelve days to cover the fifty-three miles up to the Yarkon. From there to the capture of Jerusalem, a distance of twenty-two miles, it became a slow, slogging, costly action of twenty-one days.

A portrait in relief of Sargon II.

10 JUDAH THROUGH THE REIGN OF UZZIAH

The first wars of the kingdom of Judah after the defection of Israel and Shishak's invasion can all be described as a futile trial of strength with Israel. King Asa's desperate step of calling in Ben-hadad I of Damascus against Israel has already been mentioned. In contrast to the long-range damage apparent to us, Asa's policy brought him the desired immediate respite. In building the fortresses of Geba and Mizpah, Asa bowed, at least for the time being, to the inevitable acceptance of the partition of the United Monarchy. However, while King Baasha of Israel had his hands full warding off the Damascenes, Asa was able to establish the border with Israel on a topographically secure line that leaned on the deep ravines of Wadi Beth-haninah and Wadi Suweinit, which descend the watershed plateau to the west and east respectively. To block the approach to Jerusalem even on this narrow strip of plateau, Asa (or one of his successors) renewed the fortifications of Gibeah of Saul, three miles north of the capital. Consequently, for the immediate defence of Jerusalem from the north, a quadrilateral of fortifications comprising Geba, Mizpah, Gibeon and Gibeah was created.[1]

According to archaeological evidence, another quadrilateral was created no later than the eighth century BC by building the fortress of Ramat Rahel (biblical Beth-hakerem). Together with Etam, Bether and Bethlehem, this quadrilateral guarded the immediate southern approaches to Jerusalem.[2]

Hemmed in by formidable powers and vassal-states, as well as by nomadic tribes from the desert, Judah was continually compelled to look to its defences. When Asa had completed the urgent task of securing his northern border, he continued his fortifying activities by filling in the gaps in Rehoboam's fortress belt.

And he built fenced cities in Judah: for the land had rest, and he had no war in those years ... Therefore he said unto Judah, Let us build these cities, and make about them walls and towers, gates and bars, while the land is yet before us; because we have sought the Lord our God ... and he has given us rest on every side. So they built and prospered. (2 Chr. 14:6–7)

We are not yet in a position to ascribe with certainty most of the additions to the Rehoboamite fortifications to any one of his successors, but the following incomplete list gives an idea of the extent of the network: En-gedi, Arad,

The city gate of Mizpah, a fortress which formed one corner of a quadrilateral defence network to the north of Jerusalem.

Tell Yeshua, Ira, Tell Khluweilfe (Ziklag?), Beth-shemesh and Gibeon, all within the orbit of the mountain redoubt. One may deduce from the tenor of the above-cited passage that Asa's fortifications were completed with the full co-operation of the entire population in a continuous, common national effort. The inhabitants of each city to be fortified may have contributed labour and material aid, according to royal assessment, once they had volunteered to share the burden. The success of this enterprise was explicitly stressed in the above passage.

Further large-scale fortifications were recorded from the time of Jehoshaphat: 'And Jehoshaphat waxed great exceedingly; and he built in Judah castles and cities of store' (2 Chr. 17:12). In contrast to his father, Asa, Jehoshaphat concentrated on the double task of plugging up the gaps between the main defences – the fortified towns – with forts, strongpoints and other minor works and refurbishing the logistic infrastructure of the national defence. The latter task was accomplished by operating logistic bases, the 'store cities', on much the same lines as in the United Monarchy. In addition, special attention was paid to making the main towns independent in their capability to produce and maintain arms and armament, including the servicing of war chariots.

A good example of a fort that served as link between major installations is Horvat Rasham, between Lachish and Azekah.[3] In townless areas, such as the zone between Jericho and Zoar (with only the oasis of En-gedi as a major, permanently occupied settlement), a series of forts such as Ein el-Turabe and Mugheir have come to light. An ever-mounting number of watchtowers and signal stations is still being uncovered. Some of these may belong to Jehoshaphat's great enterprise.[4]

Fortifications and siegecraft

The standard pattern of Judean and Israelite fortresses was squarish, with square protruding towers and crenellated battlements. Special attention was paid to the gates. In fortified towns where the walls followed the contours of the elevation they were built on, the gates were usually in the form of a strong tower with a narrow gateway that could be closed by two sets of doors and heavy bolts, and could also be secured in the passage between its internal compact units. The Bible sums all these up apropos Solomon's fortifications: 'and he built ... fenced cities, with double walls (thus in the Hebrew text), gates and bars'.[5]

Excavation, stray biblical passages and a host of murals and other paintings and reliefs from Egyptian, Assyrian and other sources permit us to reconstruct the Israelite fortifications and elaborate the above considerably. From Dan on the Aramean border to Kadesh-barnea on the confines of Sinai a special pattern of Israelite fortifications evolved which more often than not proves that building was carried out according to standardized techniques and specifications. The frequently used type of curtain-wall was the so-called 'casemate wall'. It is a double wall connected by internal partition walls that divide the space in between them into square compartments, 'casemates'. These might, at least in times of stress, be filled up with rubble, earth or the like, and provide the walls with considerable width and resilience. This mode of construction aimed at minimizing the effects of undermining and breaching devices. After the improved battering-ram was introduced by the Assyrians, the chances that this latest development in weaponry would either be caught within the filling of the casemate or would batter it into an even more solid mass were reasonably good. Furthermore, the flat roofs of the casemates served as a much wider battlement area than the necessarily narrow single wall, the *chemin de ronde*. Finally, the width of these walls created a new secure zone for movement on the inside, since it was nearly impossible to cover this by enemy missiles, which made for easy movement in the immediate rear of the battle zone.

Yet by no means all Israelite walls were of the casemate type. Many strong fortifications had at certain times solid curtains which were often built in segments that protruded and regressed in turn while following the contours of the topography. This arrangement ensured that the breaching effect of the battering-ram did not spread over a wider area than the segment that was assaulted. If the battlements were crowned by the above-mentioned wooden galleries, as depicted on the Lachish reliefs from Assyria, the protruding and regressing wall segments permitted some kind of enfilade. In other words, archers mounting the galleries could shoot more or less parallel to the adjacent wall section and cover its approaches, complementing the enfilading 'fire' of the towers, discussed below. Arad is one example where the earliest (tenth century BC) wall is casemated, the later one is solid, and the latest (sixth century) again casemated. Beersheva's tenth-century BC walls were solid, and then a century later they were changed into casemate walls. Kadesh-barnea, which was built in the ninth or eighth century BC, was always a casemate structure; and more examples could be given. It seems that there was no consensus of opinion about the relative value of the solid and the casemate curtains: at different times opinion shifted. Casemate fortresses continued, however, to be built in Palestine down to the end of the Byzantine period. In late Roman times they spread out from the east over all of the Roman Empire, and fortresses in Roman Britain or Germany were very much akin to those of the Israelites from a thousand years before.

The main drawbacks endemic in any type of fortification are the lack of depth in comparison with battle in the open field as well as the lack of flexibility. Fortifications are all there and easily visible. To minimize the tactical effect, the following devices were applied, one or more together: double walls like those at Lachish, sallyports and passages as at Ramat Rahel (Beth-hakerem), a glacis at the foot of the wall, and a moat. Both the latter, which were found at Lachish and Mizpah, had the joint purpose of stopping the hostile assault short of the walls, beneath lines within adequate distance for the accuracy and effectiveness of bow and sling, and protecting the base of the walls from easy undermining and breaching.

Among the major components of all major fortifications were the towers that protruded from the curtains and dominated their battlements. The towers' purpose was manifold. When at the climax of any siege the defenders on the battlements were unable to hit the enemy at the foot of the walls without exposing themselves dangerously to the attackers' missiles, the men posted on the towers could shoot along the walls and their immediate area from relatively secure positions. This enfilading or flanking fire has retained its decisive quality even in present-day field fortifications which are so designed as to afford a flanking field of fire to as many positions as possible. The placement of towers within bowshot distance of each other was obviously the rule to ensure a full enfilade.

No less important was the towers' height, for this afforded a wider field of vision and consequently a wider range of accurate 'fire'. Moreover, the height lent additional penetrating power to a discharge at a close-range target and enabled the defenders to hit enemies who had reached the crest of the walls. The towers also divided the curtains into separate compartments. Even if the curtain was either breached or carried in any of these sections, as long as the pair of towers at its sides was in good fighting order the defenders stood a fair chance of pushing back the attacker with the aid of the harassing fire provided by the men on the towers, which might feasibly serve as a base for the counter-attack. Moreover, there was no way of spreading out along the battlements before the flanking towers were subdued. To ensure that the towers were difficult to assail even from the battlements, from classical times easily-withdrawn wooden bridges or ladders connected

(*Opposite*) A casemate wall, from the ruins at Ramat Rahel (Beth-hakerem).

the two. This device could well go back to the First Temple period.

Special attention was paid to the gates, the most vulnerable spot in any fortress. In its most sophisticated form the approach to the gate was guarded by a double set of gate towers, such as in Megiddo, Samaria and Lachish. If he penetrated the outer gate, the attacker would find himself channelled into the passage between the gates, which had firing positions all along, exposing him to crossfire from two, three or four directions. Even if the entrance was defended by a single gate tower, it was usually a very strong and deep structure with internal guard rooms and upper-floor firing apertures so as to harass the enemy inside the gate. The gate towers had

The underground water tunnel at Megiddo.

at least a double set of gates on the outside and on the inside. The gateway passage could also be blocked in a third manner between the partition walls of the chambers flanking it.

Larger towns had citadels in which the defenders could make a last stand. These served as quarters for the regular garrisons quartered in the towns as well as arsenals of weapons for the population in times of trouble. Their elevated position and towers served as command posts for the direction of the overall defence (see for instance the arrangements at Hazor, Megiddo and Lachish).

A secure water supply could make all the difference in withstanding a siege if the assault failed. The engineers were able to tap very deep subterranean water tables, or even to tunnel hidden passages to outside sources of water: Hazor, Megiddo, Gibeon and Azekah are good examples.

Roads leading up to the gates were planned so that the attacker had to wheel round, which made him lose impetus and expose his right side (unprotected by his shield and so doubly vulnerable to the defenders). In situations like this the left-handed Benjaminites came in very handy since they could use their slings and still guard themselves from the right with a buckler.

Which brings us to the matter of siegecraft. To the military man it goes without saying that the art of defence and siege are complementary. It is difficult to decide whether Vauban (AD 1633–1707), possibly the greatest of all fortificatory engineers, or the Dutchman Coehorn (AD 1641–1704), his close runner-up, are to be remembered more as the builders of fortifications or as the inventors of means and ways to destroy them. It is thus almost axiomatic that, hand in hand with the development of the art of fortification, the Israelites from the days of the United Monarchy onwards became adept in all forms of siege warfare.

The procedure of a siege is very concisely described by Ezekiel in a warning of the fate awaiting Jerusalem: 'Lay a siege against it, set the camp also against it and set battering rams against it round about' (Ezek. 4:2). When prophesying Tyre's doom at the hands of Nebuchadnezzar, he says: 'He shall make a fort against thee and lift up the buckler against thee, and he shall set engines of war against thy walls and with his axes he shall break thy towers' (ibid., 26:8–9).

Jeremiah visualizes the siege of Jerusalem as follows: 'Hew ye down trees and cast a mount against Jerusalem' (Jer. 6:6). Strengthening the ramp of soil and stones either by a wooden skeleton or by the insertion of planks of wood remained a common device down to the Middle Ages. The ramps or banks were built to fill up any obstacles, such as moats, to gain enough height to apply scaling ladders and rams. Dislodging stones from the lower portion of the walls was not always the best means of battering a way into a beleaguered fortress; if the ram could be aimed higher, the crumbling wall would carry with it a proportion of the battlements and its defenders. Moreover the fallen debris would form a continuation of the ramp, which would afford a traversible approach into the breach.

But the biblical narrative has left almost no account of Israelite sappers at work, although there is a passage from Joab's siege of Abel Beth-maachah which proves that the Israelites applied all the above methods, and as early as David's time: 'And they came and besieged him [the rebel Sheba ben Bichri] in Abel . . . and they cast a bank against him and it stood in the trench and all the people that were with Joab battered to cast it down' (2 Sam. 20:15).

The ram was of course used from earliest times. When it was first used to batter down walls, we do not know. It is first represented upon an Egyptian fresco of the 12th Dynasty (twentieth century BC). In the Davidic period it might well have been developed into a device with a hardened, often ram-shaped head (hence its name), frequently metal-capped, which was either swung in a harness secured to a fixed wooden scaffolding or by a group of resolute men charging whatever they wished to breach. The Beni Hasan ram might well have been of another type, the kind with a sharp edge which can pry loose bricks and masonry by breaking the joints. These are the *hara-vot* of Hezekiah 26:8. How far the Jewish kingdoms were able to follow the Assyrian lead in using more and more elaborate rams installed in 'armoured' carts and towers is beyond our knowledge.

Siege warfare, which necessarily drew into its orbit the entire non-combatant population of the besieged town, was governed by a strict rule: before any hostile action, 'peace' was offered in return for surrender to the besieging army. If this offer was refused, the town's adult male population was liable to death and its property to confiscation. The same law remained valid until the nineteenth century AD, when for instance Jaffa, which had refused to surrender to Napoleon in March 1799, was handed over for plunder to the victorious French besieger.

Another Old Testament law governing siege warfare must be mentioned: 'When thou shalt besiege a city . . . thou shalt not destroy the trees thereof to force an axe against them . . . to employ them in the siege' (Deut. 20:19). The explanation given for this ruling is contained in the straightforward reading of the biblical original, 'for is the tree a human being so that you make war against it?'; or in the interpretation given to it by the English translators 'for the tree of the field is man's life'. While the Hebrew injunction bases itself on ethical and what we would call today 'ecological' considerations, the Authorized Version stresses the economic approach: what value will the captured town have if its sources of livelihood are undermined by destroying its agricultural plantations? It could be that both factors played their part in formulating this law.

Fortresses and fortress towers had their great stores both for victuals and the panoply of war. The elongated store houses ranged alongside each other in Beersheva covered an area of 600 square yards. Similar installations were found in Megiddo, Hazor and at Tell el-Hesa and Tell Gasileh. In other places the casemates served as depots and magazines.[6]

Nor was food for the spirit neglected. Excavations at Arad, Lachish and Beersheva have proved that even the centralist clergy of the Temple in Jerusalem bowed to the demand of the Jewish soldiers who were confined to long periods of service on frontier bases, and provided them with legalized 'military chapels'. The writer is inclined to see in this phenomenon the first step in the chain that later gave birth to that revolutionary institution which became the prototype for all subsequent monotheistic places of worship – the Jewish synagogue.[7]

Another function of these garrison sanctuaries was probably what we would call in modern parlance 'bases for army education units'. One may even postulate missionary activities among peoples and tribes on the borders. As in later times, political and military activity was backed up and followed by cultural and religious domination. As with the actions of the Levites during the United Monarchy, the border sanctuaries must have operated both internally and externally to teach and propagate Old Testament religion, law and culture. This assumption is supported by the sensational discovery of what is in all probability a large religious centre and place of worship inside

Ruins of some of the storehouses at Beersheva, which covered an area of 600 square yards.

a strong casemate fortress on the border between Judah and intermittently independent or Egyptian-dominated northern Sinai.

The army manning the defences and operating from inside this vast fortified system comprised, as in the United Monarchy and in the Northern Kingdom, both a regular nucleus and the national levy, the people in arms. The regulars included the royal guards, the picked infantry (named the 'runners') and, of course, the charioteers. It seems feasible that the 'runners' were trained to fight as a team with the chariots in mutually supporting formations. Foreign mercenaries from among the Sea Peoples (such as the Chereti and Pelethi) continued their traditional service with the House of David. Excavations at the fortress of Arad uncovered ostraca (pottery shards) pertaining to their quartermaster. They include the order to furnish Greek (?) mercenaries with certain victuals and have been dated by their discoverer, Yohanan Aharoni, to the time of Zedekiah, the last king of Judah.[8]

The size of the regular army must have varied in accordance with the state of the country's economic prosperity. Troops were deployed in the fortresses partly as stationary garrisons, partly as mobile forces to patrol, manœuvre and fight mainly in the open. The largest contingent of mobile field forces was quartered, as before, with the king in Jerusalem. The forces were formed in the by-now familiar tactical divisions of 'thousands', 'hundreds', 'fifties' and 'tens'.

The major difference between Judah and Israel was the Judean preponderance of the infantry as the main offensive arm. The defence of the Judean mountains made the emphasis on foot-soldiers mandatory, much as the broad valleys and plains of the north demanded the development of chariotry. Still, Jehoshaphat's words when placing himself at Ahab's command—'my horses as thy horses'—and the same phrase uttered by Jehoshaphat to Jehoram, Ahab's son, on the eve of their combined Moabite campaign, as well as other biblical allusions, prove the existence of Judean chariotry. The chariot was in fact the royal vehicle of war, from which the Judean king, like the kings of Egypt, Assyria, Babylon and later Persia, led his troops in battle. No single chariot could go into combat alone, a fact which indicates the existence of a force of fighting vehicles, however small. And mention of the captains of the charioteers and the chariots of King Jehoram (see below) proves the existence of more than a token force. This was only logical, for whenever Judah extended its sway over the Negev into Edom and the Mediterranean coastal plain, mobile chariotry in sizeable numbers could hardly be dispensed with.

As to the importance of the infantry in the Judean armies at all times, we possess an unfortunately severely mutilated inscription from the war of the Syrian coalition headed by King Uzziah of Judah against Tiglath-pileser. The Assyrian annalist ascribes his master's victory to the great feat of vanquishing the Judean infantry.[9] These troops certainly included levies from the national service army, about which we also have some information: 'And

Asa had an army of men that bare targets and spears, out of Judah three hundred thousand; and out of Benjamin, that bare shields and drew bows, two hundred and fourscore thousand: all these were mighty men of valour' (2 Chr. 14:8).

The traditional tribal proficiencies in warfare were evidently carried on. The tribe of Judah provided the phalanx of pikemen, while the Benjaminites continued their tradition as archers. The numbers quoted are nevertheless greatly overestimated. With a total population of one million inhabitants, it is questionable if even one-tenth could be marshalled for war at one and the same time.

An army list from the days of Jehoshaphat enumerates five main divisions of the people's army under their commanders: Adnah of Judah, commander over 300,000 men; Jehohanan of Judah, commander over 280,000 men; Amasiah of Judah, commander over 200,000 men; Eliada of Benjamin, commander of 200,000 archers; Jehozabad, commander over 180,000 archers. 'These waited on the king, beside those whom the king put in the fenced cities throughout all Judah' (2 Chr. 17:14–19). The people's army was therefore built in five divisions which may, like the twelve divisions of the former United Monarchy, have furnished, according to a fixed schedule, 'reserves on active service' for a fixed period every year. If we cross out one nought from each of the figures given above, the whole of the 'people in arms' amounts to 116,000, which is indeed possible.

The five divisions seem to have been combat divisions which were recruited from the twelve administrative divisions of the kingdom. Jehoshaphat was able to reconstruct the Solomonic infrastructure of basing the upkeep of his administration and army on twelve districts, each of which was responsible for the provisions for one month. As the limited manpower in each of these districts did not suffice for the formation of twelve district divisions, however, two or more districts had to combine to furnish the five divisions, which served either with a full complement for about eleven weeks yearly or, with half their strength, served twice a year for about one month.[10]

The defence of the Negev

The combined wars of Israel and Judah during the reigns of Ahab and Jehoram of Israel and Jehoshaphat of Judah have been described in chapter 7. It remains to survey the Negev, the south of the Judean kingdom, which was solely a Judean concern, divorced from any co-operation with Israel. The term Negev means 'dry country'. It comprises about 4,800 square miles between Beersheva and Ezion-geber. With an average precipitation of six inches per annum, the Negev could support only a nomad population. Since the Negev is a climatic border zone, fluctuations in even this minimum amount of rain are frequent, as well as in the subterranean sources feeding springs and wells. In dry periods the only means of salvation for the nomads was in gaining access, by foul means or fair, to the arable country, which was endowed with more enduring sources of water and a variety of pasture-lands, as well as the crops and plants grown by the landed peasants. One of these inroads was the Midianite invasion met by Gideon in the Jezreel

Valley, some 150 years before the foundation of the kingdom of Saul.

After the foundation of the monarchy, the permanent task of its kings was to safeguard orderly and secure life in their country by maintaining a secure grip on the southern borders. In other words, a line of border defences specially adapted to repelling the raiders from the Negev and beyond was essential to the maintenance of peace in Judah. The natural line of defence is that of the largely steep-sided, deep gorge of the Besor, Beersheva and Malkhata rivers, which are tributaries of one another and form a continuous line of demarcation that can be turned, when appropriately fortified and well patrolled, into an effective line of defence.[11]

Actually, a line of fortified border strongholds can be made out along this line, including Beersheva, Tell Masos (Hormah?) and Malkhata.[12] To make this line effective, depth was needed, since the swift raiders from the desert were capable of penetrating any linear defence. We are beginning to uncover, between the main bases of the wadi line and the upper slopes of the Hebron mountains, a constantly growing number of sites which gave depth to the forward line. We have to imagine the desert raiding parties becoming enmeshed in a network of mutually supporting fortified localities. If the raiders nonetheless succeeded in penetrating the fortified belt on their way into the arable country, they became seriously vulnerable to interception when laden with loot and/or fattened flocks on their way back. That interceptions like these were possible, even without the existence of properly functioning border defences, is demonstrated by David's pursuit and interception of the party that had raided Ziklag while he was still a feudal *condottiere* in Gittite pay (1 Sam. 30). How much more effective an action of that kind would have been had it evolved out of a permanent routine of border forces!

The major value of the Negev beyond the wadi line was as a connecting link between the land and sea commerce that converged upon Edom and the Gulf of Eilat on one side, and the Philistine plain on the other. Fittingly, when Strabo, about a thousand years after Solomon, describes Gaza, he states: '... There is said to be a passage thence across of 1,260 stadia to the city of Aila [Eilat], situated on the innermost recess of the Arabian Gulf ... Travelling is performed on camels through a desert and sandy country' (*Geography* XVI.II.30). And again: 'Aelana [Aila-Eilat] is a city ... opposite to Gaza' (ibid., XVI.IV.4). Pliny the Elder, in about AD 75, mentions the other main trade centre with which Gaza and the Philistine coast was connected: '... Next are the Nabateans inhabiting a town named Petra [which was the biblical Selah, capital of Edom]. At Petra two roads meet, one leading from Syria to Palmyra and the other coming from Gaza' (*Historia Naturalis* VI.II.144).

The districts of Edom, the Negev and the Philistine coast were always linked by common commercial interests. Both Edomites and Philistines were interested in maintaining good relations with the nomads in the Negev, who already included Arab tribes, so as to ensure the flow of goods from one commercial centre to the other. The establishment of the Israelite monarchy added a fourth interested party. Israelite supremacy over the whole Negev could be exploited passively by demanding a share in the profits of the existing trade, and actively by the development of new trade routes through the diversion of part of the flow of trade into or via the Israelite dominions. Both methods were employed, the second by diverting part of the north–south (or vice versa) trade along the Palestinian land-bridge into an easterly direction and by capturing part of the Egyptian Red Sea trade monopoly through the development of Ezion-geber or nearby Eilat and channelling off some of the Red Sea traffic from Egyptian ports.

All the other interested parties were united in their desire to sabotage the newly arrived Israelite competitors. To safeguard the desert routes and the trade stations from Solomonic times onwards, the Israelites were forced to fortify and control the trans-Negev desert routes and the main sources of water in the wilderness. The first system of fortified desert routes was clearly Solomonic, and much of Pharaoh Shishak's campaign of 924 BC was directed against it.[13] The reoccupation of the southern Negev (to its natural boundary with Sinai, the River of Egypt?) was the achievement of Jehoshaphat: 'Also some of [the latter two words are inexactly translated][14] the Philistines brought Jehoshaphat presents, and tribute silver; and the Arabians brought him flocks, seven thousand and seven hundred rams, and seven thousand and seven hundred he goats' (2 Chr. 17:11). We note that the tributes of the Philistines and the Arabs are mentioned together. They were brought to heel not only by the exercise of military power, but by the economic pressure brought to bear by the Judean mastery of the Negev.

The third factor in the Negev also has a place in Jehoshaphat's activities. The Bible mentions, almost in a parenthetical way, that, 'There was then no king in Edom: a deputy was king' (1 Kgs. 22:47). The Edomite problem evidently was solved by complete annexation of the kingdom.

With the stage thus set, the way was open to renew the Red Sea trade. 'Jehoshaphat made ships of Tharshish to go to Ophir for gold: but they went not; for the ships were broken at Ezion-geber. Then said Ahaziah the son of Ahab unto Jehoshaphat, Let my servants go with thy servants in the ships. But Jehoshaphat would not' (1 Kgs. 22:48–9). Rather than let the Northern Kingdom become too closely involved in the Negev, Jehoshaphat declined the offer of the men of Israel, who had, by then, gained some valuable nautical experience.

Though the Bible does not mention it, either Jehoshaphat or perhaps Uzziah must have renewed the Solomonic naval venture in the Red Sea after all. Scholars agree that the frequent winds blowing inland at Ezion-geber were responsible for the destruction of the Judean fleet and interpret the subsequent building of Eilat as the shifting of the naval base to a more secure spot. Surely no one would have taken this trouble if ships had not been launched?

The excavations of Tell el-Kheleifeh (biblical Ezion-geber) have now proved the existence of fortifications from the period of Jehoshaphat. Two other sites, the fortress of Kadesh-barnea, on the southern approaches to the Negev from Sinai, and Arad, in the rear of the wadi line (Wadi Besor–Beersheva–Malkhata), have definite strata of construction connected with this king. Once again, the spade has sustained the biblical account.[15] Recently another Jewish fortress was identified at Qureiye, about thirty miles south of Kadesh-barnea. Its location suggests that the southernmost border of Judah in its heyday was established along a topographically sound line of escarpments and wadi beds that skirts the ancient road from Eilat to El Arish and Gaza, respectively. Thus we can imagine that much the same dust that was stirred up along this border track by Egyptian patrol cars until 1967 swirled in the wake of Judean chariots 2,800 years ago.

Jehoram's campaign against Edom

Jehu's revolt and the subsequent weakening of Israel had its immediate repercussions in the south.

In his [Jehoram, son of Jehoshaphat's] days Edom revolted from under the hand of Judah, and made a king over themselves. So Joram [Jehoram] went over to Zair, and all the chariots with him: and he rose by night, and smote the Edomites which compassed him about, and the captains of the chariots: and the people fled into their tents. (2 Kgs. 8:20–1)

At first reading, this passage does not make sense. Why, if the king was victorious, did the people abandon the battlefield and disperse in flight? But on closer inspection the following solution suggests itself.

After a difficult and tiring approach march, which necessitated manhandling the chariots and possibly even dismantling them so as to negotiate narrow, rocky and steep passages,[16] the Judean army redeployed in the plain south of the Dead Sea (the biblical Kikar). Because of the many cracks, crevices and dry wadi beds in the marly soil it was still hard going for the chariots, the infantry, the train and the auxiliary services. At night the army camped in or near the oasis of Zoar. Because of general fatigue, the soldiers were probably less alert than usual, and the guard details – who each had to stand watch one-third of the night – similarly less attentive.

To the rebellious Edomites the appearance of chariots was most unwelcome. With their largely irregular insurgent forces, they knew that they had little chance against chariots in the open field. Admittedly, Jehoram had risked his chariots in difficult terrain, broken country and, behind that, the mountains of Edom. Yet the Judean charioteers were themselves mountain men and were probably better at manœuvring in adverse topographical conditions than most. So Jehoram thought that his risk in building his expedition around 'armour' was well calculated and worthwhile – the more so since we know of no reason why the 'runners' (the choice infantry), well versed in co-operation and mutual supporting actions with the chariots, were not taking part in this campaign.

Hence the Edomites were rightly troubled, but they did not panic. A cool appreciation of the situation had convinced them that, as was the case with the Israelites until Davidic times, their sole salvation lay in surprising the enemy in a situation where he could not exploit his superior armament. The opportunity presented itself on the night of the exhausted Judean halt at Zoar.

Under cover of darkness, the Edomites crept up to the Judean camp and jumped off for a sudden assault from a point quite close to the negligently guarded perimeter. Their main objective was the person of the king, the commanders of the chariots (in whose company he was camping), the chariots and the horses. By concentrating on these objectives, the attackers hoped to strike their enemy's offensive arm decisively. Luckily for Jehoram, he was alerted in time to wake, arm and organize the defence of his dismounted charioteers. If the Judean camp followed the usual pattern that night, the 'runners' must have camped in the vicinity of, or around, the chariots. They, too, may have been able to make use of the last-minute alarm to grasp their arms and rush to the defence. It seems that the king and many an unsung hero acquitted himself very well that night, and through many deeds of personal valour the Edomites were beaten off. Their defeat was such that Jehoram could make an unmolested retreat with the forces that had fought under his personal command.

While the king had been surrounded by attacking Edomites, he could exercise no command over the rest of the camp. There, with no knowledge of his fate, and in the absence of appropriate leadership, the sudden surprise in the dark of the night changed into sheer panic, and the stricken soldiery dispersed in headlong flight. Deprived of a large portion of his forces, Jehoram was forced to call off his campaign, and when domestic troubles focused attention on the home front, Edom made its independence final.

Edom was able to preserve this independence for two generations, about

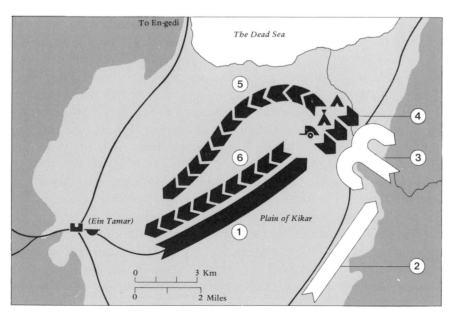

Jehoram's Campaign Against Edom

1 The Judean approach route.
2 Edomites from Selah.
3 The Edomites surprise the Judean camp in the night.
4 Jehoram repulses the Edomites.
5 Part of the Judean army, ignorant of Jehoram's success, panics and flees.
6 King Jehoram and his corps make an orderly retreat.

thirty-five years. Judah was at its nadir. Deprived of Israel's shield against the Arameans, because of the disastrous aftermath of Jehu's revolt, Judah stood alone against the full might of Damascus at the zenith of its power. Hazael of Damascus was about to implement the age-old dream of making Damascus mistress of the Palestinian land-bridge by bringing all its highways under his direct control. If successful, his dominant position in world trade would have brought him to a position in world affairs equal to that of David and Solomon.

The 'neighbour's neighbours' were, as so often in a geopolitical setting, once again a natural ally. Moab and Edom in the east and the Philistines in the west much preferred some kind of distant Aramean hegemony to living, albeit independently, in the shadow of the Jews. In his campaigns during the last two decades of the ninth century BC, Hazael captured first the King's Highway in Trans-Jordan, linking up at the Arnon River with Moab, and then the Via Maris, linking up with the Philistines at Gath. Both the Moabites and the Philistines, as well as the Edomites, were certainly happy to act as carriers and intermediaries in any trade activities emanating from Damascus.

At this point, Hazael failed to carry his plan through to its logical conclusion. It could be that he correctly judged himself unable to do so, for by abstaining from conquering the Cis-Jordanian central massif of Judah and Samaria, he left the Jews in command of the watershed road in the centre of the natural mountain bastion. Moving on this central interior line, the Jews continued to command the approaches to the flanks of both the King's Highway and the Via Maris. Consequently, they could bide their time until the appropriate moment presented itself to issue forth from their mountain redoubt and re-establish their authority over the lost territories and trade routes.

Amaziah's reconquest of Edom

The first to take the initiative this time were the Judeans. With Aramean attention focused upon the Assyrian front in *c.* 785 BC Amaziah of Judah staged a campaign to reconquer Edom. It seems that his planning followed that of Jehoram, while learning the lessons of the latter's campaign so as to avoid its pitfalls. When the armies met in the Vale of Salt, some six miles south of Zoar, the Judeans inflicted a crushing defeat on the Edomites that paved the way for the reconquest of all of northern Edom, including the capital of the country, Selah (the Rock), whose name Jehoram changed to Joktheel (2 Kgs. 14:7).

There are three interesting sidelights to the biblical narrative of Amaziah's Edomite campaign, as given in the parallel account in 2 Chronicles, 25. The first is that there was an official census of the male population in Judah which may have been updated at fixed intervals, but was definitely taken prior to planned large-scale military activities. The second is that the age of compulsory national service was fixed at twenty. The reason for this is not hard to guess. The seventeenth- to twenty-year-olds were needed to take over the jobs vacated by the national levy and to help the elders and women keep up their farms, workshops and other enterprises. In doing so, they were able to develop their physical strength to full maturity. In an age when the primary training in the exercise of arms was passed from father to son, these youngsters may not yet have been considered dextrous enough to join a major military expedition. On the other hand, their presence on the home front assured that the rear was not completely denuded of males capable of defending the homesteads in unforeseen contingencies.

Amaziah was a very strong-minded and strong-willed ruler, with far-reaching aspirations. In his time we have the first strong, albeit indirect, evidence for a corps of cavalry in the Judean army. For all his successes and drive, however, Amaziah failed to wrest from Israel the status of primacy among the Jewish kingdoms. Nevertheless, the outcome of this competition was the re-implementation of the active alliance between the two kingdoms, which served as basis for the second Golden Age of biblical Israel. Its external expression was, as indicated earlier, the re-extension of Jewish dominion over the major part of the territory of the former United Monarchy.

The tombstone of King Uzziah; the Aramaic inscription reads: 'Hither were brought the bones of Uzziah King of Jordan. Do not open.' They had been brought from the Tombs of the Kings where Uzziah was first buried.

Uzziah

Amaziah was to Uzziah, his son, what Philip later was to Alexander – the forger of the tools to be used by his son and heir to bring the kingdom to a high standard of prosperity and strength. Apropos Alexander, it has become the Western custom since the Hellenistic age to bestow upon outstanding rulers the attribute 'the Great'. Surely Uzziah deserves to be called 'Uzziah the Great' because of his achievements in many branches of government. Since national security is always influenced by many more factors than military matters, which are the subject of these pages, we must remember that cultural, social, religious and economic forces were all instrumental in enabling Uzziah to achieve his feats of arms.

And he [Uzziah] went forth and warred against the Philistines, and brake down the wall of Gath, and the wall of Jabneh, and the wall of Ashdod, and built cities [castles] about Ashdod, and among the Philistines. And God helped him against the Philistines, and against the Arabians that dwelt in Gur-baal, and the Mehunim. And the Ammonites gave gifts to Uzziah: and his name spread abroad even to the entering in of Egypt; for he strengthened himself exceedingly. (2 Chr. 26:6–8)

Uzziah thus reduced the Philistines once more to a state of absolute vassaldom. To ensure his grip, he dismantled the fortifications of some of their main towns and put Judean garrisons in Philistine towns and territory, for whose protection he erected special castles.

The geopolitical and geo-economic inter-relationship between the Philistines, the Arab tribes of the Negev and Southern Trans-Jordan (Edom) has been described earlier in these pages. With the reduction of Philistia, the Negev tribes were economically at the mercy of Judah for their trade outlets. In the circumstances they did the only rational thing possible and accepted Judean hegemony with all the strings attached.

Their submission was the more complete as in a further Bible passage (2 Kgs. 14:22) Uzziah is said to have 'built Eilat and restored it to Judah'. The chronology is not clear but, either before or after the conquest of the Philistine coast, Uzziah completed the reduction of Edom begun by his father and crowned his achievements by refurbishing the naval base at Eilat. An inscribed pottery shard from the market and store-city excavated at Tell Qassila on the outskirts of modern Tel Aviv bears the inscription: 'Gold of Ophir to Beth-horon ... thirty *shekels*.'[17] The simplest interpretation of this intriguing document is that the regimental chest of the garrison then stationed in the Israelite fortress of Beth-horon received an assignment of Ophir gold from the commander or paymaster stationed in the royal store-city, which was the forerunner of present-day Tel Aviv. The most direct way for the Ophir gold to become legal tender in Israel was through a renewed alliance with Judah, which had revivified – either with or without Israelite co-operation – the naval ventures in the Red Sea from Eilat.

The 'Mehunim' (Menuim) have traditionally been identified with those semi-nomadic tribes that inhabited the country around present-day Maan in Jordan. Mention of them as well as of the Ammonites emphasizes Judah's

(Opposite) The 'hilly, wooded and sparsely settled terrain' near Gibeon, which allowed Joshua to approach the besieged city and launch a surprise attack on the Amorite enemy.

The 'Gold of Ophir' tablet, an ostracon which appears to have been an invoice registering the delivery of gold to the Israelite fortress of Beth-horon from the paymaster at the store-city at Tell Qassila.

control over not only the King's Highway, but also the by-passes along the fringe lands in the east, between the plateau and the Arabian Desert. Much of the resilience of the Ammonites or any other people subsequently holding these desert-fringe tracks grew out of the conquerors' inability (due to inferior knowledge of the desert) to control these by-passes. The special importance of Ammon lay in its position as guardian over the Wadi Sirhan, the highway from Arabia to the Palestinian land-bridge. With the triangle Ashdod and Philistia–Eilat–Petra (Selah or, at the time we are discussing, Joktheel) firmly in Uzziah's hands, the Ammonites well knew where their economic interests lay.

Lately, the Mehunim have been identified with tribes mentioned in Assyrian documents as inhabiting northern Sinai or the Kadesh-barnea region.[18] This work cannot help to establish their identity. They fit the latter identification equally well, since Uzziah had extended Judah's sphere of influence even beyond the Brook (or River) of Egypt (Wadi El Arish). It is impossible to fix the exact location of the 'entering into Egypt', but the region

(Opposite) The River Harod and the mountains of Gilboa, scene of Gideon's defeat of the Midianites.

was between the fortresses of Pelusium and Migdol, in the area between Tine, Romani and Kantara. Ptolemies and Seleucids, Crusaders and Saracens, Turks and Mameluks, British and Turks, Israelis and Egyptians and many more have subsequently clashed in this area, where often a line of fortifications along the isthmus of Suez guarded the 'entering into Egypt'.[19] Uzziah's achievement was the control over the two branches of the Via Maris that crossed northern Sinai, and possibly its southern detours as well. The control was achieved by garrisoning the fortified water-sources that have forced the roads to adhere to their original layout throughout history. This task was, as we observed when discussing the Exodus, usually undertaken by the Egyptians, from both commercial and strategic considerations. Only the coincidence of Pharaonic weakening and Judean mounting strength forced the Egyptians to relinquish their hold over the vital approaches to their country, and thus enabled the Judeans to step into their position along the desert roads.

The rural Negev militia

Another of Uzziah's great achievements concerns the Negev proper:

Also he built towers in the desert, and digged many wells: for he had much cattle, both in the low country, and in the plains: husbandmen also, and vine-dressers in the mountains, and in Carmel [on the Ziph ridge of the southern Hebron mountains]: for he loved husbandry. (2 Chr. 26:10)

Archaeological research, especially since Nelson Glueck's exploits in the 1950s, enables us to elaborate upon the terse Bible sentences.

Policing the Negev and maintaining its roads and traffic meant maintaining a wide-ranging network of forts, strongholds, towers, check-posts, protected water-sources, signal stations and the like.[20] Maintaining all these meant the deployment of a permanent force of many thousands. The problems involved were manifold. Especially after the division of the Solomonic empire, how could Judah muster enough troops on a permanent footing, or even reserves on a rotation schedule, just for this one task without neglecting other no less vital commitments? Furthermore, with all the difficulties of maintaining a logistic military presence in the Negev even in our day, how much more difficult it must have been then. True, we cannot compare the sophisticated needs of a twentieth-century army with those of its counterpart 3,000 years before. Yet even then it was a major effort to bring all the supplies from Beersheva and the north and have all basic maintenance, servicing and, of course, the production of equipment – from composite bow to chariot axle, and from shoe to helmet – referred to the zone of permanent settlement from Beersheva northwards.

Last but not least, there was the human element. Even if the Judean soldier of biblical days was much more frugal and less demanding than his modern counterpart – who is kept in good spirits by canteens, concerts and shows, radio and even television, as well as with a quick and constant postal connection with home – ways and means had still to be found to enable the troops stationed in the wilderness to go on leave and visit their homes and families in the settled parts of the country.

The answer to all these difficulties was the prototype of the solution to the same problems in all subsequent ages: the permanent settlement of the Negev and the imposition of the defence of the area upon the settlers themselves.[21] The traveller in the Negev observes in many places a typical trinity of construction: a fortress or fort on a well-chosen, tactical position, usually upon a hilltop with a good all-round field of view; a village on the slopes, under the walls of the fortress; and extensive water-catchment and storage works on the lower slopes and in the valleys at the foot of the fortress hill. While the settlers provided the soldiers with their victuals and all other daily needs, the fortress and its garrisons provided the protection for the agricultural settlement, as well as for the waterworks vital to the existence of both. Again, with the roaming nomad tribes around, only through constant vigilance and the existence of the fortress both as a deterrent and a refuge was civil life possible. Thus mutual concern for survival made the defenders and the farmers a homogeneous, close-knit community. In fact, the natural development would have been – if not from the beginning then soon after – that the members of the garrisons were recruited from among the settlers of the attached villages.

We know that in the Second Temple period the Negev farmers were a rural border militia owing their lands to the government; in return for ownership or usufruct of their plots, as well as other sundry benefits, they were required to undertake the watch over the border. This duty was passed on from father to son. In the First Temple period, similar arrangements may well have existed. In fact, taking as evidence the passage quoted from 2 Chronicles 26, together with archaeological finds, this is exactly the picture we have. All these installations appear to have been planned according to a single blueprint, and their construction seems to have been simultaneous. The extensive water-catchment, storage and irrigation works, which even today stir the admiration of the most sophisticated observer, also could not have been built and maintained by private enterprise. The hand of the central government is everywhere in evidence.

Uzziah was most probably not the initiator of the Negev border militia. Jehoshaphat is a much likelier candidate. To Uzziah nonetheless goes the renewal and possibly the extension of this vast enterprise. The ingenuity of it all lies in the joint solution to many different problems; each alone was 'problematic', but combined they made the whole scheme feasible. We may take, for example, the overpopulation of Judah. Whenever Judah prospered and the population grew above a certain maximum, the problem of reserves of arable land arose. Hemmed in by the sea, Israel and the desert bordering on Edom, the only land reserves available to Judah were in the Negev. By directing the overflow of the population into the Negev, the Judean kings simultaneously eased the pressure on the settled parts of their realm, created new homesteads for the needy, multiplied the amount of land under cultivation, created a secure logistic infrastructure for trade and defence of the Negev, gave additional depth to the network of fortifications built to prevent the nomad raids, and created the manpower to undertake the border and road defence and to finance these efforts at least partly by their own handiwork.[22]

There is another case where Uzziah followed the precepts of Jehoshaphat, who in turn carried on the Solomonic tradition. Although the Philistines were subdued, and probably more securely than ever before, Uzziah made no attempt to exterminate or even decisively to weaken the hereditary enemy and the most dangerously sited of Judah's neighbours who had never missed an opportunity to attack Judah in its rear when it was attacked by superior forces elsewhere. The reason for this was that the Philistines served Judah much as the Tyreans served Israel, as the maritime carriers of their national trade. With commercial connections guarded as trade secrets, much of the overland trade through the Negev was also in Philistine hands, and Uzziah, like his ancestors, was afraid to cut off the branch that made much of his trade enterprises meaningful. It could well be that by according towns like Gaza and Ashkelon preferential treatment, by not razing their walls, Uzziah hoped to induce the Philistines to a more positive working relationship.

Uzziah's general staff and army

Every student of matters military remembers Wellington's complaint that he could do either of two things: comply with all the administrative red tape, as demanded by the British secretary of war, or lead his troops and try to win his battles. Every old soldier will agree with Wellington that red tape has bedevilled many a tactical operation. On the other hand, they will agree that sound staff work is one of the prerequisites of victory. So we are thankful to get even a very small glimpse of Uzziah's general headquarters. Three functionaries are mentioned: a chief-of-staff, called Hananiah, who commanded the army in the king's absence, Jeiel the 'Adjutant General', according to British nomenclature, or 'G 1 – Chief of the Personnel Section', who kept the army rolls and was in charge of all clerical work (his Hebrew title *sofer* – literally 'scribe' – denoted the additional duty of chief of intelligence); and the *shoter*, whose duties included the overseeing and enforcing of the orders emanating from GHQ and possibly the running of the logistics department, or parts of it.

Uzziah's forces were armed with the traditional Judean weapons: 'And Uzziah prepared for them throughout all the host shields and spears, and helmets and habergeons and bows and slings to cast stones' (2 Chr. 26:14). From Davidic times onwards, we have records of repeated preparations of arms and armament for the Judean army. This repetition is, of course, explained both by wear and tear and the loss of weapons in exercises as well as in action. Though we do not know of any radical change in 'small arms', minor changes and adjustments may have been introduced from time to time, and these would demand re-equipment. Lastly, there was much to be said even in those days for a unification of armament. Besides, it was impossible to force the poorer soldier to equip himself with the prescribed weapons out of his private purse. Uzziah was the first king who brought about a complete unified rearmament of the entire national army, or at least the first to have this act recorded. Among the items of armament mentioned are *shiryoniyot*, translated in the King James version as habergeons (coats of mail) but meaning body armour in general. We may deduce that according to their various types of offensive armament and tasks, each corps wore different armour. The famous Judean phalanx may have worn helmets, mail shirts and heavy sandals much like their Assyrian counterparts.

One more component of Uzziah's military establishment deserves mention: the hereditary caste of the *gibborei hayil*, the 'mighty men of valour' in the King James translation. These seem to us at least partly the offspring of David's élite guard of *gibborim* ('heroes'), who were given land by the king, either permanently or as fiefs, and who formed a knightly caste that served as the backbone of the army – though, being landowners, they were rather more a part of the 'people in arms' than of the regulars. As men of means and certain leisure, they had the time to exercise in the use of arms more diligently than ordinary citizens. Their number is given plausibly at 2,500 families, and 'under their hand' was the national levy (2 Chr. 26:12–13).[23]

With these forces Uzziah achieved his many military victories. At their head he proudly stepped into the place of the deceased Jeroboam II of Israel as chief of the Syro-Palestinian coalition and led his army and that of his allies as far north as Hamath on the Orontes to meet the Assyrians. As at Qarqar, the outcome of the battle of Hamath in *c.* 739 BC seems to have been an impasse.[24] This time, however, the might of the Assyrians was not broken. In 738 Tiglath-pileser renewed his invasion, and as the coalition had broken up, he was able to capture the whole of Syria.

According to the Assyrian annals, even Uzziah was compelled to pay homage to the victor. Yet it seems certain that healthy respect for the Judean armed forces was among the reasons why Tiglath-pileser refrained from pressing his advantage home and penetrating further south. Even when he began his southern campaigns in 734, Tiglath-pileser stopped short of pushing into Judah proper.

The logistics involved in Uzziah's Syrian campaign were the same as we discussed when considering Ahab's march to Qarqar. What do we know about the order of marching, camping, communications and tactical evolutions of the Judean field forces? Luckily, the Book of Numbers has preserved interesting details of the exodus from Egypt which certainly may be applied to practice in the Judean kingdom.

The army on the move

According to Numbers chapter 10, the march through potentially hostile territory was in four major combat formations divided into three divisions each. The headquarters and the staff moved after the first division, and the field sanctuary, presumably together with the train, moved between the second and third divisions. The main column was preceded by an advance guard that had among its duties the choice and marking out of the camp for the next night.

These arrangements are not basically different from those followed until modern times. The posting of the headquarters behind the first combat formation allowed for its immediate security if the head of the column came upon the enemy. Enough troops were forward to deal with the most immediate problems and the commander was both sufficiently advanced to gather first-hand impressions of the situation and sufficiently removed from the first contact with hostile forces to deliberate and decide on the most appropriate line of action while the bulk of his troops were as yet uncommitted. In fact, the advance guard would frequently provide an even earlier warning.

To make good use of the time and men available, and not only in battle but in all circumstances, the commander needed to deploy and direct his troops with short conventional signals. The Israelites used for this purpose both standards and wind instruments, as was the custom with all armies until the introduction of the field telephone.

Numbers 10:4–6 has the following standing orders, translated in modern language: (1) one blast of trumpet – gathering of the 'O Group' – e.g. the meeting of the commanders with the commander-in-chief to receive orders and instructions; (2) one sounding of the alarm (a different tone from the above) – eastern wing of your battle – advance; (3) two soundings (or second sounding) of the alarm – right wing advance; (4) the wings alerted shall acknowledge the reception and execution of the order by an answering blast.

The use of standards and ensigns to transmit tactical movements is evident from such passages as Jeremiah 5:26: 'And he will lift an ensign ... and they shall come with speed' or ibid., 11:12: 'And he shall set up an ensign ... and gather together.' Jeremiah mentions a different flag-signal, to bring about a retrograde movement: 'Set up the standard towards Zion, retire, stay not' (Jer. 4:6). Instruments and standards were used in combination if only to draw attention in the heat of battle to the signals flashed by the voiceless ensigns (Isa. 18:3).

When moving into camp each unit marched off directly to the area assigned to it by the advance party which had the exact sites marked distinctly by the respective ensigns. This, and the fact that the formations camped as a rule in the same part of the camp, did a great deal to reduce the time taken to pitch camp and disorders arising out of this, one of the most vulnerable moments in any campaign. A sufficient example comes from the siege of Jerusalem in AD 70 when twice the tenth Roman legion was subject probably to the greatest danger of the whole war, when it was attacked by massive sallies from Jerusalem while pitching camp.[25]

Rather curiously the Israelite camp as described by Numbers chapter 2 is very similar to the famous Roman *castra*, which has been called the greatest logistic achievement of the Roman army. The Israelite camp is described as divided into four, the Roman either into three or four major parts, which are permanently allocated to the same forces. Both camps have their headquarters, shrine and commander's tents in the centre, and both use the unit insignia for demarcation purposes.[26]

What form and shape had the Judean standards? Modern lore has endowed the twelve tribes with heraldic symbols taken from Jacob's blessing (Gen. 49). The ancient Israelite tribes might well have had tribal symbols, but unfortunately we have no idea if these insignia were related to the symbols used by Jacob. Professor Yadin recently conjectured that the winged beetle forms and other similar discs carried upon long poles were the royal standards of Judah. The standards are depicted on metal dishes, now in the British Museum, that Professor R. D. Barnett has established came from Judah as part of the tribute paid to one of the Assyrian kings. They are carried by ensign bearers in a procession.[27] One wonders if those standards, which were clearly at least partly made of metal, could not have been used in battle, *inter alia*, to flash signals by reflected sunrays, much as Joshua had done either with his sword, spear of shield at the battle of Ai.

11 JUDAH'S LAST DECADES

There was no hope of Judah's being able to withstand Assyrian pressure without outside aid. But whatever the reason, Ahaz, Uzziah's grandson, refused to join Aramean Damascus and Pekah ben Remaliah of Israel in their league against Assyria. Perhaps Ahaz felt that as long as he preserved an alliance with distant Assyria and did not interfere with any Assyrian designs, such as free movement along the Via Maris in any future conflict with Egypt, it would not be in Assyria's interest to become entangled in the Judean mountains. It was certainly not foolhardy to try to ride out the impending mutual blood-letting of the Great Powers in the relative security of Judea and to await further developments. The situation of Damascus and Israel was otherwise. Both were on the direct axis of Assyrian operations, and in any future Assyrian bid for more direct control of the Palestinian land-bridge, their existence would be in peril. Consequently, when Ahaz refused to join the league of Rezon of Damascus and Pekah of Israel, both kings invaded Judah with the intention of coercing Judah into an alliance. They went so far as to try to depose Ahaz and the Davidic dynasty.

Although the prophet Isaiah tried to imbue Ahaz with confidence against 'the two tails of these smoking firebrands', Ahaz panicked and called Tiglath-pileser to his assistance. During this period of lost confidence and internecine warfare with Israel, Edom, Philistia and much of the Negev were once more lost to Judah (2 Kgs. 16, 2 Chr. 28, Isa. 7).

A nation's destiny is often shaped by its ability to stand up to challenges of the severest nature. The very gravity of these challenges acts as an invigorating and unifying factor and spurs the nation on to major exertions. The fall of France, Dunkirk and the German Luftwaffe's bombing of Britain in 1940 were the factors that broke the shackles of British lethargy and set Britain on the road to victory over the all-powerful Nazis and their allies. In many ways, the fall of Samaria in 722 BC had a similar effect upon the Judeans, who were torn by internal strife and apathetic to outside events. Out of the trauma of the loss and deportation of ten out of the twelve tribes that made up the Jewish people arose a spiritual renaissance that made the Judeans ready for physical sacrifice and exertions not only to preserve their national identity and independence, but to try to spread their spiritual and physical sway over as much of former Israel as possible.

It requires, of course, the right people in the right places and the right leader at the right time to make good use of a national upsurgence and steer it in the direction of national salvation. Hezekiah, the son of Ahaz, was such a man. His thirty-year-long reign (which began *c.* 724) has rightly earned the highest biblical praise. The biblical chronicler goes so far as to claim that, '. . . after him was none like him among all the kings of Judah, nor any that were before him' (2 Kgs. 18:5).

The reign of Hezekiah

In his internal reforms, Hezekiah, like Jehoshaphat before him, followed the Davidic precedent and made the Levites the harbingers and agents of his cultural, administrative and religious reforms. In security affairs, his first efforts were aimed at re-establishing his sway over the Negev and Edom. To achieve a permanent and secure presence in both, he fostered the expansion of the surplus Simeonite population into these areas and their permanent settlement there. His advance into the former Northern Kingdom was preceded by religious emissaries who destroyed altars as far as Bethel and Samaria and called upon the remaining Israelites to sacrifice in Jerusalem and accept it as their spiritual centre. Furthermore, to strengthen the population in Judah, he transplanted Israelites from as far north as Asher and Zebulun into his dominion.[1]

At a certain stage, Hezekiah proclaimed open rebellion against Assyria:

And the Lord was with him; and he prospered whithersoever he went forth: and he rebelled against the king of Assyria and served him not. He smote the Philistines, even unto Gaza, and the borders thereof, from the tower of the watchmen to the fenced city. (2 Kgs. 18:7–8)

The relations with the Philistines were somewhat more complicated than that.[2] From extra-biblical evidence we know that the overriding danger of the common foe had served to alleviate the mutual hatred existing between Judah and the Philistines which had been kindled anew when, in the dark days of Ahaz, the Philistines had occupied the Judean piedmont between Gimso, Ajalon and Socoh. Moreover, the various Philistine communities, which were by now exposed to conflicting political promises and pressures from the Great Powers, had developed divergent, even conflicting attitudes. Hezekiah was able to exploit these, and the league with anti-Assyrian Ashkelon was formed. This enabled Hezekiah to recapture most or all of the lost territories and to bring much of the domains of Gaza under his sway. Together with Zidka of Ashkelon, Hezekiah deposed King Padi of Ekron and confined him in Jerusalem, placing an anti-Assyrian ruler in his stead. In this way the future field of battle was cleared for the inevitable contest with Assyria.

It is possible that by that time Hezekiah had already opened up negotiations with the Babylonians,[3] who began to pose a serious threat to Assyria's dominion by an uprising within Mesopotamia, which was a mainstay of Assyria's power. At all events, with the large Jewish deportations to the interior of the Assyrian Empire and to Babylon, Hezekiah certainly had good and constant information about happenings in Assyria.

The third partner in the Judean–Ashkelonite alliance was, of course, Egypt. The Pharaohs, who had never recovered their former might, were nevertheless always sensitive to the fact that permanent occupation of the Palestinian land-bridge by any other Great Power was a potential preliminary step towards the conquest of the country of the Nile, famous for its fabulous resources and riches. Pharaoh Shabaka was thus an active member of the alliance.[4]

Hezekiah was clearly conscious of the grave danger to which he was committing the Judean kingdom by throwing down the gauntlet before Sennacherib, king of Assyria. He made ample provisions for the Assyrian onslaught and spared no effort to put Judah in a state of highest preparedness.

Among his fortifications, Jerusalem was foremost: 'Also he strengthened himself and built up all the wall that was broken, and raised it up to the towers, and another wall without, and repaired Millo in the city of David, and made darts and shields in abundance' (2 Chr. 32:5). In other words, he repaired the breaches in the walls of Jerusalem, which had been made in the days of Ahaz and, either because of a false feeling of security or destitution, had not been mended since. The basic enlargement of the Jerusalemite defences and the inclusion of the new quarters in the girdle of the walls had already been achieved by Hezekiah's great-grandfather, the great Uzziah, and this work was continued by Jotham: 'Moreover Uzziah built towers in Jerusalem at the corner gate, and the valley gate and at the turning of the wall, and fortified them. He [Jotham] built the high gate of the house of the Lord, and on the wall of the Ophel he built much' (2 Chr. 26:9; 27:3).

We see that major attention was paid to strengthening the natural weak points of any fortress: the entrances and the angles in the walls that create dead ground for the defender. The remedy applied was the construction of protruding towers that would expose the flanks of assault parties to the missiles of the defenders stationed in and above them. According to the traditional translation of the chronicler, Uzziah armed these towers with missile-shooting engines: 'And he had made in Jerusalem engines, invented by cunning men, to be on the towers and upon the bulwarks, to shoot arrows and great stones withal' (2 Chr. 26:15).

The Hebrew passage 'khesbonoth makhasheveth khoshev', which the King James version has rendered as 'engines invented by cunning men', is obscure and open to various interpretations. If we accept the traditional translation, which follows the Septuagint, the above passage becomes the first mention in written records of artillery ordnance. It is 500 years earlier than any proven, and 300 years earlier than any assumed missile-shooting contraption. But this fact does not automatically challenge the Septuagint translation. With our growing knowledge and appreciation of ancient Jewish dexterity in technical skills, one cannot deny that a small country – because of its ever-precarious security – was forced to apply its inventiveness to military innovations. How else could it survive in this cockpit of the ancient world? By the way, Roman tradition tells us that the invention of missile-shooting engines is credited to the Syro-Phoenician region. Yet among the arguments against the identification of *khesbonoth* as catapults or the like is the fact that not a single mention or pictorial representation from the vast amount of written and graphic material from Assyria, the foremost military power of the day, can be cited for these. Surely, if the Assyrians had not themselves invented these machines, they would have adopted them (if serviceable) or at least mentioned their capture and destruction?

With this in mind, Professor Yadin has proposed that we recognize in the word *khesbonoth* the Semitic root for 'wood' and translate the passage as 'wooden galleries and breastworks', which we know so well from ancient pictorial sources. These were wooden structures built on scaffolding that were added to the walls and towers so as to give additional height to the defences and gain extra space to marshal troops wherever necessary.[5] To protect these wooden structures against fire-bearing arrows and sundry combustibles, as well as to safeguard the troops manning them against hostile missiles, the soldiers' shields – and, if necessary, additional shields, bucklers and targets – were fastened to the wooden beams. Similar structures were known to reinforce castles and town defences as late as the sixteenth century AD. The main problem is that because of the easy inflammability of wooden structures in the East, the negative influence of the hot summer sun and winds on their stability, and the desire to mount these structures (one of the few devices of surprise available to the defenders) only upon the actual approach of the enemy, this original and captivating interpretation is not fully convincing either.

Whatever Uzziah's constructions and devices, we trust Hezekiah to have incorporated them in his fortifications. Intriguingly, the above-quoted passage from Chronicles 32, which records Hezekiah's military works in Jerusalem, includes the construction of 'darts and shields in abundance'. This enterprise fits the preparation of additional shields for wooden scaffolding and of an ample reserve of missiles for the defenders. On the other hand, the 'darts' could also have served as necessary ammunition for catapults and ballistas.

To prevent the fall of the country's fortresses for want of food during long sieges, Hezekiah provided his 'fenced cities' with 'storehouses also for the increase of corn and wine, and oil; the stalls for all manner of beasts, and cotes for flocks' (2 Chr. 32:27). In the absence of ample stores of meat and other preserved foods, the installation of a reserve of livestock as iron rations was a well-founded move. But probably the greatest feat was the provision of a permanent source of water for Jerusalem in case of siege: 'This same Hezekiah stopped the upper water course of [the] Gihon [Spring] and brought it straight down to the west side of the city of David' (ibid., v. 30). What Hezekiah's engineer did was to close the outlet of the Spring

of Gihon at the foot of the City of David and divert the spring water through a subterranean tunnel over 1,700 feet long and between 11 and 3 feet in diameter into a specially constructed pool inside the city walls. In 1880 the now-famous inscription, which was placed in the tunnel to commemorate its completion, was found.[6] The existing fragment reads as follows:

> . . . and this was the matter of the boring: when yet the hewers were lifting the pick, each towards his fellow, and when yet there were three cubits to be bored, heard was the voice of each calling to his fellow; for there was a fissure even from south to north. And on the end of the boring, the hewers struck each to meet his fellow pick against pick, then went the waters from the issue to the pool for two hundred and a thousand cubits, and a hundred cubits was the height of the rock above the head of the hewers.

Hezekiah's manifold preparations served him well when the Assyrian avalanche started moving in 701 BC. The course of Sennacherib's campaign, his division of forces and prolonged sieges and his subsequent withdrawal from Judah with loss of face, leaving the kingdom independent, have been related in chapter 9.

One pre-arranged, last-minute step of the Judeans must be cited:

> And when Hezekiah saw that Sennacherib was come . . . he took council with his princes and his mighty men to stop the water of the fountains which were without the city: and they did help him. So there was gathered much people together, who stopped all the fountains, and the brook that ran through the midst of the land, saying, Why should the kings of Assyria come, and find much water? (2 Chr. 32:2-4)

(*Opposite*) Hezekiah's tunnel, which ensured a permanent supply of water to Jerusalem in case of siege. The tunnel diverted the water from the Spring of Gihon into a pool within the city walls.

A relief from the palace of Nineveh shows Sennacherib, 'King of the universe, king of Assyria . . . while the booty of Lachish passed before him'.

Although these steps are no 'scorched-earth policy' in the full sense of the term (e.g. as it was practised by the Russians in 1812 and again in 1941–2), they were very severe and had detrimental consequences for the rural population, farmers and shepherds alike. To carry out these steps effectively, Hezekiah required the co-operation of the populace, which he received. Instrumental in this enterprise were the *gibborim*, the 'feudal' landlords. By acquiring their consent to be an example to the entire population in plugging the sources of water on their lands, the goodwill of the small yeomen farmers was gained and the invaders were further hamstrung by the dearth of water.

Historical narrative often lacks the description of the attitude and reactions of individuals of the rank and file. A stroke of luck brought to light a hiding place of some Judeans during Sennacherib's siege of Lachish.[7] These people, who hid in a spacious burial cave in the vicinity of the fortress town, gave vent to their pent-up emotions by scribbling graffiti on the cave's walls. Their fear was expressed by the cry of distress, 'God almighty deliver us'; their prayer for the success and survival of the Judean realm by 'The Almighty is the God of the whole earth, the mountains of Judea belong to Him, the God of Jerusalem'; while their joy at the tidings of Jerusalem's successful stand and their delivery from this hideout found expression in: 'God almighty, the Mount Moriah thou hast favoured as Thy dwelling!'

These graffiti also include drawings of ships and of three people. The ships are most probably allusions to the naval craft of the Ashkelonites with whom the Judeans were allied against Sennacherib, or Egyptian vessels, and expressed the hope for succour sent from Egypt by sea. Two of the people depicted may be Levites, one playing the lyre and the second with his hands raised in prayer. Do they represent the fugitives themselves or people close to them? In this context the third person is even more intriguing: a man wearing a coat of mail and plumes, indicating the crest and plumes of the helmets common to the armies of those days. Was it the effigy of the enemy the scribblers on the cave wall were scratching or have they preserved by chance the crude image of the Judean 'Tommy', 'GI', 'poilu' or whatever name is used for the anonymous combat soldier, on whom, when the chips are down, the outcome of all military engagements depends?

The Bible mentions one item of psychological warfare used by the invaders that strikes us as rather modern: the Assyrian harangue of the besieged Jerusalemites in Hebrew. In a succession of arguments – using terror, ridicule, promises, slanted information and 'logical' proof of the futility of it all – the Assyrians tried to break the defenders' will to resist. Both the Book of Kings and the Book of Chronicles quote the chief Assyrian commanders as addressing the defenders personally in Hebrew. If they really were able to parley without the assistance of interpreters, we would have proof of the relative weight of the Jewish commonwealth in international affairs in the closing years of the eighth century (2 Kgs. 18; 2 Chr. 32).

The choice of the spot for the attempted 'brainwashing' was opposite the upper pool, the receptacle for the Gihon waters flowing through the recently completed tunnel. It is possible that this spot was chosen to impress the Jerusalemites with the fact that, all their efforts and preparations notwith-standing, there was no escape from Sennacherib. Some of the arguments seem to be rather beside the point. The Assyrian general derided Hezekiah's failure to have built an adequate corps of cavalry. One wonders whether the defenders on the walls didn't bless their king's foresight in refraining from competing with the Assyrian horsemen, a rather futile attempt at any time, and in concentrating instead, among other measures, on making Jerusalem immune from thirst.

Sennacherib's retreat did much to enhance Judah's prestige, so much so that Merodach-baladan, king of Babylonia, sent an official envoy to Hezekiah with letters and gifts.[8] However, Assyria's strength was far from broken. On the contrary, Sennacherib and Essarhadon (681–669 BC) renewed their relentless campaigning with the goal of conquering Egypt. But the outcome and experience of the 701 BC campaign had paved the way for a tacit *de facto* understanding with the Judeans. While Judah abstained from inter-ference with Assyria's designs and military operations along the Via Maris, Assyria refrained from attacking Judah.

In 669 Essarhadon succeeded in conquering Lower Egypt from Pharaoh Tirhakah, and in 663 Ashurbanipal completed the Assyrian conquest by cap-turing upper Egypt as far as the first cataract of the Nile. Assyria's power was now supreme, and King Manasseh of Judah, Zedekiah's son, saw no choice but to toe the line and accept Assyrian overlordship, even to the extent of providing Assyria with auxiliary forces for its military enterprises. In his wish to appease his masters, or at their insistence, as well as in his anxiety to be on good terms with his neighbours, he threw Judah wide open to pagan practices. This compromise, combined with the strongly fortified borders, preserved the integrity of the Judean heartland and enabled Manasseh to undertake comprehensive military preparations and reorganizations on the eve of his fifty-five-year-long reign, when internal troubles loosened Ashurbanipal's grip over the far-flung empire.

The true heir to Hezekiah's policy was Josiah (628–609 BC), who cleverly *Josiah* exploited Assyria's growing weakness by making his religious emissaries the spearhead of his political expansion. The discovery of the Book of Deu-teronomy in the Temple served as an incentive for cleansing the country of alien influences, and Judah underwent a rapid process of religious rejuvena-tion. The spirit of national elation served as a magnet for the leaderless Is-raelite rural population on both sides of the Jordan, as well as for the foreign ethnic groups who had been transplanted in Israel and had adapted them-selves to the Jewish cult. Consequently, during the first decade of his reign, Josiah achieved virtual rule over most of former Israelite Cis-Jordan, as well as over parts of Gilead.

The Bible does not speak of his fortifications, but archaeological activity has brought to light a strong fortress on the seashore, about $7\frac{1}{2}$ miles north of Ashdod, that can definitely be identified as Josiah's building. Its purpose was twofold: guarding the frontiers with the Philistines and blocking hostile movement along the coastline.[9] The latter task indicates Josiah's uneasiness about Egypt's revival and possible designs. His fears were not unfounded. Judah's security depended on a balance of power between 'the Big Three' of those days: Egypt, Assyria and Babylon. As long as these three cancelled out much of each other's surplus aggression, there was a good chance of more than mere survival for the smaller states. None was more keenly aware of this situation than the king of Judah, whose realm was situated on the traditional warpath of the Great Powers.[10]

Hezekiah had already played his part in bringing about this balance of power. Manasseh's temporary captivity had made Assyria paramount in his time. But since then, Assyria had been torn by internal rivalries, Babylonia and Media having combined to deprive her of most of her eastern possessions including Nineveh, the capital. At the same time, Egypt regained her liberty, and Psamtik, first Pharaoh of the 25th Dynasty, strove hard to tip the new tri-partite power-balance in his favour. By coming to the aid of the Assyrians, who seemed to him to have lost their preponderance for the foreseeable future, he hoped to quench any Babylonian aspiration to become the formal successor as the sole or main power. He wished to acquire this position for Egypt.

Necho's campaign

As it was precisely this Egyptian objective which Josiah feared and tried to frustrate, he refused Pharaoh Necho free passage through the Judean territories when the Pharaoh embarked in 609 BC on his campaign to aid Assyria in its last stand against the 'Neo'-Babylonians. Josiah was playing for very high stakes. Not only did he disregard the Egyptian offer of neutrality, but he chose not to impede the progress of the Egyptian army through the coastal plain, or its passage through the notorious Iyron Pass which traversed the Carmel mountains. Instead, he took up his own position in the open country near Megiddo, where the Iyron Pass gave out into the Jezreel Valley. The setting was the more dramatic as, for the first time since the Exodus, Jew and Egyptian crossed swords in a major battle. In choosing his battlefield, Josiah was well aware of the psycho-political advantages. His plan was to prove the military superiority of Judah over Egypt in a set battle in the open field. He hoped that by doing so he would create a lasting deterrent impression on any would-be invaders. Tactically, he banked on catching his enemy disorganized and off balance as it emerged from the pass, and on making the Carmel range a huge anvil against which to pound and crush the Egyptians with a general attack of chariots and infantry. A flight or even retreat through the Carmel and then all the way back to Egypt, with exposed flank towards the Judean mountains, would have meant disaster.

Josiah's plan was certainly audacious. Religious fervour may have accounted for the moral strength to take this calculated risk. However, one cannot but assume that Josiah judged both the size and quality of his army a match for that of Necho. That evaluation in itself is a good indicator of

his having brought the Judean armed forces up to a high pitch. By the way, Josiah seems not to have overlooked what he thought would be the unlikely case of a Judean reverse. In this contingency, the fortress of Megiddo was at hand to serve as a safe harbour for the defeated, as were the many natural caves in the Carmel mountains.

Necho must have sensed the Judean intention to attack before he could effect an orderly, full deployment in the valley. Presumably he formed his massed archers into an advance screening force to break, or at least slow down, the expected Judean attack on his deploying formations. Moreover, like Hazael, he directed his archers to try to identify the Judean king and concentrate their fire on the royal chariot. As at Ramoth, this stratagem worked. We have to imagine Josiah erect in his war chariot, charging conspicuously at the head of his troops, being mortally hit by an Egyptian arrow in the initial stages of the battle.

With the death of the king, the battle was lost, and with the lost battle, Judah's plans to maintain the international equilibrium came to nothing. Seen from this angle, the obscure archer who killed Josiah in 609 at Megiddo fired the first shot in Judah's final downfall.

In about 605 BC the Judean kingdom, humbled and weakened by the unexpected death of its charismatic leader, became a vassal-state of Nebuchadnezzar, king and master of the mighty Neo-Babylonian Empire. But even in this abject situation, the nation did not lose its belief in its strength and

The Iyron pass through which Pharaoh Necho's army passed en route to Assyria in 609 BC.

(Opposite) The Judean mountains provided an ideal base for Maccabean guerrilla activity, and insuperable tactical problems for the Seleucid armies.

ability to shake off the foreign yoke. The religious enthusiasm brought about by Josiah's reforms (precipitated by the discovery of the Book of Deuteronomy) was so persistent and deep-rooted that people from all walks of life refused to take matters at their face value. Against the isolated voice of the prophet Jeremiah, who preached temporary submission to Babylonia as a divinely sanctioned step within the concept of diplomacy as the art of the possible, many a 'false' prophet called for active measures and rebellion.

To quench this spirit of rebellion on the strategic land-bridge, in 598 Nebuchadnezzar despatched a special army which succeeded in laying siege to Jerusalem and forced the complete submission of Jehoiachin, who accepted personal exile and the total despoliation of the Temple in order to save Jerusalem from utter destruction. Together with the king, 10,000 captives were carried off, including the great nobles and officers of state, the *gibborim* and 'all the craftsmen and smiths'. The obvious intention was to deprive Judah both of its leaders and its technicians and craftsmen, to prevent her from mounting another rebellion.

Yet Nebuchadnezzar's step was of no avail. It took only an Egyptian naval demonstration off the Phoenician coast and some Egyptian landing parties in the year 591 to induce Zedekiah, the new king, to prepare another uprising. One cannot but wonder at the magnitude of resilience and physical resources in what had become a minor country. The preparations were once more spurred on by religious fervour, which this time was also used as a lever for social reforms, so as to make every citizen see that his cause was worth fighting for. Egypt's assistance was enlisted, and the anti-Babylonian alliance began to mature. But Nebuchadnezzar sensed the need to act before this alliance could make comprehensive preparations, and in 588 he hurried down through Syria to subdue the rebellious Jews.

Judah's defences were reduced after heavy fighting. Of this epic struggle a faint but nonetheless pathetic and vivid echo has come down to us. Excavations at Lachish have brought to light a number of ostraca that were despatches from the commander of a small outpost by the name of Hoshayahu, who came under the command of Yaush, the military governor of Lachish. One terse message was penned during the crucial phase of the assault upon the Judean heartland: '... for the signal stations of Lachish we are watching, according to all the signs which my lord gives, because we do not see [the signals] of Azekah'.[11]

Azekah had thus already fallen, and the Babylonians were marshalling their vast forces for the assault upon Lachish and other strongholds. They knew better than to penetrate into the mountains before having cleared the approaches. In the end, Jerusalem came under its last siege prior to the Babylonian exile. A futile Egyptian attempt at relief only strengthened Nebuchadnezzar's conviction that as long as the Judean state existed, the Babylonian position on the Palestinian land-bridge was not secure. The defenders in their turn understood only too well the gravity of the situation and held out for over two years: 'And the city was besieged unto the eleventh year

A fragment of the 'Lachish Letters' written during the time of the Babylonian invasion by Nebuchadnezzar.

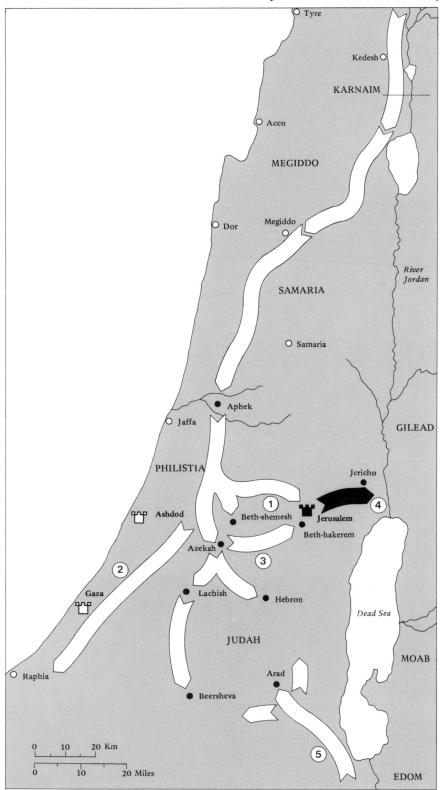

Tyre

Kedesh

KARNAIM

Acco

MEGIDDO

Dor

Megiddo

River
Jordan

SAMARIA

Samaria

Aphek

Jaffa

GILEAD

PHILISTIA

Jericho

Ashdod

Beth-shemesh

Jerusalem

Beth-hakerem

Azekah

Dead Sea

Gaza

Lachish

Hebron

JUDAH

MOAB

Raphia

Arad

Beersheva

EDOM

0   10   20 Km

0   10   20 Miles

The Fall of Judah

1 Nebuchadnezzar's army
captures Judean cities and
lays siege to Jerusalem.
2 The Babylonian hold
around Jerusalem is weakened
when the Egyptians move up
to join forces with Judah.
3 The siege of Jerusalem is
renewed after the Egyptians
are defeated; Jerusalem is
captured.
4 Zedekiah is taken captive
while fleeing to the Judean
mountains.
5 Hostile neighbours such as
the Edomites make raids into
weakened Judah.

of king Zedekiah. And on the ninth day of the fourth month, the famine prevailed in the city, and there was no bread ... and the city was broken up ...' (2 Kgs. 25:2–4).

The king made a last attempt at preserving the resistance and escaped at the head of some of his household troops to carry on the fighting, possibly from the Judean desert. Before getting to the safety of this natural refuge, however, Zedekiah was intercepted and taken captive. The leaderless city was systematically destroyed by the Babylonian army under the command of Nebzaradan's 'captains of the guard', who also burned down the First Temple.[12]

The exiles and emigrants who left Judah in the wake of the Babylonian conquest preserved their warlike character even in their new settlements in foreign lands. Jews began to figure prominently in armies and military settlements both in Babylonia and in Egypt and their dependencies down to the Roman period. These martial qualities were also one of the main reasons why Cyrus, king of Persia, permitted and actively promoted the return of the Babylonian exiles to Judah. After capturing Palestine in the wake of the great Persian conquest that wrested supremacy from Babylonia in about 540 BC, he wished to have the country secured by a population at once warlike and loyal, but not strong enough to make itself independent. What better way than to grant the Jews the right to return to a very curtailed Judah, with hostile neighbours checking any attempt at throwing off benevolent Persian overlordship? Thus in 537 BC the first wave of repatriates were able to lay the foundations for the Second Commonwealth, built around the Second Temple.

PART II

12 EARLY MACCABEAN BATTLES

The origins of the
Maccabean revolt

The battles of the Maccabees brought forth one of the great captains of history, Judah the Maccabee. They were the first battles in recorded history to be fought over the issue of religious freedom. What distinguishes them is the military genius of Judah the Maccabee, who departed radically from the tactics universally applied at the time and instinctively adapted the principles of war in an entirely novel manner.

The Maccabean revolt opened in 167 BC after an extended period in which no organized Jewish force had engaged in warfare. Indeed, the last battle in which a major Jewish force had taken up arms had been in 586 BC, over 400 years earlier, when the Jewish defenders of Jerusalem fought a losing battle against the invading forces of Nebuchadnezzar. From time to time Jews fought in the armies of other nations. But for 400 years the hills of Judea had not echoed to the sound of Jewish armies on the march.

In the middle of the second century BC, Judea was a small province of the Syrian-based Seleucid Empire. It had been so since the Seleucid monarch Antiochus III wrested the area of Palestine from the Ptolemies of Egypt and incorporated Judea into his empire in 198 BC. In the days of Judah the Maccabee, the province was a rectangular-shaped area covering about 1,000 square miles, each side of the rectangle measuring some thirty to forty miles. The area itself was mountainous, broken by villages or wadis running down to the Mediterranean Sea in the west or to the Jordan Valley and the Dead Sea in the east. The population of the province at the time is estimated in the region of 200,000 to 250,000.

In 332 BC Alexander the Great of Macedonia, one of the greatest generals in history, defeated the Persians and took control of the Persian Empire, which extended deep into Asia, including Judah, latinized as Judea. On the untimely death of the youthful Alexander in 323 BC, the lands he had conquered, from Egypt and Asia Minor in the west to India in the east, were divided among his Macedonian generals, who fought over the inheritance. Ptolemy was assigned the satrapy of Egypt, where he soon established himself as a monarch based in Alexandria. Seleucus, who had been apportioned the satrapy of Babylon, likewise crowned himself king, with his capital in Seleucia. He later extended the area under his control into Syria, establishing a new capital at Antioch, on the Mediterranean, in the north-west corner of Syria.

The long-standing rivalry between the ruling power in Syria and that in Egypt manifested itself once more. For obvious strategic reasons, the area of Palestine was coveted by both the Ptolemies in the south and the Seleucids in the north. For over a hundred years, Jerusalem and Judea remained part of the Ptolemaic Empire. But in 198 BC Antiochus III, the father of the emperor against whom the Maccabees were to revolt, took Palestine from the Ptolemies, making it part of the Seleucid Empire.

The Jews had enjoyed a fairly benevolent rule under the Ptolemies. Apart from the requirement of a heavy annual tribute, Judea was in effect an autonomous region. The first-century AD historian Josephus Flavius describes how the Jews were free to administer their own affairs in peace, to practise their religion without molestation and to conduct the traditional Jewish rites in their Temple in Jerusalem. This policy of tolerance towards the practice of the Jewish religion and respect for the domestic autonomy of the Jews in Judea was maintained when the Seleucids, under Antiochus III, gained control of Palestine.[1] But it changed with the accession of his son Antiochus IV Epiphanes.[2]

When Antiochus IV came to power in 175 BC, he realized that while he would undoubtedly find himself in conflict with his southern neighbour, Egypt, the main threat to the Seleucid Empire would inevitably come from the growing power of Rome, which he respected and feared. Judea therefore assumed added importance, because of its proximity to Egypt and the fact that from the Judean hills it dominated the historic coastal route connecting Syria with Egypt. Judea did not pose a military threat to Antiochus, nor did he fear any military problems from this area. However, with the danger threatening him on his southern and eastern borders, where the Medes and the Parthians posed a constant threat, he resolved to secure the vital strategic province of Judea by imposing Greek culture and rites on its population, thus ensuring a common loyalty and uniformity of practice throughout his empire. This was the method he proposed to adopt in order to weld his subject peoples together, thereby, he believed, unifying his empire. The instrument for unity would be Hellenism, and this process would be carried out not only for religious and social ends but for political purposes.

The process of Hellenizing Judea and especially Jerusalem; the Seleucids' assumption of the authority to appoint a High Priest, who was the spiritual leader of Jewry; and the split between the 'Hellenized' Jews and those who remained true to their traditions and faith, caused a rebellion to break out in Jerusalem. News of this uprising reached Antiochus in 168 BC as he was withdrawing northwards along the coastal road from Egypt after abandoning the siege of Alexandria. The withdrawal had been a humiliating move, as he had left Egypt under the threat of Roman intervention. It was therefore in a mood of anger that he despatched forces under one of his generals, Apollonius, to deal with this new situation in Judea.

(Overleaf) The Judean hill homeland of the Maccabee

The Seleucid troops engaged in a massacre of the Jewish population in Jerusalem. They burned and pillaged and broke into the Temple, stealing many of the precious holy vessels. Thereafter the Temple was converted into a Hellenist shrine dedicated to the Olympian Zeus, and the sacrificial offering of a pig crowned this profane act of desecration.

A fortress known as the Acra or Citadel was constructed on a hill facing the Temple and commanding it, and a permanent Seleucid garrison was stationed there. Steps were soon taken to impose the will of Antiochus on the rebellious Jews and eradicate the influence of Jewish rites and customs. Jews were forbidden, on penalty of death, to congregate in prayer, to observe the Sabbath and religious festivals, to carry out circumcision or to adhere to the dietary laws. They were obliged to participate in pagan rituals, including sacrificing pigs and partaking of their flesh.

The rise of the Maccabees

After subduing Jerusalem, Antiochus pursued his goal of 'de-Judaizing' Judea by moving into the countryside with troops under orders to enforce the regulations against Jewish religious practices. One of these units, under an officer named Apelles, arrived in the village of Modiin in the foothills of Judea, north-west of Jerusalem. An altar was set up in the village, and before the assembled population Mattathias, the Jewish priest, was ordered to perform a sacrifice and eat of the pig's flesh. With him were his five sons. When Mattathias did not move from his spot, one of the assembled Jews moved forward to the altar to obey the order and perform the sacrifice. Mattathias thereupon rushed forward in a fury, slew the traitor, and killed Apelles. His sons led the villagers against the Greek unit, wiping it out. Thus began the revolt of the Maccabees.

Mattathias led the people of his village into the hills of Gophna, a section of the Judean hills immediately north-west of present-day Ramallah. This area was chosen because of its relative inaccessibility to the Seleucid garrison in the coastal plain and because the mountainous terrain lent itself to defensive measures and evasion. There the small band of farmers who had taken up arms could organize as a guerrilla group, train, defend themselves and plan and develop the course of the revolt. They numbered about two hundred, of whom probably not more than fifty were able-bodied men, and they lacked any military training whatsoever.

For approximately a year the rebels made their preparations in relative peace. They trained in guerrilla warfare and recruited new members to their ranks. Emphasis was laid on the re-affirmation of the principles of Judaism for which they were fighting. They defended themselves whenever necessary but initiated few operations while organizing their base. At the same time, they strengthened contacts with the villages in the countryside and spread the story of the revolt. Soon an effective intelligence-gathering organization was developed as a people's militia grew under the leadership of Judah the Maccabee. Mattathias had designated Judah, his middle son, to succeed him before the aged priest died during the first year of the revolt.

Armed with farm implements of a primitive nature and home-made weapons such as the mace and the sling, Judah's small group prepared to give battle to an up-to-date Greek army. The Seleucids were well trained, well organized and tried in battle. Their ranks were composed of heavy and light infantry, heavy and light cavalry, chariots, elephant units and 'artillery' units operating ballistas (engines for hurling huge stones), not to mention the various service units. Their weapons included swords, javelins, spears, bows, slings, ballistas and battering-rams.

Judah analysed the seemingly hopeless situation and instinctively enumerated the elements that could be put to work in his favour. Though the Seleucid troops enjoyed overwhelming superiority in manpower and arms, they were trained only for a set piece battle in conventional fighting form. They were mercenaries with little or no commitment to a cause. Facing them would be sons of the country fighting on their own soil, for their own people, and prepared to die for their religious beliefs and freedom. Since the Seleucids were trained in conventional warfare, the military reply to them must be in terms of unconventional warfare. Since they were trained to fight by day, the Jewish military reply must be to strike at night. Furthermore, Judah's forces, diminutive as they were, enjoyed one of the basic requirements of a guerrilla force. As Mao Tse-tung expressed it thousands of years later, they were like a fish in water: Judah's fighters came from the local populace in the villages and could melt back into the population when necessary.

As they proceeded with their training and gained confidence, Judah's guerrillas developed and strengthened their supply lines to the villages scattered over the countryside. By the end of the first year, the force grew to a total of several hundred men bearing arms. An elaborate informal intelligence system was developed whereby Judah commanded full knowledge of the situation in Judea and the region of Samaria to its north. Gradually offensive guerrilla activities were directed against Seleucid patrols, which were ambushed and wiped out. Soon the purpose of these hit-and-run tactics was not only to disrupt the occupying forces but also to create an arsenal of modern arms for the Jewish rebels.

Judah's activities increased, entire areas of the countryside came under the effective control of the Maccabees, and the Seleucid garrison in Jerusalem was cut off. Seeing that the situation was deteriorating and the Maccabees had gained the upper hand in Judea, Apollonius, the governor and commander of Antiochus' forces in the region, who was based in Samaria, decided to intervene. Judah and his forces were to face their first full-scale military operation.

The core of the Seleucid army was the phalanx, a tactical formation consisting of heavy infantry drawn up in close order. The troops advanced towards the enemy in a tight mass, with the men in each rank shoulder to shoulder and almost on the heels of the rank in front. The principal tactical element of the phalanx was the *syntagma*, comprising some 250 men, which could be compared to the modern company. This body comprised sixteen

Seleucid battle tactics

ranks with sixteen men in each rank, in other words a unit measuring fifteen yards square. Four such *syntagmae* created a *chiliarchia* of over 1,000 men. Two such *chiliarchiae*, numbering some 2,000 men and extending over a width of 120 yards and to a depth of 15 yards, constituted the smallest phalanx used in warfare at that time.

As the phalanx advanced on the enemy force, the first five ranks held their spears horizontally, while the remaining eleven held them vertically. All of them were ready to engage the enemy. The entire phalanx would press against the enemy once battle was joined. It thundered forward crushing everything in its path when the enemy was weak, and meeting in a fearful, head-on clash when the enemy was equal to it. The complex was protected on the flanks by cavalry and light forces, which skirmished before the main forces.

The weakness of this organization lay in the fact that it was cumbersome and precluded exploiting the element of surprise. As a result, one of the main tactics of war was absent in this deployment. The progress of a marching column deployed as a battle-ready phalanx was a slow and tedious one. Both

The Campaigns of Judah the Maccabee, 167–164 BC
1 The Maccabeans retreat into the Gophna mountains.
2 The Seleucid governor of Judah, Apollonius, advances to quell Jewish resistance.
3 Judah's forces ambush and defeat the Seleucid army.
4 General Seron leads a second army to subdue the rebellion.
5 165 BC. the battle of Beth-horon. Again, Seleucid forces are ambushed in a narrow pass and defeated.

(cont. opposite)

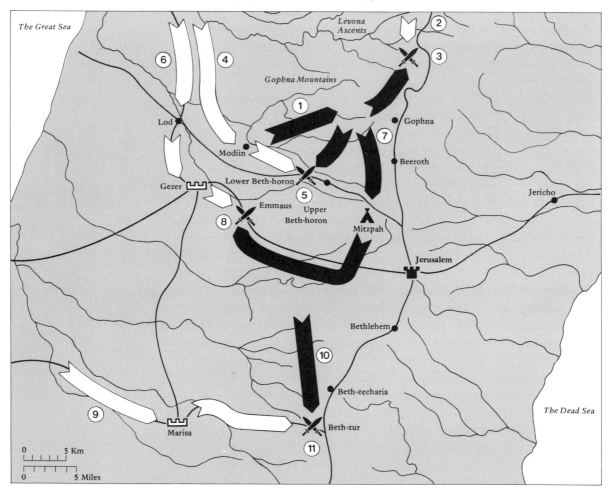

sides were in full view of each other and, when battle was joined, the developments were in accordance with fixed tactical principles. The concept of achieving tactical or even strategic advantage by interfering with the enemy's deployment did not exist. It was simply not done at the time.

Judah's natural military instincts saw the advantages to be gained from refusing to allow the enemy to dictate the field and style of battle. Basically, his approach was influenced by the political and social problems facing his people at the time. Just as today the reserve and militia systems that exist in Israel reflect social, economic and political considerations, so then did the organization of Judah's forces reflect similar problems among the Jewish population of Judea.

In 166 BC Apollonius' force moved along the mountain watershed from Samaria southwards towards Jerusalem. He took the direct Samaria–Jerusalem route, which passes along the flank of the Gophna area. According to Major-General Avisar's detailed book on the Maccabean battles published in Hebrew,[3] Apollonius advanced into Judea with a force numbering some 2,000 men, while facing them was a Jewish force under Judah of approximately 600. As Judah analysed the problem facing him, he resolved to take advantage of the element of surprise and make use of the terrain to neutralize the effect of the Seleucid superiority in both manpower and weaponry. The Seleucids' advantage would be on open, flat ground; Judah therefore decided to attack in a defile or a valley. The large force assumed the normal preparation for a set piece battle; Judah would attack them on the march, when they were neither prepared for battle nor able to assume the positions in which they had been trained to fight.

The site Judah chose for the engagement was in Nahal el-Haramiah, some three to four miles north-east of Gophna. At this point the route southwards from Samaria enters a narrow defile that winds uphill for more than a mile. The enemy was approaching in columns of four. Judah decided to block the march and then push the Seleucid troops into a situation that would force them to create a front on one of their flanks. This would place the enemy in a position for which he was least prepared and in which he would be most vulnerable.

Judah divided his forces into four units. One was to act as a sealing unit at the southern end of the defile. A second unit would be the main attacking force along the eastern side of the defile, towards which the main force of the enemy would be compelled to turn. A third unit would attack from the western side of the defile, while a fourth would be held at a short distance north of the main attacking unit on the eastern side, ready to close the northern entrance to the defile and thus complete the trap.

It was late afternoon when the Seleucid forces came marching into the defile in columns of four. The Seleucids marched in two separate *chiliarchiae* of approximately 1,000 men each, with the commander Apollonius riding in between. The forces advanced tightly bunched up in a compact group, with the men behind actually bumping the men in front. At the signal, the

The defeat of Apollonius

6 A third army, under generals Ptolemy, Nicanor and Gorgias, is sent by Antiochus. They avoid the Judean mountains and set up camp at Emmaus.
7 Judah collects his forces at Mizpah and sets out to meet the Seleucids.
8 The Seleucids are defeated at Emmaus.
9 A fourth army, under Lysias, approaches Judea from the south.
10 Judah's forces move to intercept them.
11 164 BC: Lysias is defeated at Beth-zur.

sealing unit at the southern end of the defile fell upon the leading troops of the Seleucid column. The main body, unaware of what was happening at the head of the column, pressed forward, as the entire Seleucid force was jammed into the defile. At this point the unit on the eastern slope appeared and attacked the column from its flank. Encumbered by its heavy weapons, which were unsuitable for fighting in the narrow defile, the Seleucid column turned to meet this new onslaught, while the rear element of the column continued to press into the defile. At this point the forces on the western slopes emerged and attacked from the rear. The Seleucids were now trapped under devastating fire from both east and west.

Hearing the noise of battle, Apollonius, who was leading the second *chiliarchia*, spurred his horse forward in order to see what was happening. He was killed by the murderous fire from both hills. When the entire Seleucid force was in the defile, Judah led the fourth force and closed off the northern entrance to the defile. The Seleucid troops were completely trapped, fighting leaderless under conditions for which they had never been prepared. The entire force was destroyed and all its weapons and equipment fell into the hands of the Jews.

Judah's victory had an electrifying influence on the Jewish population of Judea. He was accepted as the national leader and was now able to impose discipline upon his people. Moreover, volunteers rushed to join his forces. His tactics had been vindicated, as was his decision to ignore the accepted methods of warfare. He had proved that a small and weak people could fight successfully against a mighty army and that the spirit can be mightier than numbers. In essence, Judah had demonstrated the importance of that great principle of war – morale. His approach to battle, with its inherent flexibility and adaptation to circumstances, gave full play to his capabilities as a commander – as opposed to the set piece approach followed by the enemy. In addition, Judah learned the great importance of eliminating the leader of the opposing side as early as possible in the battle, particularly when the enemy is committed to an inflexible approach.

After the defeat of Apollonius' troops, Antiochus realized that he faced a serious situation in Judea. No tactical conclusions were drawn from the battle, but it was clear that the emperor could not allow a group of rebels to flout his authority in such a blatant manner. Rather than embark upon a re-evaluation of the political and military situation in Judea, however, Antiochus decided to undertake a major operation to restore law and order in the province and to take firm and unequivocal action against those who opposed his forces.

The battle of Beth-horon

Antiochus thereupon despatched to Judea General Seron, who conceived his mission of avenging Apollonius' defeat as a means of enhancing his military reputation in an easy campaign against a group of lightly armed guerrillas. He set out early in 165 BC, marching southwards to Judea. Rather than fall into the trap that had led to Apollonius' downfall, he resolved to advance along the coastal road. This route guarantees a safe approach march.

(*Opposite*) The Levona Ascents (left of the picture), where Judah ambushed Apollonius.

(*Opposite, top*) Beth-horon pass, looking towards Upper Beth-horon.

On reaching the general area of Jaffa, Seron turned inland, advancing eastwards past the site of the present-day international airport at Lod, and reached the foothills of Judea. His force was now some fifteen miles, or a day's march, from Jerusalem and the nearest Seleucid garrison. His plan was to join up with the Jerusalem garrison and then, based in Jerusalem, to fan out across Judea in a punitive expedition that would destroy the Maccabean revolt and crush all Jewish resistance.

According to 1 Maccabees 3:16, Seron made for the pass of Beth-horon. This same pass, a secondary route to Jerusalem, was taken by the British 90th Division under General Allenby advancing on Jerusalem against the Turks in 1917. It was also the route chosen by Israeli forces to advance on Jerusalem in the 1967 Six Day War in order to move on the Old City from the north.

Judah was heavily outnumbered. Seron's force was approximately double that of Apollonius, namely a guard phalanx of four *chiliarchiae* numbering some 4,000 troops, while Judah had approximately 1,000 men. Indeed 1 Maccabees describes the atmosphere of apprehension with which the Jewish forces, entrenched in the Judean hills, viewed the approach march of the Seleucid forces across the Valley of Ajalon, and Judah's sharp reminder to them that they were fighting for their homes, their families and their belief in God.

Beth-horon pass, looking south : the scene of Seron's flight.

Once again Judah decided to ambush the advancing forces in terrain that would neutralize the enemy's advantage in organization, numbers and

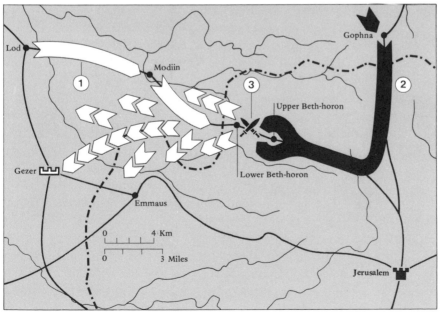

The Battle of Beth-horon

1 Seron's troops advance through the Judean hills.
2 Judah's army moves down from the Gophna mountains to attack the Seleucids.
3 The battle of Beth-horon.

weapons. The ascent to the pass of Beth-horon runs through a long defile commanded on both sides by steep slopes. Judah would again seal the exit from the pass and then attack the column from both flanks.

This time the Seleucid general, Seron, rode at the head of his troops. For Judah, the elimination of the enemy commander early in the battle was a primary mission because of the effect it would have on the morale of the enemy forces. According to the Jewish historian Josephus, Judah's orders to his troops were that 'regardless of the numbers of the enemy, who is mighty, we will advance together and reach Seron'.

This time Judah could not hope to trap the entire enemy force, as he had done with Apollonius' troops, for the Seleucid forces now marched into the hills with wide gaps between their units. Thus their column was over a mile long. To have attempted to trap this entire column would have meant dispensing with the element of surprise – because of the time factor – and this Judah was unwilling to do.

Seron's forces set out at dawn on what was to be their last day's march before reaching Jerusalem. The front *syntagma* of the first *chiliarchia* began the long winding ascent into the hills towards Beth-horon. It was a slow advance, as the troops were weighted down by their equipment and heavy weapons. Judah's look-outs, hidden among the rocks and the olive-tree covered hillsides, watched silently as the Seleucid forces advanced slowly up the ascent to the Beth-horon pass.

This time Judah, wielding the sword he had taken from Apollonius (which was to remain with him in all his battles), led the sealing unit. As the Seleucid vanguard approached the ambush, Judah's men charged the enemy forces. They cut down the leading Seleucid ranks, which had been immobilized by the surprise, and made for Seron. The rear units of the leading *chiliarchia* advanced, pushing forward, while the lead units staggered backwards under the fierce attack of Judah's sealing unit. At this point, the flank units on both slopes launched a barrage from their bows and slings, increasing the confusion in the pass, and then attacked the Seleucids with swords in close combat.

With the leading *chiliarchia* decimated, and Seron dead, the Seleucid forces broke and fled. As panic spread, the following *chiliarchiae* turned and fled towards the coastal plain, leaving over 800 men, the bulk of the first *chiliarchia*, dead on the battlefield. Judah led his men in pursuit of the fleeing troops, following them 'down the pass of Beth-horon as far as the plain . . .'.

Judah had now destroyed two Seleucid armies and caused heavy losses in equipment, which he put to good use in arming his own forces. He had reinforced his prestige in the eyes of the populace and was able to create an army which, it is estimated, numbered 6,000 men. He had made full use of the principle of surprise and morale, had dictated the battlefield, and had struck first at the enemy command. He now stood at the head of a well-trained force, bolstered by the taste of victory, strengthened by combat experience against overwhelming odds, and confident in the knowledge of mass popular support.

It was finally clear to Antiochus that his forces in the province of Judea *The battle of Emmaus* faced a major rebellion. The emperor was about to embark on a campaign against the rebellious elements in the eastern part of the Seleucid Empire when the news of Seron's defeat reached him. He realized the gravity of the situation in Judea just as he was about to leave on his own campaign to ensure additional revenues for his dwindling coffers. Accordingly, he appointed Lysias, a member of the royal family, as his viceroy and guardian of his son Antiochus (later Antiochus V Eupator) until his return. He had no option but to transfer a considerable proportion of the forces assigned to his campaign to Lysias for operations against Judea.

Antiochus' orders to Lysias were to destroy Judah's forces by the use of any and all means at his disposal and 'to uproot and destroy the strength of Israel and the remnant of Judea, to blot out all memory of them from the place, to settle strangers in the territory and allot the land to the settlers' (1 Macc. 3 : 35–6). Lysias chose three generals to lead the expedition against Judea: Ptolemy, Nicanor and Gorgias. Under them the Seleucid expedition set out along the coast in the spring of 165 BC and reached Emmaus, where a major base camp was established. This time they were obviously not going to be lured into the Judean mountains to be trapped, as in the case of the two previous expeditions.

The camp at Emmaus (present-day Imwas, adjoining the village of Latrun) was located in the foothills just above the Valley of Ajalon and was sited in such a way as to ensure the topographical conditions for battle required by the Seleucid forces. The Seleucid strength employed in this campaign is given in 1 Maccabees at 40,000 infantry and 7,000 cavalry, while 2 Maccabees puts the force at some 20,000 troops. (The latter figure is generally believed to be the more acceptable.) The Seleucid plan was to develop operations against Jerusalem from this base camp, aided, no doubt, by the garrison inside Jerusalem itself, and thereafter gradually extend activities throughout the province of Judea.

Judah had in the meantime taken advantage of his victory at Beth-horon to prepare his men to face this new expedition, which comprised approximately half the total strength of the Seleucid army. He intensified the recruiting campaign, raising a force of some 6,000 men, and began to organize his army into sub-units, which bear a remarkable resemblance to those used in modern armies. He divided his force into units equivalent to battalions, numbering 1,000 each. These in turn were sub-divided into company-like units of 100 men each. Each such unit was again divided into platoon-like units of 50 men each, while each platoon was divided into five section-like units of 10 men each.[4]

So confident were the Seleucids of victory (they were now joined by reinforcements from Idumea, on the southern border of Judea, and from the coastal plain) that their command invited large numbers of camp followers and slave dealers to join the troops at Emmaus. According to 2 Maccabees

Emmaus – the Seleucid camp was situated at the back left of the picture, where the modern square building is. Judah moved from the east (the right-hand side) with his main force along the foot of the central hill towards the enemy on the left. His secondary force moved behind the central hill (later the site of the Crusader fortress of Latrun), to attack the enemy from the rear.

8:11, Nicanor offered Jewish slaves to the coastal towns 'undertaking to deliver them at the price of ninety to the talent'. Slave merchants brought large quantities of gold and silver, together with chains, in anticipation of profitable trade.

On the Jewish side, Judah prepared his forces by dividing them into four equal groups of 1,500 men. Each of the first three groups was commanded by one of his brothers – Simon, Johanan and Jonathan – while he took personal command of the fourth unit. He assembled his army at Mizpah, some five miles north-west of Jerusalem on the road to Beth-horon. Here he consolidated his forces and devoted time to raising their morale, for once again they were severely outnumbered. In addressing his forces, Judah emphasized their links with the past and issued orders in accordance with biblical custom: for example, following biblical law, he released from service newly-weds or those who had built a new home.

At Mizpah Judah was well located to cover any approach by the enemy forces into Judea, for it became clear to him from the reports of his patrols that the enemy was basing himself at Emmaus. Accordingly he moved his forces to the south-east of Emmaus, concentrating in the hills above present-day Latrun.

The two camps were now clearly visible to one another, with the Seleucid forces under constant observation. This time Judah decided to let the enemy make the first move for, from the patrol activity and preparations being made by the Seleucids, it was clear that they were planning to initiate an attack

A closer view of the site of the
Seleucid camp at Emmaus,
where the phalanx formed up.

on the Jewish base.

Gorgias decided to imitate the tactics Judah had used earlier. His plan was to lead a force up into the hills of Judea under cover of darkness, surprise the Jewish camp and destroy Judah's forces. He naturally assumed that Judah would not expect a Seleucid attack at night, as the Seleucids were unaccustomed to night fighting. Accordingly, Gorgias moved up into the hills at the head of 5,000 infantry and 1,000 cavalry troops.

Judah was obviously well informed of these plans when he prepared his counter-attack. He decided to employ a ruse to draw Gorgias' contingent deeper into the hills of Judea and away from the main body of the Seleucid force. First he ordered a large number of bonfires to be lit in the Jewish camp, indicating the existence of a large concentration of troops there. But under cover of darkness, Judah withdrew his forces from the camp, leaving it occupied by only a small rearguard of some 200 men.

When Gorgias' forces attacked the camp at night, they found to their surprise that it was empty, but they observed the rearguard withdrawing – as they were intended to. Believing it to be the main force, Gorgias urged his forces in pursuit of this rearguard, which withdrew into the main valley leading up to Jerusalem, known today as Shaar Hagai (Bab el-Wad). As Gorgias' forces advanced up the defile, he was attacked by the units Judah had stationed there in advance.

Meanwhile, 15,000 infantry and 3,000 cavalry had been left at the enemy camp at Emmaus. Judah now prepared to attack this camp and take it by surprise. He sent one group of 1,500 men to wait in an area north of the Seleucid camp and move into action once the camp had come under attack by the main force, with Judah in command. Leading 3,000 men, Judah

The Battle of Emmaus
(phase one)

1 Seleucid forces advance and camp at Emmaus.
2 Judah assembles his army at Mitzpah.
3 On reports of the Seleucids' halt at Emmaus, Judah advances his forces to the south-east of Emmaus.
4 Gorgias decides to make a surprise attack on the Jewish camp at night.
5 Warned of this, Judah orders bonfires to be lit in the Jewish camp and then withdraws, leaving only a rearguard of 200 men.

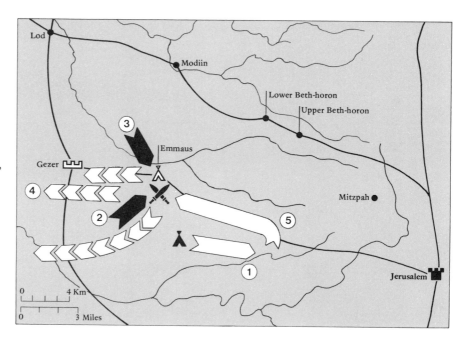

moved against the enemy camp at dawn but found, to his surprise, that the enemy forces had been alerted and were formed up for battle in a phalanx on the plain before the camp.

Judah could no longer attack the camp as he had planned, for he had to deal with the Seleucid forces drawn up in battle array facing him. The element of surprise had been lost, and for the first time in the wars of the Maccabees he was up against an organized phalanx and obliged to fight a type of battle for which his forces were not particularly well trained. But Judah nonetheless surprised the enemy, this time tactically, for to have followed the accepted pattern of a military engagement would have spelled doom for the Jewish forces. He again revealed a flexibility of thought unusual in military leaders of that time. He sized up the situation and immediately adapted his moves to it.

The enemy force was arrayed in a phalanx facing south. Judah's forces were to the west of the phalanx. He therefore decided not to meet the phalanx head on, as would be expected, but to attack it on its western flank, where the phalanx was protected by light cavalry, and to try to roll it up. Judah divided the forces under his command into three groups of 1,000 men each. One of these sub-units engaged the cavalry in battle, while at the same time the remaining two units each insinuated themselves into the enemy's flank and began to penetrate the ranks of the phalanx in small groups. The phalanx, which had been trained to give battle on its front in direct confrontation, began to disintegrate as its ranks were engaged in bitter hand-to-hand fighting.

At this point the northern group of 1,500 men – unaware of Judah's battle with the phalanx and assuming that Judah's forces had attacked the base

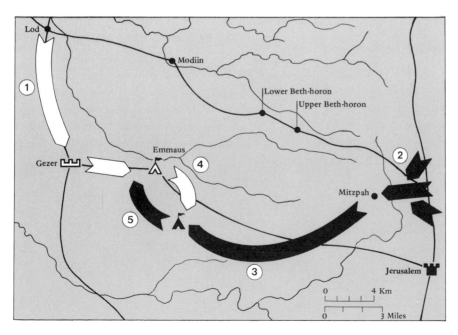

The Battle of Emmaus (phase two)

1 Gorgias, believing the whole Jewish army to be there, attacks the camp. Seeing the rearguard withdrawing up the main valley towards Jerusalem, he follows it. He is then harassed by the rearguard.

2 Meanwhile, Judah prepares to attack the Seleucid camp, and sends a force of 1,500 men to the north of Emmaus; he then attacks the phalanxes from the south-west.

3 The northern group attacks the Seleucid camp from the north.

4 The Seleucids flee towards the coast.

5 Gorgias' army returns towards their base camp but, on seeing the rout, also flees towards the coast.

camp of Emmaus, which still contained approximately 10,000 infantry men and 2,000 cavalry men – attacked the camp from the north. The forces in the camp were unprepared for battle, having assumed that Gorgias' forces in the hills to the south had taken care of the comparatively small Jewish force and confident in the knowledge that a protective phalanx was covering the approach to the camp. The Jewish force thus penetrated the camp and engaged its surprised occupants in battle. In this way, Judah succeeded in fragmenting the Seleucid forces. Gorgias with 6,000 troops was chasing an elusive force in the mountains; Judah's forces had broken into the flank of the phalanx and were engaged in hand-to-hand fighting, and the force under his brothers' command was battling against the surprised troops in the base camp.

The phalanx broke and fled towards the camp. There pandemonium reigned, as horses and elephants milled around amongst fighting troops while the large numbers of slave traders and camp followers began to run as the panic spread. Nicanor's forces broke and fled towards the coast. Some 3,000 of them were killed. At this point Judah again proved himself to be an outstanding commander, controlling the battle at all times, for he stopped the pursuit and issued orders forbidding the taking of booty. Judah knew that he had yet to contend with Gorgias. He therefore concentrated his forces at Emmaus and set fire to the enemy camp.

Gorgias soon received reports that his base camp was aflame. He turned back his forces, which were being harried by the light Jewish forces in the hills. But as the scene in the valley below was revealed to Gorgias' men, they, too, were seized by panic and fled to the coast, this time with Judah's forces in hot pursuit.

The defeat at Emmaus constituted a most serious blow to Antiochus and, indeed, prejudiced his entire campaign in the eastern provinces of the empire. In fact the very existence of the Seleucid dynasty was now threatened, for this defeat was to have serious consequences in the future. Judah, for his part, had again gained time and was in fact in total control of Judea, with the exception of the Seleucid garrison in Jerusalem (which was to all intents and purposes cut off). Another large Seleucid army had been destroyed, and considerable quantities of weapons and equipment, in addition to much wealth and valuable booty, had fallen into his hands. As a result Judah could equip his army, which by now numbered some 10,000 men.

13 FROM FREEDOM TO INDEPENDENCE

The battle of Beth-zur

The Seleucids were not long in preparing to avenge the defeat. Lysias himself set out from Antioch at the head of a force determined once and for all to put an end to the humiliating situation in which the Maccabees had inflicted one defeat after another on the mighty Seleucid armies. This time Lysias made for Jerusalem in order to join up with the garrison in the Acra fortress. Based in this fortress, his plan was to fan out into Judea, mount punitive operations and finally crush the Jewish forces.

Lysias marched his army on the traditional route along the coastal plain. But he did not enter the hills of Judea along the routes previously taken by the Seleucids, where Judah's forces had waited in ambush. Instead he outskirted Judea, marching southwards on the coast to the general area of Ashkelon, turning inland towards Marisa (Mareshah) and thence to Hebron. His route traversed territory friendly to the Seleucids. The last section passed through the land of the Idumeans, who were hostile to the Jews and friendly to the Hellenist rulers. Then his forces continued northwards to Beth-zur, a Judean border fortress some six miles from Hebron, where they set up camp.

Lysias' army has been estimated in the region of 20,000 infantry and 4,000 cavalry troops, approximately the same force that Judah had engaged at Emmaus. Facing Lysias at Beth-zur was a Judean force of some 10,000 men. Judah had followed the progress of Lysias' army closely, keeping pace with it as it finally moved up from the south. He realized that he could not rely on splitting the enemy camp, as he had succeeded in doing when he encountered Nicanor and Gorgias.

A direct assault on Lysias' forces would be fraught with great danger because of the relative strengths of the forces. He therefore resolved to make full use of the terrain on the road leading northwards to Jerusalem and chose a sector in which he would meet the Seleucid phalanx not in battle array but marching in columns and therefore most vulnerable to attack.

He sought a sector whose topographical nature could be exploited to offset the enemy's numerical superiority and chose an area immediately north of Beth-zur, probably in the vicinity of what is today Hirbet Beth-heiran. The route northwards traversed high ground bisected at many points by ravines

Beth-zur, site of Lysias'
defeat by the Maccabees in
164 BC.

and wadis, which afforded excellent cover for ambushing forces. At the same
time, the narrow route, by its very nature, confined the advancing forces
and prevented them from lining up in battle formation.

Judah divided his forces into four groupings, the first consisting of 3,000
men; the second and third of 1,000 men each; and the fourth consisting
of 5,000 men. He estimated that, despite the difficult nature of the terrain,
Lysias would be in a position to concentrate up to 10,000 men in certain
sectors. That is why Judah held back the fourth group of 5,000 men as a
reserve, ready to intervene and turn the tide of the battle.

The Seleucid forces moved northwards in a column of march. They
entered a long defile, and as they emerged from it Judah's first force issued
forth from the ravine where it lay in ambush and launched a surprise attack
on the left flank. The Seleucid lead unit was severely mauled by the sudden
heavy assault, and the leading phalanx was thrown into confusion as Judah's
first formation spread out and engaged the enemy follow-up units from both
sides of the gully. Now the second and third groups of Judah's forces began
their advance, moving forward along a front approximately half a mile wide.

As units of the lead Seleucid phalanx were beaten back, panic spread
among the following phalanxes when they discovered that they were trapped

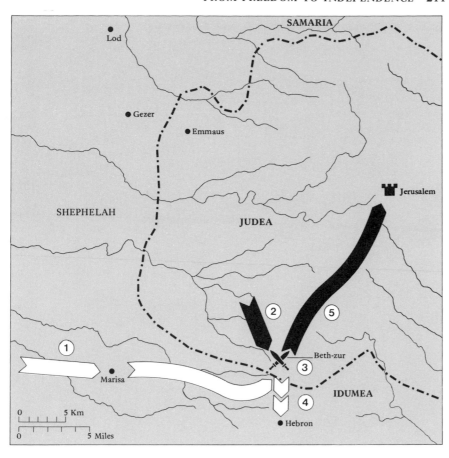

The Battle of Beth-zur

1 Lysias approaches Judea from the coast, via the fortress of Marisa, thus avoiding the difficult and dangerous terrain of the Judean mountains.
2 Judah's forces move to meet Lysias.
3 The Seleucids are ambushed at Beth-zur.
4 Lysias' troops flee towards Hebron.
5 Judah travels to Jerusalem; the Temple is rededicated.

in a gully with Judah's forces arrayed along the slopes of both sides. Lysias' forces included a large number of untested recruits, and before long his lead units were in full flight. The fleeing forces reached the base camp, in which there were still some 8,000 troops. For this encounter Judah had set aside his reserve force of 5,000 men, but the base troops panicked and fled with the remainder before the reserve unit began its attack.

Judah decided against pursuit of Lysias' forces, which fled towards Hebron, because despite his success he hesitated to be drawn into hostile country. Lysias, discouraged by the low fighting quality of his mercenaries, retired and withdrew to Antioch. His army had been soundly defeated with a loss of some 5,000 men. But his withdrawal without any attempt to put up a fight was due primarily to political reasons rather than military weakness. It was obvious to Lysias that he would require a stronger army to fight Judah. On the other hand, he was primarily preoccupied with pressing internal problems and a renewed struggle for power in the Seleucid Empire. And though Judah had again scored a remarkable victory, he had no illusions about the real reason for Lysias' quick withdrawal.

The battle of Beth-zur had been the most serious defeat that the Seleucid army – led by the viceroy himself and enjoying considerable superiority in

The rededication of the Temple

An excavated wall on the eastern side of Jerusalem, showing a second-century tower built during Maccabean rule over sixth-century ruins.

men and weapons – had suffered at the hands of the Maccabees. Judah estimated that he had gained a breathing spell, that Seleucid prestige had waned and that, internally, the empire was now in a very unstable and precarious situation. As a result, he assumed, he had won his struggle for the time being and that some time would pass before the Seleucid forces would return to Judea. The Maccabees had achieved religious freedom for their people, and now Judah's thoughts turned to the achievement of political independence. His first step in that direction would be to go to Jerusalem, rededicate the holy Temple, and affirm before the entire Jewish nation the attainment of freedom of religion.

Once in Jerusalem, Judah decided to postpone an attack on the Acra, the formidable Seleucid fortress facing the Temple Mount. Upon arriving at the Temple area, his forces were engaged at a distance from the Acra by the Seleucid garrison. Judah's forces contained them while the Jews entered the Temple, removed all the profanations, built a new altar, restored the interior of the Temple and consecrated it. On the twenty-fifth day of Kislev (the ninth month of the Jewish calendar) in 164 BC, the Temple was dedicated. The Talmud relates the story of the miracle that followed. A single cruse of pure oil, found in the Temple, sufficient for one day, burned in the candelabrum for eight days. This event is commemorated annually in the Jewish festival of Hanukkah.

The emergence of Jewish nationalism and the expression it received in the province of Judea, where the Maccabees held military sway, created a reaction in the entire region bordering on the province. Pro-Hellenist forces, unable to stand up to the Maccabees in the field of battle, turned their wrath on the Jewish communities scattered throughout the region, across the Jordan River and in Galilee. In an attempt to demonstrate Jewish vulnerability, they persecuted the local Jews, assuming that they could act with impunity.

Urgent pleas came from Galilee reporting that 'Ptolemais [Acre], Tyre and Sidon had mounted their forces to make an end of us'. The local powers had attacked the Jews in Gilead, across the Jordan, and desperate calls for help came from Dathema, a fortress some twenty miles east of the Sea of Galilee (on today's border between Syria and Jordan), advising Judah that an army under the command of Timotheus was besieging the fortified town and that the losses to the Jewish communities were very heavy.

Judah realized that his reaction to this new situation would be a test of his ability to command the struggle for religious and national independence. He decided that in this campaign to save the Jews in the surrounding lands,

The rescue expedition

The Jordan Valley in the Gilead region, where Judah and Jonathan defeated Timotheus and rescued persecuted Jews.

his troops would operate as a guerrilla army and would avoid weighing themselves down with heavy equipment and supply trains. He also realized that his proven ability to maintain forces in Judea while at the same time operating with expeditionary forces outside its borders would have the desired effect on all the powers observing the struggle in and around Judea – above all on the Roman Empire, which was taking an increasing interest in developments in the Seleucid and Ptolemaic spheres.

Judah sent his brother Simon into Galilee on a relief expedition with 3,000 men, while together with his brother Jonathan he moved across the Jordan River into the Trans-Jordanian desert at the head of a force of 8,000 men *en route* to Gilead. Simon's forces, unhindered by Seleucid reinforcements, defeated the local forces in Galilee and rescued the Jews of the area, bringing them back triumphantly to Judea. Meanwhile, Judah made his way to Gilead, where the Jewish populations were being held prisoner in fortified towns such as Bostra, Bosora, Alema, Kaspein, Maker and Karnaim. These towns in northern Gilead were concentrated primarily east and south-east of the present-day Golan Heights.

Judah opened his campaign with an attack on Bostra, some sixty miles north-east of Philadelphia (present-day Amman). He waged his campaign successfully, moving from one town to the next until he came to Dathema. This was the main centre of Jewish resistance and was invested by Timotheus' forces. Approaching the town from an unexpected direction, Judah arrived at dawn to find the enemy already scaling the walls and fortifications of Dathema. The situation of the beleaguered Jews appeared hopeless when Judah suddenly launched his attack, taking the besieging forces by surprise from the rear. The besieging units were defeated, the city was saved and Timotheus' army fled. Timotheus then attempted a counter-attack at Raphon, twenty miles north-west of Dathema, but Judah again defeated his forces and sacked the city. He gathered all the rescued Jews of Gilead and, fighting his way back through hostile territory, brought them safely to Judea.

Following his campaign in Trans-Jordan, Judah carried out a number of punitive expeditions against the hostile Idumeans (through whose territory Lysias had passed *en route* to Beth-zur) and against Jaffa, where he burned the harbour with all the shipping in it in reprisal for the drowning of its small Jewish community. He had now asserted himself as the leader of a military force to be reckoned with not only in Judea but throughout the surrounding area. He was also in absolute control of Judea (with the exception of Acra), and the borders were comparatively secure. Judah could now begin to guide his people towards the concept of national independence.

Meanwhile, the fortunes of the Seleucid Empire were at a low ebb. Before his death, Antiochus IV appointed Philip as regent over his empire until Antiochus Eupator came of age. But rather than securing stability, this final act precipitated a struggle for power between Philip and Lysias, who had previously been entrusted with the guardianship of Antiochus' son. Judah decided to exploit this situation – which obviously hampered the Seleucid forces – and attack the Acra fortress and the Hellenist Jews in Jerusalem. Aided by the siege equipment he had captured, he proceeded to invest the citadel.

It had been obvious to Judah that he could not acquiesce indefinitely in the presence of a Seleucid fortress in the heart of Jerusalem. By its very presence, the Acra reminded the Jews that the area was not entirely free and reminded the rulers of Antioch that its imperial garrison had to be maintained and strengthened. Early in 162 BC Judah mounted an attack on the fortress, but it failed and his troops were beaten back. He then proceeded to lay siege to the Acra. Emissaries from the besieged garrison hurried to Antioch and pleaded with Lysias to save them. Influenced by his desire for

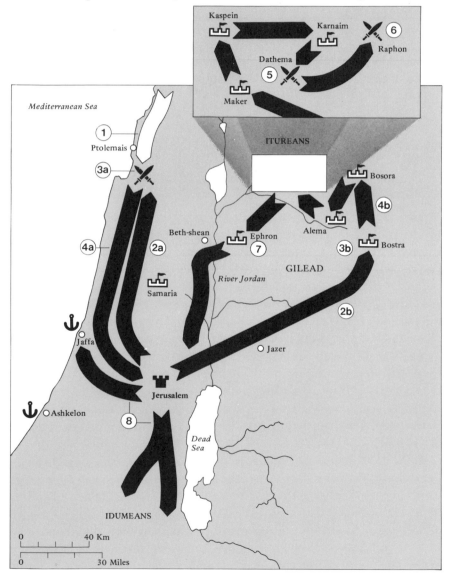

The Rescue Expeditions of Judah and Simon

1 Forces from Tyre and Sidon join with those of Ptolemais to persecute local Jewish communities.
2a On receiving reports of this, Judah sends his brother Simon to Galilee.
2b On similar reports of persecution from Gilead, Judah and Jonathan set out through Trans-Jordan.
3a Simon defeats the Phoenician allies and rescues the Jews of Galilee.
3b Judah's force relieves Bostra.
4a Simon returns to Judea with rescued Jews.
4b Judah moves on to relieve Bosora, Alema, Maker, Kaspein and Karnaim.
5 Judah defeats Timotheus at Dathema.
6 A counter-attack by Timotheus at Raphon fails.
7 Judah returns with the rescued Jews, through hostile territory, to Judea.
8 Judah carries out punitive expeditions against Jaffa and the Idumeans.

One of Antiochus v's elephants grapples with a soldier. The Seleucids had been forbidden by Rome to use elephants in war, but disregarded the agreement in their efforts to subdue the rebellious Jews. Judah's younger brother, Eleazar, was crushed to death by an elephant in the battle of Beth-zechariah.

revenge against Judah, Lysias decided to risk the possible return to Antioch of his rival, Philip, who was campaigning on the eastern borders of the empire, and leave for Judea in order to mount a renewed offensive against Judah.

Judah had for the first time made a serious error of military and political judgment. He had gambled on Lysias being tied down in Antioch by the internecine struggle for the Seleucid crown. But Lysias had set out for Judea, accompanied by the young Antiochus v Eupator, and brought with him a unit of war elephants – in defiance of a treaty with the Romans whereby the Seleucids had renounced the use of elephants in warfare. He decided to take the risk of incurring the wrath of the Romans in the hope that the elephants, which the Maccabees had never before faced, would prove to be the factor that could turn the tide of battle and bring about the quick defeat of the rebels.

At the head of more than 30,000 troops, some thirty elephants and a force of cavalry and chariots, Lysias took the same route he had taken a few years earlier and approached Jerusalem from the south. Upon reaching Beth-zur, he placed the town under siege, forcing Judah to abandon his own siege of the Acra in order to meet this threat. Having analysed all options open to him, Judah apparently came to the conclusion that this time the only viable tactic was to face the Seleucids in a conventional set piece battle, because the enemy would be expecting every form of strategy but the conventional one. He therefore left the garrison at Beth-zur to fend for itself and decided to make a stand at Beth-zechariah, some six miles north of Beth-zur and twelve miles south of Jerusalem.

The Beth-zur garrison eventually surrendered, and Judah's troops had meanwhile taken up positions on the high ground at Beth-zechariah along the road to Jerusalem. The sight of Lysias' forces marching across the plain to Beth-zechariah was calculated to instil fear in the hearts of the opposing army. The scene is described in 1 Maccabees. Leading the army were the elephants, the light infantry and the light cavalry. Behind them marched the heavy infantry, ready to form up in phalanx formation, with the heavy cavalry protecting their flanks. Each elephant 'had a strong wooden turret fastened on its back with a special harness by way of protection, carrying four fighting men as well as an Indian driver. The rest of the cavalry Lysias stationed on either flank of the army to harass the enemy while themselves protected by the phalanxes. When the sun shone on the gold and bronze

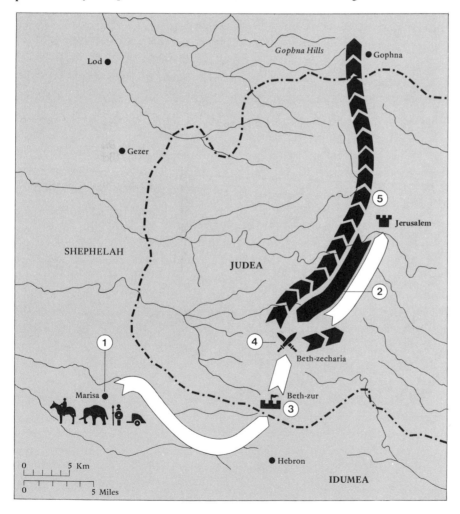

The Battle of Beth-zechariah

1 Lysias' army.
2 Judah moves to intercept the Seleucids, halting at Beth-zechariah.
3 Lysias takes Beth-zur.
4 The battle of Beth-zechariah: Eleazar the Maccabee is killed by an elephant, and the Maccabean army is defeated.
5 Judah flees back to the Gophna mountains, and Lysias advances to Jerusalem to storm the Temple Mount.

Beth-zechariah, seen from the direction of Lysias' attack.

shields, they lit up the hills which flashed like torches' (1 Macc. 6:37–9).

It is evident from this description that Lysias had learned his lesson from the previous encounters with Judah, for this time he retained control of the high ground flanking his axis of approach. The same 1 Maccabees describes how part of his army 'was deployed over the heights and part over the low ground. They advanced confidently and in good order. All who heard the din of this marching multitude and its clashing arms shook with fear. It was a very great and powerful array indeed'.

For the first time the Maccabees were to fight from defensive positions. Judah sited his forward units with the intention of causing attrition to the enemy and gradually wearing him down. Thereafter the phalanxes would be engaged by the main Maccabean forces arrayed in the rear. Lysias, on the other hand, planned for his advance units, supported by the elephants, to weaken the fighting capacity of the Maccabees, wear down the forward units and then make way for the phalanxes, which would move up and crush the main Maccabean army.

When the two armies clashed in fierce battle, the elephants had an unnerving effect on the Judeans and created a psychological disadvantage. Observing this situation, Judah's younger brother Eleazar realized that he must demonstrate to his men that the elephants were vulnerable. Sighting an elephant bearing the royal arms, he fought his way through the protective forces surrounding the beast, came under the elephant, thrust his sword into its underbelly and killed it. But as he did so, the elephant fell on him and he

was crushed. He was the first of the Maccabean brothers to fall in battle. Yet his sacrifice was in vain, for Lysias' phalanxes pushed on inexorably. Reading the battle and seeing that the situation was hopeless, Judah decided to save the bulk of his army. He broke off contact and withdrew his forces across the mountains to Jerusalem.

The battle of Beth-zechariah emphasized to Judah the mistake inherent in the attempt to imitate the enemy's tactics. The Jewish army would continue its successful career as long as it remained true to its original guerrilla-type tactics instead of adopting tactics for which the enemy was better equipped, adapted, organized and trained. The Seleucid army was a regular one and could therefore train over long periods to fight in phalanx formations. Judah's army, however, was a civilian reserve militia that was called to the colours as circumstances required.

But even in retreat Judah had demonstrated his mettle as a leader in war. His greatest quality remained his ability to adapt himself to new and changing circumstances in the heat of battle. Appreciating his error and the direction of the tide of battle, Judah remained master of the situation and, without hesitation, drew his conclusions and issued his orders, painful though they may have been.

After Judah's withdrawal, Lysias pressed on to Jerusalem, which was now wide open before him. Judah had passed through Jerusalem, fortified the Temple Mount, and then withdrew to Gophna with the remaining forces, so that they could live to fight another day. When Lysias reached Jerusalem and stormed the Temple Mount, the forces Judah had left behind fought valiantly. The attacking forces were thrown back, and Lysias found himself compelled to resort to siege.

The Maccabees prepared for a prolonged resistance. Unknown to Lysias, however, their situation was desperate because of a shortage of food and supplies. They were saved literally at the last moment when news reached Lysias that Philip was moving back towards Antioch with a view to taking over the government. Lysias faced a bitter dilemma. Victory was within his grasp but now he would have to withdraw. Accordingly he decided to make the best of the situation and offer a peace agreement granting the Jews liberty of conscience and freedom of worship.

His proposal is recorded in 1 Maccabees:

So let us offer these new terms and make peace with them and their whole nation. Let us guarantee them rights to follow their laws and customs as they used to do, for it was our abolition of these very customs and laws which aroused their resentment, and produced all these consequences. (1 Macc. 6:58-9)

When Judah accepted his proposal, Lysias hurried back to Antioch, engaged Philip, defeated him and resumed his power as ruler of the Seleucid Empire.

Many of the Jews in Judea felt that they had now achieved their objective. They felt the time had come to return to their homes and their old patterns of living and proposed dissolving the armed forces. But Judah had come to the conclusion that only by attaining political freedom and independence would the Jews of Judea achieve true freedom of worship. Therefore the army had to be maintained intact and adopt as its primary aim total national independence. He believed that the weakness of the Seleucid throne, the intrigue in the court at Antioch and the watchfulness of the Romans offered great and exciting possibilities. Accordingly, he resolved to continue the fight.

In the meantime, a bitter and bloody struggle for the Seleucid throne developed in 162 BC. Ultimately Demetrius, cousin to the nine-year-old Antiochus V Eupator, returned from Rome (where he had been held hostage), gained the support of the local population and seized power, putting Lysias and Antiochus V Eupator to death. Demetrius then appointed a new High Priest, Eliakim, in Jerusalem, who – contrary to expectations – executed many Hasidim[1] (Orthodox Jews). At the same time the Seleucid general Bacchides, whom Demetrius despatched to Judea to bolster the new High Priest's authority, killed many Jews in the area of Gophna suspected of Maccabean sympathy.

This return to an oppressive policy roused Judah to renewed action. Together with his brothers and battle-tried commanders, he reactivated the Jewish militia and began to harass Eliakim and his Hellenist supporters. The latter appealed to Antioch for aid, whereupon Demetrius immediately despatched a force led by Nicanor, the general who had been routed by Judah at Emmaus three years earlier, to deal with the Maccabees.

Reverting once again to guerrilla tactics, Judah's forces ambushed Nicanor at Capharsalama (Kfar Shalem), on the road between Jerusalem and Beth-horon, and routed the Seleucid forces. Nicanor withdrew to Jerusalem and awaited reinforcements from Antioch. When they finally reached the borders of Judea, he moved his forces down from Jerusalem in order to meet and protect them as they moved through the Beth-horon pass.

Judah bided his time and only when the two armies had met and merged did he ambush the combined force at Adasa, five miles north of Jerusalem, attacking from the right flank. The Seleucids, over-confident because of their combined strength, were taken by surprise. Nicanor fell early in the battle. His troops panicked and, being cut off from Jerusalem by Judah's forces, fled towards the coastal plain. The Jewish villagers joined Judah's army in the pursuit, harassing the Seleucid forces as they withdrew in defeat.

Following the victory over Nicanor in the spring of 161 BC, Judah again became master of the country and once more reviewed the political situation in the Seleucid Empire. In view of the attempt by Timarchus, satrap of Media and Babylonia, to renounce his allegiance to Demetrius, it was clear that Demetrius did not enjoy the support of Rome. Judah therefore decided to make overtures to the Roman Senate. The embassy which he despatched to Rome met with success and concluded a treaty of alliance between Rome and Judea (1 Macc. 8:23–30). For the first time since the Babylonian Exile, Judea was regarded as an independent power – and by none other than the major power in the world at the time!

Ironically enough, however, the Roman alliance, which was perhaps Judah's greatest political success, proved to be the immediate cause of his downfall.[2] The Seleucids could view a periodically successful guerrilla outbreak in Judea with equanimity, for they were convinced that, given the right opportunity, they could easily master the situation. But when Judea allied itself to Rome and, indeed, became a protégé of that imperial power, the court in Antioch could not help but perceive great danger inherent in the situation. Furthermore, an independent Judea, supported by Rome, would enhance the threat to the Seleucid Empire from Egypt, for this new constellation of power could ultimately lead to an alliance between the Ptolemies in Alexandria and Judea, a development which would bring the rival dynasty in Egypt almost to the Seleucids' doorstep.

With this imminent danger threatening him, Demetrius did not hesitate to act. His decision was strengthened by reports from Judea indicating that the Jewish resistance had weakened, because it was no longer motivated by the drive to overcome the sources of religious oppression. By granting religious toleration Demetrius' predecessor, Lysias, had removed the source of Jewish discontent. Thus Demetrius was able to concentrate on the rebellious Maccabean forces and weaken the Jewish revolt. Indeed, his evaluation was vindicated by events. In the spring of 160 BC, Demetrius despatched Bacchides at the head of a force of some 20,000 infantry and 4,000 cavalry through eastern Galilee taking the direct route to Jerusalem. As Demetrius

Judah's last battle

had rightly calculated, Judah was unable to muster more than '3,000 picked men'.

Bacchides based himself some eight miles north of Jerusalem in an area that today includes the town of Ramallah. As he moved northwards, Judah manœuvred his forces in a south-western direction in an attempt to bypass him and cut him off from his base. However, Bacchides countered his manœuvre and the armies clashed at Elasa, some six miles east of Beth-horon. The sight of the Seleucid army's overwhelming superiority in numbers caused the courage in Judah's ranks to fail. Many deserted, leaving Judah on the battlefield with 800 men, and I Maccabees describes how, faced by impossible odds, this brave leader urged on his small band desperately calling on them: 'Let us move to attack and see if we can defeat them.' His men tried to dissuade him from attacking, urging him to resort to their early guerrilla tactics, melt away in the hills and return to fight later. But Judah is recorded as having replied: 'Heaven forbid that I should do such a thing as run away. If our time is come, let us die bravely for our fellow-countrymen and leave no stain on our honour.'

Judah estimated that, were his most loyal forces to flee before the enemy, following the numerous desertions that had already occurred, it would bring on the demoralization of his people and could mean the end of the Jewish resistance movement. Instead he believed struggle to the death against impossible odds would inspire those who followed him. His decision was a classic example of a commander weighing the principle of morale against other principles in war and deciding that the spirit of his men was his most effective weapon in a political as well as a military context.

At the head of his 800 valiant men, Judah engaged Bacchides' 20,000 troops. The battle is described in 1 Maccabees as follows:

The [enemy] cavalry was divided into two detachments; the slingers and the archers went ahead of the main force, and the picked troops were in the front line. Bacchides was on the right. The phalanx came on in two divisions. When Judah saw that Bacchides and the main strength of his army was on the right flank, all his stout-hearted men rallied to him, and they broke the [enemy's] right; then he pursued them . . . When the [enemy] on the left saw that their right had

(*Opposite*) Adasa, site of Judah's defeat of Nicanor.

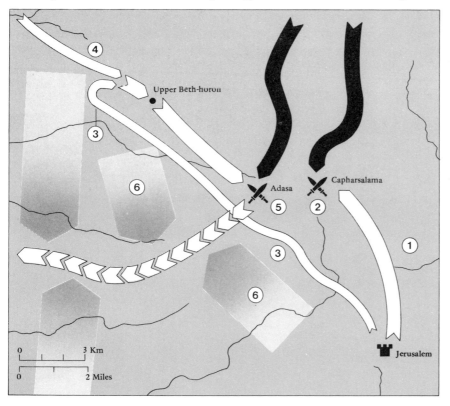

The Battles of Capharsalama and Adasa

1 Nicanor sets out from Jerusalem to subdue the Maccabeans.
2 Judah ambushes and defeats him at Capharsalama.
3 Nicanor sets out to meet reinforcements from the plain.
4 The Seleucid armies meet near Upper Beth-horon.
5 The combined forces are ambushed en route to Jerusalem at Adasa.
6 The fleeing Seleucids are harassed by Jewish villagers.

been broken, they turned about and followed on the heels of Judah and his men, attacking them in the rear. ... (1 Macc. 9:11–16)

Judah had concentrated his attack on the enemy's right flank, which was being led by Bacchides. His attack was successful, but he did not achieve his main purpose, namely to kill the Seleucid general. When the right flank under Bacchides broke and fled, Judah and his men followed them in hot pursuit. But the Jewish forces assigned to hold the enemy's left flank were overwhelmed, and the Seleucid left flank wheeled and pursued Judah's forces, who in turn were pursuing Bacchides and his right flank forces. Then Bacchides turned to give battle. Judah was sandwiched in between the forces facing him and the pursuing left flank. A bitter battle ensued with many casualties on both sides. Judah the Maccabee was among the fallen. 'All Israel made great lamentations for him and mourned many days and said "How is the mighty one fallen, the Saviour of Israel!"'

By his self-sacrifice and example, Judah had inspired his people to continue the fight. The leadership passed on to his brothers, first Jonathan[3] and later Simon, who, after a long and bitter struggle, achieved Judah's dream of independence.[4]

Judah's military genius is evident from the accounts of his battles. In all the major clashes his force was outnumbered by his enemies. Indeed, his strategy and battlefield tactics were dictated to a very considerable degree by the adverse ratio of forces which he invariably faced. A cold military analysis of Judah's battles leads one to the conclusion that they were the result of a combination of Judah's innate military genius, the bravery of his forces and the moral principles which activated them.

An analysis of Judah's tactics reveals that his main principle of war was

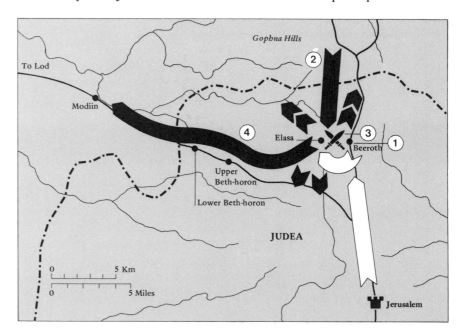

The Battle of Elasa and the Death of Judah

1 Bacchides camps at Beeroth.

2 Judah moves south.

3 The battle of Elasa: Judah is defeated and killed. The Maccabeans flee.

4 Judah's body, rescued from the battlefield, is taken back for burial in the family village of Modiin.

to attack – on every occasion and in every circumstance. He appreciated that only an offensive military policy would guarantee success against the Seleucids, bound as they were to a set piece type of warfare based on the inflexible phalanxes. A second principle which guided Judah was that of keeping the initiative in his hands. He invariably endeavoured to use local terrain to his advantage and thus never to allow the enemy to dictate the field of battle.

The Seleucid strategy was based on a policy that required the Jewish revolt to be subdued. This required the Seleucids first to discover the whereabouts of the Jewish forces, by seeking them out, and then to engage their enemy in the only manner they knew, bound as they were to the traditional phalanx-based tactics. Conscious of this inflexible strategy, Judah relied on influencing the enemy's approach route and the location of the battle area; and, of course, he could put to brilliant use the principle of surprise, on which he based much of his tactics.

The Maccabean strategy required a highly organized and effective intelligence effort. It is obvious from all the accounts of Judah's battles that he had perfected a military intelligence system which served him well. Indeed, without an efficient intelligence network, the principles of war on which he based his moves would have proved ineffective. Judah also benefited from the fact that the Seleucid forces avoided movement at night. He realized that by putting the darkness to good use, he could offset the enemy's numerical superiority and, at the same time, retain a greater measure of battlefield initiative in his hands. But it was Judah's flexibility of thought and approach, above all, that stood him in good stead. The Seleucids never managed to learn this lesson from their encounters with the Maccabees. For instance, they continued to make use of cavalry forces, although these were never very effective in the mountains and valleys of Judea. As long as Judah took advantage of the rigid means of warfare adopted by his enemy, he was victorious. However, as his army grew and acquired modern, sophisticated weapons, he tended to copy the enemy's tactics. This proved his undoing at Beth-zechariah, although he saved his forces just as imminent defeat loomed before him. The Seleucid forces maintained their battlefield strength. On the other hand, the Jewish forces, which had reached a peak strength of 15,000, began to decrease as internal political differences eroded their ranks. Only 800 men fought with Judah in his last battle. But faithful to the last to the principle of morale, he insisted on entering battle at the head of a hopelessly outnumbered force rather than withdraw in retreat.

Judah was destined to rouse his people, to forge the nation and prepare it to implement his dream of independence. For the first time in history, he led a nation in a struggle for religious freedom. He was a fighter, a hero, a general and a national leader in times of great tragedy and extreme circumstances. In Judah the greatness and courage of the spirit joined with an unusual practical ability for action and leadership of the highest quality. He was one of the great captains of history.

(*Overleaf*) Ancient tombs at Modiin, where Judah's body was taken for burial after his death in the battle of Elasa.

NOTES TO THE TEXT

The conclusions of the authors contained in this book are based on their personal military appreciation of the Bible as a factual, unbiased source. Although legitimate textual criticism has been levelled at the Bible on several grounds, the authors have followed the sequence of its account of military matters as this appears to them to be logical and convincing. Even if there are doubts as to the identity of the individuals involved, the topographical and tactical details, which are the primary concern of this book, seem factual and worthy of interpretation.

The works of recent writers on biblical matters, as well as other sources, have been invaluable in reconstructing the geographic and political setting of events, and the following chapter notes give precise references to such works. The author of Part I has, however, avoided consulting works dealing with the purely military aspects of the Bible, although previous reading may have influenced him unconsciously. Readers wishing to compare the views in this book with those held by other scholars should consult the works of Y. Aharoni, J. Liver, A. Malamat, B. Mazar, E. Oren, Y. Yadin and S. Yeivin; apologies and thanks are due to them for any influences of which the author is unaware and which are therefore not mentioned in the chapter notes.

(H) indicates published in Hebrew

Chapter 1

1 Pritchard, J. B. (ed.), *Ancient Near Eastern Texts relating to the Old Testament* (Princeton, 1969), pp. 227–8.
2 The only other country on the Palestinian land-bridge independent for any length of time, the Crusader kingdom of Jerusalem, also derived from its religious ideals and dedication, as far as they went, the strength and stamina to balance the Muslim preponderance in numbers.
3 Gichon, M., 'The influence of the Mediterranean shores upon the security of Israel in historical retrospect', in *The Sea and the Bible* (Haifa, 1970), pp. 71–96. Cf. Yeivin, S., 'Did the Kingdoms of Israel have a maritime policy?' in *Jewish Quarterly Review*, 50 (1960), pp. 193–228.
4 See notes 17 and 18 below.
5 For the physical geography of biblical Palestine, consult Smith, G. A., *A Historical Geography of the Holy Land* (London, 1894), and Abel, A., *La géographie de la Palestine* I and II (Paris, 1933–8).
6 For the origin and fate of the Hyksos, see Winlock, H. E., *The Rise and Fall of the Middle Kingdoms in Thebes* (New York, 1947), pp. 91ff.; Alt, A., *Die Herkunft der Hyksos in neuer Sicht* (Berlin, 1954); Mazar, B., *Canaan and Israel* (Jerusalem, 1964), pp. 64ff. (H). The earliest known war chariots, so far, are the Sumerian four- and two-wheelers of the first half of the third millennium BC. Cf. Yadin, Y., *The Art of Warfare in the Biblical Lands* (London, 1963), pp. 36ff.; Salonen, A., *Notes on Waggons in Ancient Mesopotamia* (Helsinki, 1950).
7 For Abraham and the Patriarchs, see Malamat, A., in *History of the Jewish People*, Ben Sasson (ed.) (Tel Aviv, 1969), pp. 37ff. (H); Albright, W. F., *From Stone Age to Christianity* (Baltimore, 1940), pp. 179ff., and Boehl, F. M., *Das Zeitalter Abrahams* (Leipzig, 1930).
8 McMunn, G., and Falls, C., *Military Operations in Egypt and Palestine* II, 2 (London, 1928), pp. 560–95; Gullet, H. S., *Official History of Australia in the War of 1914–1918* IV (Sydney, 1923), pp. 743–75.
9 Prophetism was one of the major counter-weights to over-centralized autocratic tendencies. Even the most high-handed of the kings tried to avoid an open showdown with the prophets. In this context, see the stories of David and Uriah (2 Sam. 11–12) and Ahab and Naboth (1 Kgs. 21). For the Israelite regime, see Sulzberger, M., *Am Ha-arez, The Ancient Hebrew Parliament* (Philadelphia, 1909); De Vaux, R., *Ancient Israel* (London, 1961), pp. 111–13.

10 Newberry, P. E., *Beni Hasan I* (London, 1893), Pl. 28, 30–31.

11 See below, pp. 84–6, and note 14, chapter 5.

12 Jarvis, C. S., 'The Forty Years' Wandering of the Israelites', *Palestine Exploration Quarterly* 70 (1938), pp. 32ff. For a completely different approach and a summing-up of all theories, see note 16 below.

13 Diodorus Siculus I, 30, 4.

14 *Geography* III, 17.

15 Frederick II, *Die Instruktion Friedrichs des Grossen für seine Generale von 1747*, Foerster, R. (ed.) (Berlin, 1936), pp. 38ff., 42.

16 Harel, M., *The Sinai Wanderings* (Tel Aviv, 1968), pp. 90ff. (H). Harel surveys all proposed routes and marshalls evidence for still another one. According to him, the Israelites took a central course from Ras Sudar to Kadesh-barnea. One of the Egyptian fortresses blocking the main road has not long ago been excavated near the Bir el Abd railway station. See Oren, E., *Qadmoniot* VI (1973), pp. 101–4.

17 For the conquest of Canaan, its background and sequence, see Malamat, *History*, pp. 51ff.; Mazar, *Canaan and Israel*, pp. 102–20; Alt, A., *Kleine Schriften zur Geschichte des Volkes Israel* I (Munich, 1953), pp. 89ff.; Rowley, H. H., *From Joseph to Joshua* (London, 1950); Yeivin, S., *The Israelite Conquest of Canaan* (Istanbul, 1971).

18 Egyptian documents cited by Simons, J., *Handbook for the Study of Egyptian Topographical Lists relating to Western Asia* (Leyden, 1937), nos. 4, 8, 17, 23; Gardiner, A. H., *Ancient Egyptian Onomastica* I (Oxford, 1917), p. 193; and *Ancient Near Eastern Texts*, p. 477, all mention the tribe of Asher as existing in Canaan from the time of Seti I onwards. The El Amarna archives contain letters dispatched by the Canaanite petty kings to pharaohs Amenophis III and IV (*c*. 1385–1346 BC) that illustrate the partly peaceful, partly aggressive infiltration of Hebrew clans into Palestine during the sojourn of their kinsmen in Egypt. Cf. note 17 above.

19 At Acre, for instance, Napoleon relied upon information gathered a dozen years before by civilians and also upon the intelligence of an officer wounded before he could fully scutinize the defences. See Gichon, M., 'Acre 1799, Napoleon's first assault' in *Army Quarterly* 89 (1964), pp. 100ff.

20 See note 17 above.

Chapter 2

1 See note 15, chapter 1, above.

2 See note 3 below.

3 Garstang, J., *Foundations of Bible History: Joshua and the Judges* (London, 1932), pp. 136–8. Earthquakes have caused many physical upheavals in Palestine since earliest times, see Amiran, D., 'A revised earthquake catalogue of Palestine' in *Israel Exploration Journal*, pp. 223–46. For the archaeological evidence of the conquest of Jericho, see Kenyon, K. M., *Digging up Jericho* (London, 1957), pp. 256ff.

4 McMunn and Falls, *Military Operations*, pp. 175–204; Gullet, *Official History*, pp. 126–63; Kressenstein, F. K. V., *Mit den Türken zum Suezkanal* (Berlin, 1938), pp. 171–91.

5 Gichon, M., 'The conquest of Ai' (*Zer L'Gevurot*), Shazar volume, *Yearbook of the Israel Society for Biblical Research* (1973), pp. 56–73 (H).

6 Joshua's device of alerting his detachments by means of flashes from reflected sunbeams was not an isolated stratagem. A famous example comes from the Battle of Marathon between the Athenians and the Persians (480 BC). Herodotus relates that Persian sympathizers contacted the Persian fleet off Marathon and set it on its course to occupy undefended Athens. Only the mad rush of the Marathon runner alerted the weak and unsuspecting garrison in the nick of time (Herodotus, VI, 115). In the Holy Land, the sun telegraph made its reappearance as a mechanically sophisticated tool in the wake of Allenby's forces in World War One. From that time until the establishment of the State of Israel in 1948, it remained an important method of communication for the often isolated Jewish settlements, which little thought they were making use of an ancient and locally inspired device.

7 See p. 204.

8 Fuller, J. F. C., *The Decisive Battles of the Western World and their Influence upon History* II, (London, 1955), pp. 72, 509.

9 Severe weather conditions critically impeded Allenby's advance into the Judean mountains. See his chief of staff's account, Wavell, A., *Palestine Campaigns* (London, 1931), pp. 160–2.

10 See notes 17 and 18, chapter 1, above.

11 For the Marianu, see Callaghan, R. T. O., 'New light on the Maryannu', *Jahrbuch für Kleinasiatische Forschungen* I (1950–1), pp. 309ff. Cf. Reviv, R., 'Some comments on the Maryannu', *Israel Exploration Journal* 22 (1972), pp. 218ff. Not only the chariots but the Canaanite military establishment as a whole was well organized and sophisticated in comparison to the Israelite tribal contingents. See, for instance, Rainey, A. F., 'The military personnel of Ugarit', *Journal of Near Eastern Studies* 24 (1965), pp. 17–27, and his *Social Structure of Ugarit* (Jerusalem, 1967), pp. 73–80. On the war chariot, see note 6, chapter 1, above, and note 25, chapter 5, below.

12 The need for time to get armed, counted and arrayed has always been the weak point of mounted and wheeled troops. For the same reason, during World War Two armoured forces camped in a circle, rather like the wagon trains of the Wild West, and in danger zones a percentage of the vehicles kept their engines running in order to be ready for immediate action.

13 There was also a town called Me-merom, named

after the adjacent rivulet. Because of its strategic importance it had been destroyed by Ramses II (cf. Malamat, *History*, p. 61). For the controversy about this battle, read Aharoni, Y., *The Land of Israel in the Biblical Period* (Jerusalem, 1962), pp. 188ff, and footnotes. Archaeological evidence corroborating our view as to the correctness of the biblical sequence has been marshalled by Yadin, Y., *Hazor* (London, 1975), pp. 254ff.

Chapter 3

1 See notes 17 and 18, chapter 1, above. For the nature of the office of judge, see Malamat, A., 'Charismatic leadership in the Book of Judges', *Magnalia Dei*, Cross, F., Lemke, W., Miller, D. (eds.) (New York, 1977), pp. 152–68.
2 Aharoni, Y., 'The battle of the Waters of Merom and the battle with Sisera' in *The Military History of the Land of Israel in Biblical Times*, Liver, J. (ed.) (Jerusalem, 1964), p. 100 (H).
3 For the problem of the identification of Haroshet Hagojim, consult *Encyclopedia Judaica*, p. 1347 and bibliography. Cf. Aharoni, 'Battle of the Waters', pp. 99ff.
4 For Canaanite war chariots, see Yadin, *The Art of Warfare*, pp. 86ff.; for Canaanite chariots together with Canaanite infantry bearing the triple sickle-shaped sword, see Yadin, p. 206; for charioteers and Canaanite pikemen, and for Canaanite mail-clad infantry, see Yadin, p. 242. On Thutmose's Megiddo campaign, see Faulkner, R. O., 'The Battle of Megiddo', *Journal of Egyptian Archaeology* XXVIII (1942).
5 See Gichon, M., 'The origin of the Limes Palaestinae and the major phases in its development', *Bonner Jahrbucher Beiheft* XIX (1967), pp. 175–93, and 'The defence of the Negev in military retrospect', *Maarachot* (April, 1963), pp. 13–21 (H).
6 The swift cross-country manœuvrability of nomad raiding parties always made their interception the task of two distinct forces. The larger and less mobile had to block as many avenues of retreat as possible so as to give the other smaller and more mobile group the chance to pursue the raiders in the right direction. For over five hundred years this strategy was the basic concept of Imperial Roman border defence on all its desert frontiers (cf. Gichon, M., *Roman Frontier Studies* (Tel Aviv, 1968), p. 191ff.). The people who, according to Judg. 7:2, were 'too many' should be understood as unnecessary for the pursuing force, which had to be as agile and light-footed as the nomad warriors. Whether their number was whittled down to only three hundred is open to argument. It should, however, be taken for granted that the rest of the people were not just dismissed but were employed with the blocking forces.
7 Only the Mameluk commander was too quick for Reynier and succeeded in shutting the gate in the nick of time before the faces of the charging French. Cf. Gichon, M., 'The sands of El Arish and Mount Tabor', *Maarachot* (July 1964), p. 160 (H).

Chapter 4

1 For the Philistines, see the summing up by Mazar, B., 'The Philistines and the rise of Israel and Tyre', *Israel Academy of Sciences and Humanities* I (Jerusalem, 1964), 7.
2 Samson's legendary exploits are outside the scope of these pages, though it should be noted that they have been set in areas of major strategic importance. Zorah and Eshtaol figure as major towns in the days of Jehoshaphat. The first was a royal fortress from Rehoboam's time (see p. 134). Amaziah and Jehoash fought here for the supremacy of their relative kingdoms (2 Kgs. 14). There was fighting in these areas during World War One as well as during the Israeli War of Independence. The Hill of Ali el-Muntar, where legend has it that Samson deposited the gates of Gaza (Judg. 16:3), figured decisively in the Napoleonic campaign (Napoleon Bonaparte, *Campagnes d'Egypte et de Syrie* II (Paris, 1947), pp. 39–40) as well as during World War One (McMunn and Falls, *Military Operations* I, pp. 270ff.) and the Israeli–Arab Wars of 1956 and 1967. Cf. Gichon, 'Carta's Atlas of Palestine from Bethther to Tel Hai', *Military History* II (1974), pp. 85, 104, and bibliography, p. 118.
3 For instance, in the battles of Ain Jalud in 1260 and Radanija in 1616. See Gichon, 'Carta's Atlas', pp. 65, 74, and Smail, R. C., *Crusading Warfare 1097–1193* (Cambridge, 1956), pp. 78ff.
4 A vivid and illuminating example of the consistency of tactical values attached to topographical features in the Holy Land is provided by the 181st Brigade of the 60th Division which was detailed by Allenby to capture Michmash on 12 February 1917. On the eve of the assault, after reading his Bible, the Brigade Major persuaded his Commanding Officer to call off the frontal assault and to copy Jonathan's approach by stealth, along the exact route taken by him.
5 See note 5, chapter 3, above.
6 1 Sam. 28–30.
7 For Philistines in the northern valleys, see Rowe, A., *The Topography and History of Beth-shen* (Philadelphia, 1930), pp. 23ff.; Garstang, *Foundations*, pp. 310ff.; Alt, A., 'Das Stützpunktsystem der Pharaonen Beiträge zur Biblischen', *Landes und Altertumskunde* LXVIII (1950).
8 The biblical term 'Seren', denoting the title of the rulers of the Philistine Pentapolis, is thought to be derived from the same root as the Greek word for 'tyrant', Τύραννος. In its present-day revival it has been chosen to designate the military rank of captain.

Chapter 5

1 The nine exemplary knights of Christendom, con-

sisting of Joshua, David, Judas Maccabeus, Hector, Alexander, Caesar, Arthur, Charlemagne and Godefroi of Bouillon.

2 For the Jebusites, see Alt, A., *Palästina Jahrbuch* 24 (1928), pp. 79–81; Mazar, B. (Maisler), *Journal of Palestine Oriental Society* 10 (1930), pp. 189ff., and *Sefer Yerushalayim*, Avi-Yonah (ed.), 1 (Jerusalem, 1956), pp. 107ff. (H); Avigad, N., *Israel Exploration Journal* 5 (1955), pp. 163ff.

3 For pre-Davidic Jerusalem, see Kenyon, K. M., *Jerusalem: Excavating 3000 Years of History* (London, 1967), pp. 9–53. The citadel has not yet been identified, but its presumed site, the northern part of the town, was not excavated (Kenyon, plan 5). The large tower – M – may belong to it and, even if it was a gate tower as Miss Kenyon believes, the location of the citadel adjacent to it could be the most logical, from the point of view of topography and fortification. Cf. Kenyon, K. M., *Digging up Jerusalem* (New York, 1974), pp. 77ff.

4 Yadin, *The Art of Warfare*, pp. 268–9.

5 For the *tzinor* see plans 3 and 4 in Kenyon, *Jerusalem*, and Kenyon, *Digging up Jerusalem*, pp. 84ff. The many far-fetched explanations for 2 Sam. 5:6–9 and 1 Chr. 11:4–6, summed up partly by Mazar, *Sefer Yerushalayim*, pp. 108–10, look unconvincing from the military point of view. Concerning the two-stage conquest of the citadel first, and the rest of the town second, as is implied by the straightforward reading of sequences in the Hebrew original, it should be pointed out that the rendering of ''Ijr David' as 'City of David' is faulty insofar that ''Ijr' has also the more restricted meaning of 'a city's fortress'. Cf. 2 Chr. 26:6 which should read 'and he built citadels in Ashdod ...'.

6 See Yeivin, S., 'The Wars of David', in *The Military History*, Liver, J. (ed.), p. 156.

7 2 Sam. 8:13; 1 Kgs. 11:9–10; 1 Chr. 18:12.

8 See Mazar, *Canaan and Israel*, pp. 245–69.

9 For the 'neighbour's neighbour' in European history, see Tsarist Russia, the USSR and Prussia, and Germany, in relation to Poland; Habsburg, Bourbon and Franco's Spain, and Germany, in relation to France; Scotland and France in relation to England, and more recently, Iran and Turkey's attitude in the Arab–Israeli conflict, despite their being Muslim countries.

10 Grateful thanks to Colonel Eric Patterson, RE, for providing these facts, and in particular the name of the regiment in question.

11 Gichon, 'Carta's Atlas', pp. 36, 37, 201 and bibliography. See also Playfair, I. S. O., *et al.*, *History of the Second World War: The Mediterranean and Middle East* 2 (London, 1956).

12 Loss of either the coastal road(s) or the King's Highway meant that hostile forces could operate along the flanks of the Jewish kingdoms or bypass them on the land-bridge. This became painfully evident whenever the kingdoms were driven back into the mountain bastions (see the following chapters), or when in a later age the Crusaders lost command of Trans-Jordan. Command of the desert-fringe tracts was all-important to the control of hostile forces accustomed to desert conditions. Their loss in about 634 BC permitted the Muslims to shift their forces from Syria to the Negev and back, as demanded. Cf. Gichon, 'Carta's Atlas', pp. 18–19.

13 See note 3, chapter 1, above. Mazar in 'The Philistines and the Rise of Israel' (see note 1, chapter 4, above), p. 19, argues for an Egyptian over-lordship of the Philistine shore at that time. From the biblical accounts it is apparent that the enfeebled 21st dynasty was no match for the Israelites, yet one may think of some kind of a common sphere of interest. Only with the newly regenerated Egypt in Solomon's declining years are overt moves to oust the latter feasible. The abstention, at the height of his power, by Solomon, and later by Uzziah, from Judaizing the outlets of the trans-Negevite trade cannot be attributed to military or purely political reasons.

14 For the Persian Order of Battle at Arbela, see Arrianus, Anabasis III, 8, 3–15; on the Roman auxilia, see Webster, G., *The Imperial Roman Army* (London, 1969), pp. 124–55. As late as the sixteenth century Genoese crossbowmen, Swiss pikemen and halberdiers and Croatian and related light-horsemen were in constant demand for their hereditary mode of fighting.

15 The absence of Gad and Asher from the list in 1 Chr. 27:16–22 must be an oversight by a later copier, possibly caused by his counting twelve for the twelve tribes and forgetting that the four half-tribes inhabiting Cis- and Trans-Jordan respectively are enumerated separately. For a somewhat divergent view of the Negiddim, cf. Yeivin, S., in *The Administration in Ancient Israel in the Kingdoms of Israel and Judah*, Malamat, A. (ed.) (Jerusalem, 1961), pp. 47–61 (H).

16 For the 'Thirty' see Mazar, *Canaan and Israel*, pp. 183–207, and comparable bibliography there. For other, partly divergent discussions of the Davidic armies, consult De Vaux, R., *Ancient Israel, Its Life and Institutions* (London, 1962), pp. 214–67, and Yadin, *The Art of Warfare*, pp. 275ff.

17 See Mazar, 'The Philistines and the Rise of Israel', p. 187. For the Cheretites, see Albright, W. F., 'A Colony of Cretan Mercenaries on the Coast of the Negev', *Journal of the Palestine Oriental Society* 1 (1921), pp. 187–99, and Loewenstaum, S., *Encyclopedia Biblica*, s.v. Chereti, col. 337–44 (H).

18 Mazar, B., *Vetus Testamentum*, Supp. 7 (1960), pp. 193–205. Cf. Alt, A., 'Festungen und Levitenorte im Lande Juda' in *Kleine Schriften* II, pp. 306–15.

19 The phalanx goes back to the third millennium BC Sumerians. Such is the evidence of the relief stele of

King Eannatum of Lagash: see Parrot, A., *Tello* (Paris, 1948), Pl. vib.

20 Divisible by four: see Exod. 12:37*; Num. 2 (all but Gad), 31:5*; Josh. 4:13, 7:4*, 8:3*; Judg. 7:8*, 20:15, 20:34; 1 Kgs. 10:26, 20:15*; 1 Chr. 27:1; 2 Chr. 14:8*, 26:13. Divisible by three, or specifically mentioned as divided into three: all those references marked with an asterisk, also Judg. 7:16; 1 Sam. 13:5; 2 Sam. 18:2.

21 Mazar, 'The Gibborim of David' in *Canaan and Israel*, pp. 189–90.

22 Gichon, M., 'The Defences of the Solomonic Kingdom' in *Palestine Exploration Quarterly* (1968), pp. 113–14.

23 See note 3, chapter 1, above.

24 Yadin, *The Art of Warfare*, pp. 86ff.

25 The Solomonic chariots, Yadin, *The Art of Warfare*, pp. 284ff. Yadin argues for a smaller number of vehicles than is quoted in the Bible. Yet if the greater number of 2,000 as quoted by the Assyrian annals for the reign of Ahab (see p. 118) is accepted, 1,400 do not seem to be out of proportion for the United Monarchy at its peak.

26 Yadin, *The Art of Warfare*, p. 366.

27 See note 4, chapter 3, above; *Ancient Near Eastern Texts*, p. 246.

28 See Gichon, 'The Defences', pp. 113–26, for a detailed account of the ensemble and of the individual fortresses of King Solomon.

29 For the Solomonic administration, consult (and note divergencies) Aharoni, *The Land of Israel*, pp. 261–4; Alt, 'Israel's Gaue unter Salomon' in *Kleine Schriften* II, pp. 76–98; Yeivin, *The Administration*, note 15 above.

Chapter 6

1 Mazar, *Vetus Testamentum*, Supp. 4, (1975), pp. 57–66.

2 Glueck, N., 'Tel el Khaleifa', *Encyclopedia of Archaeological Excavations in the Holy Land* II, p. 582.

3 For The Arameans v. Israel, see Mazar, *Canaan and Israel*, pp. 245–69.

4 1 Kgs. 15:27, 16:15.

5 For Tirzah and its fortifications, see De Vaux, R., 'La troisième campagne de fouilles à Tel-el Farah', *Revue Biblique* 58 (1951), pp. 409ff.

6 Yadin, *Hazor*, p. 199.

7 The author collected some typical sherds, such as Samaria-ware bowls and cooking-pot fragments, similar to those referred to on pp. 195ff and Pl. 75 II (a) and (b) in Amiran, R., *The Ancient Pottery of Eretz Israel* (Jerusalem, 1963).

8 For the fortresses of the Naphtali line throughout the ages, see Gichon, 'Carta's Atlas', pp. 24–5, 71.

Chapter 7

1 For the stele of Mesha, see Albright, *Ancient Near Eastern Texts*, p. 320.

2 For Samaria and its fortifications, see Crowfoot, J. W., Kenyon, K. M. and Sukenik, E. L., *The Buildings at Samaria* (London, 1942), pp. 5ff. This refers to the Reissner and Fisher excavation report. If the as yet unexcavated fortress of Yibleam (a Levite city) that guarded the approaches from the north through the Jezreel Valley and the north-west through the Dotan Valley, is added to the three strongly fortified cities of Shechem (cf. Wright, G. E., *Shechem: The Biography of a Biblical City* (London, 1950), p. 150), Samaria and Tirzah, one gets a quadrilateral of fortifications ideally designed to protect the Samarian heartland, as well as to serve as springboards and *points d'appui* for offensives from four separate directions. When this is compared with the famous Habsburg quadrilateral of eighteenth–nineteenth-century North Italy, the ancient Israelites' solution seems a better one.

3 1 Kgs. 20:7 and 14. From verse 12 it is evident that Ben-hadad was already encamped before Samaria and besieging the city. The elders and district governors must therefore have been inside the city already. In the days before the telephone it would not have been feasible for a commander to direct troops from a headquarters thirty-nine miles distant from the field of action. (Cf. Yadin, *History of Warfare*, pp. 305ff.)

4 For *ne'arim*, cf. De Vaux, *Ancient Israel*, pp. 220–221.

5 McMunn and Falls, *Military Operations* II, 2, pp. 416–546; Gullet, *Official History of Australia*, pp. 692–712; Guhr, H., *Als türkischer Divisionskommandeur in Kleinasien und Palästina* (Berlin, 1937), pp. 248–61; Gichon, 'Carta's Atlas', p. 109.

6 1 Kgs. 20:26 implies a renewal of hostilities during the year immediately following the first Aramean invasion. However this is not consistent with the time needed for the complete reorganization of the Aramean kingdom prior to the second campaign.

7 Yadin, *The Art of Warfare*, p. 309.

8 The author has had the opportunity of personally testing all four.

9 Taylor, F., *The Wars of Marlborough 1702–9 I* (Oxford, 1921), p. 213; Fuller, *The Decisive Battles*, pp. 150, 211–12.

10 For relations between Israel and Assyria, consult Malamat, *The Wars of Israel and Assyria* and *The Military History*, Liver (ed.), pp. 241ff.

11 Yadin, *The Art of Warfare*, pp. 382ff.

12 Yadin, *The Art of Warfare*, p. 297. This passage, however, could just as well mean that both rode chariots.

13 *Ancient Near Eastern Texts*, pp. 278–9.

14 Gunter, E., *The Officer's Field Note and Sketch Book and Reconnaissance Aide-Memoire* (14th edition, revised and rewritten) (London, 1912), pp. 58ff.

15 See note 13, chapter 7, above.

16 For the northern Gilead zone of clash of interests

between Aram and Israel, see Mazar, *Canaan and Israel*, pp. 245ff., and Mazar, 'Havoth Yair', in *Encyclopedia Biblica* III, pp. 66–7.

Chapter 8

1 *Ancient Near Eastern Texts*, p. 320.
2 *Ancient Near Eastern Texts*, para. (25). Aroer excavations, see *Encyclopedia of Archaeological Excavations in the Holy Land*, Avi-Yonah (ed.), pp. 99–100.
3 Kressenstein, *Mit den Türken*, pp. 181ff.
4 See Liver, J., 'The Wars of Mesha, King of Moab', *Palestine Exploration Quarterly* 99 (1967), p. 30.
5 2 Kgs. 7:6 mentions Aramean forebodings of an Egyptian threat too. Contacts between Jehoram and Egypt were in line with Egypt's policy of counterbalancing any acquisition of supremacy by one of the states on the Palestinian land-bridge, by assisting the apparently weaker party. One is reminded of Great Britain's 'balance of power' policy towards the Continent, and especially the Netherlands, a bridge country with many geographical features similar to Israel. At that stage Egypt was concerned amongst other things about its supply of cedar wood from Lebanon, which was vital for the maintenance of its navy.
6 Mazar (Maisler), B., *Untersuchungen zur alten Geschichte und Ethnographie Syriens und Palästinas* (Giessen, 1930); Tadmor, H., in *History*, Malamat (ed.), I, pp. 122ff.
7 'Lo-debar' of Amos 6:13 is wrongly translated literally by the Authorized Version as 'a thing of nought', but it is in fact the name of a town mentioned in both biblical and external sources, e.g. 2 Sam. 17:27.
8 For reliefs depicting the Assyrian new model army, see Yadin, *The Art of Warfare*, pp. 406ff.

Chapter 9

1 For a detailed account with relevant bibliographies, see Gichon, M., 'The Fortifications of Judah', in *The Military History*, Liver, J. (ed.), pp. 410–25. Cf. for some divergent ideas, Kallai, Z., 'The Kingdom of Rehoboam', *Encyclopedia Judaica* 10, pp. 246ff.
2 For Alam el-Halfa, see de Guingand, F. W., *Operation Victory* (London, 1947), pp. 139ff.
3 See note 11, chapter 11, below.
4 The Kushites of Serach are not the Ethiopians, as was assumed by older commentators, but a semi-nomadic people of the same name as that used in the Bible for Africans, who are known to have lived on the southern borders of Palestine from the second millennium BC. Cf. Mazar (Maisler), B., *Untersuchungen zur alten Geschichte und Ethnographie*.
5 *Ancient Near Eastern Texts*, pp. 255–7. The siege of Lachish is depicted in detail in a relief from Sennacherib's palace at Nineveh: see Barnett, R. D., *Assyrian Palace Reliefs and their Influence on the Sculpture of Babylonia and Persia* (London, 1960), pp. 44–9.
6 Tadmor, H., 'The Campaigns of Sargon II of Assur', *Journal of Cuneiform Studies* 12 (1958), pp. 80ff. Note that Tadmor advocates the attribution of this particular siege to Sargon.
7 De Bourienne, F., *Memoirs of Napoleon* (Edinburgh, 1830), p. 153 (should read 'Cestius' instead of 'Crassus'!) Cf. Josephus Flavius, *De Bello Judaico* (The Wars of the Jews) II, para. 542ff.

Chapter 10

1 For Mizpah, see McCown, C. C., *Tell en Nasbeh* I *Archaeological and Historical Results* (New Haven, Conn., 1947); for Gibeah, see Albright, W. F., *Annual of American Schools of Oriental Research* IV (1922–3), and Sinclair, L. A., *Annual of American Schools* XXXV (1954–6), pp. 5ff. Geba has not been excavated.
2 Aharoni, Y., *Excavations at Ramat Rahel* I and II, (Rome, 1962–4); for identification with Beth-hakerem see pp. 122–3. Eighth-century pottery was picked up at Bether by the author.
3 For Horvat Rasham, see Rahmani, L. I., *Yediot* 28 (1964), pp. 209ff.
4 Kochavi, M. (ed.), *Judaea, Samaria and the Golan Archaeological Survey 1967–8* (Jerusalem, 1972). The following Iron Age II sites could be fortresses built by Jehoshaphat or his successors: Judean desert, nos. 4, 92, 93, 145, 199, 202; Judah, nos. 28, 79, 166.
5 2 Chr. 8:5. A detailed description of all aspects of the biblical fortifications is not within the scope of this book, nor will detailed references and sources be given. For the archaeological evidence and its interpretation, see the appropriate articles in the *Encyclopedia of Archaeological Excavations*, Avi-Yonah (ed.), which includes a comprehensive bibliography. A shorter survey is offered by the *Archaeological Encyclopedia of the Holy Land*, Negev, A. (ed.) (London, 1932).
6 Herzog, Z., 'The Storehouses', *Beersheba* I, Aharoni, Y. (ed.), (Tel Aviv, 1973), pp. 23–30.
7 Aharoni, Y., *Israel Exploration Journal* 18, pp. 162ff. The existence of the sanctuaries in Northern Kingdom fortresses could have been learned from the Bible. For both kingdoms Aharoni lists Dan, Bethel, Geba, Arad and Lachish.
8 Aharoni, 'Hebrew Ostraca from Arad', *Israel Exploration Journal* 15, pp. 1–15.
9 Tadmor, H., 'Azriyau of Yaudi', *Scripta Hierosolymitana* VIII (1961), pp. 232–71; *Ancient Near Eastern Texts*, p. 282.
10 Jehoshaphat's civil administrative districts are preserved in Josh. 15:21–62. To the ten districts enumerated in the Hebrew Bible the Septuagint adds an eleventh, taken from a more complete source than that used by the canon. The twelfth district com-

prises the southern Benjaminite towns captured by his father and garrisoned by Jehoshaphat (cf. 2 Chr. 17:2). The list of these towns is given in Josh. 15:21–4. Cf. Alt, 'Juda's Gaue unter Josia', *Kleine Schriften* II, pp. 276–88; Aharoni, *The Kingdom of Israel and Judah*, pp. 123ff.

11 While on service with the Israel Defence Force, the author established the usefulness of large sections of these wadis as present-day anti-tank obstacles.

12 The excavations at Beersheva, still under progress, have already shed light on these strongholds in the triple role of defensive, offensive and administrative bases for the Judean border. See *Beersheba* I, Aharoni (ed.). With their tactical value unchanged these sites became in turn Greek, Herodian and Roman border fortresses: see Gichon, M., 'Idumea and the Herodian Limes', Israel Exploration Journal 17 (1967), pp. 27–55. As late as World War One the fate of Palestine was decided by Allenby's capture of Beersheva in October 1917 (see Gichon, 'Carta's Atlas', p. 105 and bibliography).

13 See pp. 101–2.

14 The Hebrew original could mean either 'a part of the Philistines brought ...' or 'from the Philistines did Jehoshaphat receive ...'.

15 For Ezion-geber, Kadesh-barnea and Arad, consult the relevant articles in the *Encyclopedia of Archaeological Excavations*. For the southernmost fortress at Qureiye, cf. Meshel, S., *Hadashot Archeologiot* (October 1975), pp. 51–2 (H).

16 A Judean chariot is shown on Sennacherib's relief depicting the siege of Lachish: see note 5, chapter 9, above, and Yadin, *The Art of Warfare*, p. 301. For the dismantling and man-handling of chariots, see Yadin, p. 426, after Botta, L. E., *Monument de Ninive* I (Paris, 1849), Pl. 20.

17 Mazar, B., *The Excavations at Tel Qasile* (Jerusalem, 1950).

18 Modern scholars tend to place the Mehunim beyond the southern borders of ancient Judah: see Tadmor in *The Military History*, pp. 266ff. Some scholars, for instance Albright, W. F., *Bulletin of the American Society for Oriental Research* 129, pp. 10–24, have connected the Mehunim with the Bani Main, the 'Minaioi' of classical sources whose caravan trade and commerce extended from southern Arabia to the Mediterranean sea coast. Yet even if this connection does not stand, their tribal territories seem to have extended from western to eastern Palestine.

19 Gichon, M., *Sinai as a Frontier Area in Historic Retrospect* (Tel Aviv, 1969), pp. 17ff.; Gichon, 'Carta's Atlas' for relevant maps; Abel, F. M., *Géographie de la Palestine* II, p. 218. Migdol=Tell el Kher, Pelusium=Tell Farama. A Judean fortress and sanctuary in northern Sinai has recently been excavated by Z. Meshel; see *Qadmoniot* 36 (1977), pp. 115ff.

20 For Negevite fortifications during the First Temple period, see Aharoni, 'Forerunners of the Limes', *Israel Exploration Journal* 17 (1967), pp. 1–17.

21 For this and the following see summing-up by Glueck, N., in *Rivers in the Desert: a History of the Negev* (London, 1959), pp. 168ff. His detailed accounts were published in the *Bulletin of the American Society for Oriental Research*, 1953–60.

22 Diligent survey has enabled B. Rothenberg to define a special type of Iron Age II pottery typical of the Negev, which he calls 'Midianite'. It is a safe assumption that the southernmost Jewish tribes, who remained semi-nomadic pending a centrally organized settlement policy, assimilated much of the local culture and handicrafts, especially since the autochthonic 'Midianite' population was assimilated by them.

23 De Vaux, *Ancient Israel*, pp. 69–70. McKane, W., 'The Gibbor hayil ...', *Glasgow University Oriental Society Transactions* XVII (1959), pp. 28–37.

24 For Uzziah at the head of the anti-Assyrian coalition, see note 9, chapter 10, above.

25 Josephus Flavius, *De Bello Judaico* V, para. 73–97.

26 Webster, *The Imperial Roman Army*, pp. 166ff. For a camp partitioned into three and headquarters, see plan of Novaesium; for partition into four and headquarters, see Birrens and Fendoch.

27 Barnett, R. D., *European Judaism* 8 (1968), pp. 1*–6*; Yadin, *European Judaism* 8, p. 6*.

Chapter 11

1 1 Chr. 4:41–3, 2 Chr. 30, 31:1. The text speaks extensively of Hezekiah's successful endeavours to have the Israelites of the former Northern Kingdom participate in the religious service at the Temple of Jerusalem. From 2 Chr. 31:6 we gather that he also succeeded in transplanting some Israelites permanently in Judah. As Judas Maccabaeus (see 1 Macc. 5) and more recently the first government of the State of Israel also found, Hezekiah realized it was imperative to augment his forces by enlisting Jewish manpower from abroad in order to withstand foreign pressures.

2 For Hezekiah v. the Philistines and Assyria, see Tadmor, *The Military History*, pp. 138ff.

3 2 Kgs. 20:12–13; 2 Chr. 32:31.

4 Maspero, G., *The Passing of the Empires 850 BC – 330 BC* (London, 1900), pp. 251–3 (obsolescent but still worth while reading); Breastead, J. H., *A History of Egypt* (London, 1964), pp. 460–1.

5 Yadin, *The Art of Warfare*, pp. 326–7.

6 *Ancient Near Eastern Texts*, p. 321. My quotation is from Baikie, J., *Lands and Peoples of the Bible* (London, 1932), p. 33.

7 Naveh, J., 'Old Inscriptions in a Burial Cave', *Israel Exploration Journal* 13 (1963), pp. 74–92.

8 See note 3 above.

9 For Mezad Hashaviahu, see Naveh, J., *Israel*

Exploration Journal 12, pp. 89–99 and 10, 129–39.

10 For the political background of Josiah's reign, consult Malamat, *The Military History*, pp. 296ff. His military reforms were extensively dealt with by Jung, E., in *Beitrage zur Wissenschaft der Alte und Neue Testaments 1937: der Wiederaufbau des Heerwesens des Reiches Juda unter Josia* (Stuttgart, 1937). This work was not available to me when preparing this book. Note divergencies in our respective views concerning interpretation of various problems.

11 Torczyner, H., *et al.*, 'The Lachish Letters' in *Lachish* I, Harding, L. (ed.) (London, 1938): Ostracon 4; Ancient Near Eastern Texts, p. 322. It should be noted that, as with present-day regulations, already in biblical times there was a proper procedure for switching to an alternative method of communication when signalling direct was impossible. Fire and smoke signals had been used by the Israelites since the times of the Judges, in addition to the other methods of oral and visual communication described previously (see Judg. 20:38). Their use was usually confined to stationary posts. Napoleon used fire and smoke signals in Galilee as late as 1799. See also Vegetius Renatus, *The Roman Military Manual* III, 5: Per noctem flammis per diem fumo' – flames by night and smoke by day, to communicate with one's allies. For the ancient East, compare Dossin, G., 'Signaux lumineux du pays du Mari', *Revue Archéologique* XXXV (1938).

12 The political and strategic background of Judah's last decades have been described by Malamat, A., 'The twilight of Judah', *Supplements to Vetus Testamentum* 28 (Edinburgh, 1974).

Chapter 12

1 Although the Temple treasury of Jerusalem was plundered on the orders of Seleucus IV (187–176 BC) when he had to raise the tribute Rome had imposed on his father, Antiochus III (2 Macc. 3:7ff.).

2 The story of Antiochus and the Maccabean revolt is recounted in the First and Second Books of Mac-

cabees, which are by different anonymous authors. Antiochus' persecutions are echoed in the Book of Daniel and Josephus also recounts the story of the Maccabees.

3 Avisar, E., *The Wars of Judah the Maccabee* (Tel Aviv, 1965).

4 Following the organization attributed by the Bible to Moses (see chapter 1), and also used by David (see Chapter 5).

Chapter 13

1 Literally 'pious ones'. Though they were thoroughly opposed to any attempts to Hellenize Judaism, it is unlikely that they took up arms. The *Psalms of Solomon* call the Pharisees 'Hasidim'. The name 'Hasidim' may be the origin of 'Essenes', the pietistic groups who lived around the shores of the Dead Sea about a century or so later and were themselves opposed to the successors of Judah the Maccabee, who had become the Hellenizing Hasmonean dynasty. Later Jewish revivalist groups in Germany in the Middle Ages and Poland and Lithuania from the eighteenth century were also called Hasidim.

2 Although the source of this alliance is the strongly pro-Jewish writer of 1 Maccabees, there is no reason to doubt its existence. The agreement was renewed by Judah's successors, the Hasmoneans, but in itself it became a source of conflict within Judea when it was supported only by the upper classes – the rulers, priests and their rich and influential supporters, the Sadducees.

3 Jonathan was appointed High Priest by the Seleucid ruler, Alexander Balas, an appointment which Judah had never tried to secure because his family did not have the hereditary qualifications for the office. Jonathan's appointment was later the source of tension in Judea.

4 In 142 BC. From then on the descendants of Mattathias became the Hasmonean dynasty, taking the hereditary title 'High Priest and Ethnarch of the Jews'. The Romans renewed their agreement with the Jews through Simon in 139 BC.

CHRONOLOGICAL TABLE

27th–22nd century BC	The Old Kingdom in Egypt.
c. 2350 BC	Uni invades Canaan.
18th–16th century BC	Canaan part of the Hyksos Empire.
16th–8th century BC	The New Kingdom in Egypt.
1468–1436 BC	Thutmose III fights seventeen campaigns in and north of Canaan.
14th century	18th Dynasty in Egypt. Penetration of the Hebrew Tribes into Canaan. Sojourn of the Israelites in Egypt.
13th century	Moses – Exodus from Egypt.
	Joshua – Conquest and Settlement of Canaan (=Palestine).
12th–11th century	The Judges. The Philistines and other 'sea peoples' settle on the shores of Canaan.
c. 1050	Samuel
c. 1025–1006	Saul
c. 1006–968	David – The empire extends from the borders of Egypt to the Euphrates.
c. 968–928	Solomon – Solomon builds the Temple in Jerusalem. Alliance with Tyre.
c. 925	Division of the United Monarchy.

	Kingdom of Israel		Kingdom of Judah
		c. 928–911 BC	Rehoboam reigns in Judah.
c. 925–907 BC	Jeroboam reigns in Israel. Invasion of Shishak.	c. 924	Shishak I of Egypt invades Judah and Israel.
		c. 908–867	Asa, King of Judah, consolidates the Kingdom including the great defence works of Rehoboam.
c. 882–870	Omri reigns in Israel. Builds Samaria, renews alliance with Tyre.		
c. 870–851	Ahab reigns in Israel. Beats off Arameans. Heads coalition against Shalmanezer III. Battle of Qarqar (853). The prophet Elias active.	c. 867–851	Jehoshaphat reigns in Judah – offensive and defensive alliance and co-operation with Israel.
c. 858–824	Shalmanezer III of Assyria succeeds in repeated campaigns to subdue the Arameans and reaches Gilead and Galilee.		

Kingdom of Israel		Kingdom of Judah	
c. 852	Mesha, King of Moab re-establishes independence from Israel.		
c. 850–842	Jehoram reigns in Israel.		
c. 850	Israel and Judah invade Moab without lasting success.		
c. 842–814	Jehu rebels, is crowned king over Israel with the assistance of the prophet Elisha. The internal struggles make Israel practically dependent upon Damascus ruled by Hazael.		
		c. 812–810	Jehoash, King of Judah under pressure from Damascus.
		c. 799–785	Amaziah reasserts Judah's independence and recaptures Edom.
c. 800–785	Jehoash reaffirms Israel's independence.		
c. 785–750	Jeroboam II in alliance with Uzziah of Judah re-establishes the Solomonic borders. The prophet Amos active.	c. 786–758	Uzziah reaffirms Judah's ascendancy over its neighbours to the east, south and west. The prophet Isaiah commences his activity which continues well into Hezekiah's reign.
c. 745–727	Tiglath-pileser III of Assyria invades and subjugates the Palestinian land-bridge during several campaigns. Only Judah seems to have guarded a modicum of independence.		
c. 722	Samaria captured by Sargon II of Assyria after a three-year siege by his predecessor, Shalmanezer V. Large parts of the population exiled into remote parts of the empire ('the lost ten tribes'). The remnants mingle with transplanted gentiles and form the Samaritans – not accepted as orthodox Jews.	c. 724–697	Hezekiah rules Judah. He beats off Sennacherib's invasion (701).
c. 722–628	Israel an Assyrian province.		

Kingdom of Israel		Kingdom of Judah
	c. 628–609	Josiah – last expansion of Judah which, owing to Assyria's weakness, incorporates much of former Israel.
	c. 609	Josiah killed at Megiddo in battle against Pharaoh Necho.
	c. 605	The Neo-Babylonian Empire established, which includes nearly all of the Assyrian realm.
c. 604–539 Israel a Babylonian province.	c. 586	Nebuchadnezzar captures Jerusalem, and the First Temple is destroyed. Large parts of the population are exiled to Babylonia. Subsequent flight of Jewish troops into Egypt accompanied by the prophet Hezekiel. Foundation of the first Jewish military colonies in Egypt.
c. 539 Israel a Persian province.		

537–332 BC	The Persian Period.
537	Under Persian rule, Jews allowed to return from Babylon to Judea.
515	Restoration of the Temple (henceforth called the Second Temple).
c. 440	Nehemiah arrives from Babylon and rebuilds the walls of Jerusalem.
c. 435	Ezra the Scribe joins Nehemiah in rebuilding the city of Jerusalem and the community in Judea.
332–134	The Hellenistic Period.
332	Alexander the Great conquers the Persians and gains their territories, including Palestine.
301–200	Palestine under the Ptolemies of Egypt.
198	Seleucid emperor Antiochus III of Syria wrests Palestine from the Ptolemies.
190	Antiochus III loses decisive battle of Magnesia to Romans.
188	Under treaty of Apamea, Antiochus' son (the future Antiochus IV) is sent to Rome as hostage.
187	Accession of Seleucus IV, son of Antiochus III.
175	Accession of Antiochus IV Epiphanes, brother of Seleucus IV. Onias III (Honya), traditionalist Jewish High Priest in Jerusalem, is ousted by the emperor; pro-Hellenist Jason installed in his stead. This marks the start of Seleucid attempts to Hellenize Judea.
172	Jason dismissed, flees to Trans-Jordan, and extreme Hellenist Menelaus appointed High Priest in his place.
170	Antiochus IV launches first campaign in Egypt.
168	Rome conquers Macedonia. Antiochus IV, on his second campaign in Egypt, is about to complete his conquest of the country when Rome orders him to retreat. Uprising in Jerusalem. Antiochus sends punitive expedition to Jerusalem. Many

Jews massacred; the Temple looted; the formidable Acra fortress built as a Seleucid military base.

167   Antiochus IV issues anti-Jewish decrees.

December 167   Desecration of the Temple.

167   Incident at Modiin. Mattathias and his sons raise banner of revolt. Judah creates guerrilla force. The Book of Daniel given forth.

167–166   Death of Mattathias. Judah succeeds him as leader of the Maccabees. Apollonius defeated near Gophna in first Maccabee battle against Seleucid forces.

165   Seron defeated at battle of Beth-horon. Antiochus IV departs on his eastern campaign. Nicanor and Gorgias defeated at battle of Emmaus.

164   Lysias repulsed at battle of Beth-zur.

December 164   Maccabees rededicate the Temple. Inauguration of Festival of Hanukkah.

163   Judah's expedition to rescue the Jews of Gilead. Simon's relief expedition to western Galilee. Judah campaigns in coastal plain and Idumea. Death of Antiochus IV Epiphanes. Succeeded by his young son Antiochus V Eupator, with Philip as regent

162   Judah's brother Eleazar killed in battle of Beth-zechariah. Lysias reaches Jerusalem. In the name of Antiochus V, Lysias annuls anti-Jewish decrees. High Priest Menelaus removed and executed. Demetrius escapes from Rome, becomes new Seleucid emperor (Demetrius I Soter). Antiochus V and Lysias put to death. Eliakim (Alcimus) appointed High Priest. Nicanor repulsed at battle of Capharsalama.

161   Nicanor killed at battle of Adasa. Judah's treaty of friendship with Rome.

160   Maccabees defeated by Bacchides at battle of Elasa. Judah killed. Jonathan succeeds Judah as Maccabee leader. The eldest Maccabee brother, Johanan, murdered by Trans-Jordanian tribe.

ACKNOWLEDGMENTS

The illustrations in this book are supplied or reproduced by kind permission of the following:

Antichita Egittologia, Turin 146;
Ashdod Expedition 65;
Werner Braun 152;
British Museum 115, 117 (above), 128, 143, 179;
Burgerbibliothek, Bern (photo by Gerhard Howald) 75;
Department of Archeology, Hebrew University, Jerusalem 47;
Department of Archeology, University of Tel Aviv 138;
Werner Forman 117 (below), 132;
Giraudon 216;
Sonia Halliday Photographs *41* (above), *44*, *166*, 178, *183*, *184*, 192–3;
Sonia Halliday Photographs (photos by Jane Taylor) 58, 73, 78, 105, 109, 113, 135, 155, 185, 198;
David Harris 26, 50, 64 (above), 72, 93, 99, 116, 119;
Hillel Heiman 32, 34, 37, 70, 79, 200, 201 (above), 204–5 (above), 205 (below), 218–19;
Israel Department of Antiquities and Museums 30, 90, 118, 142, 148, 186;
Israel Museum 48, 108, 163, 167;
Jerusalem Excavation Fund 212;
Lachish Archeological Expedition 136;
Zev Radovan 38, 56–7, 64 (below), 210, 213, 222, 226–7;
Rijksmuseum, Leiden 19;
Ricarda Schwerin 91;
Ronald Sheridan *41* (below), *42–3*, *165* and jacket picture;
Staatliche Museen, Berlin 17;
Weidenfeld and Nicolson Archives 151;
Robert B. Wright 94.

Numerals in italics indicate colour illustrations

Picture research by Joy Jacques
Maps drawn by David Worth and Jennifer Mexter

The authors wish to thank Ms Miro Tillo and Ms Michaela Koppel for their help in drafting the maps for this book.

INDEX